Educational Leadership

Second edition

Together creating ethical learning environments

The second edition of *Educational Leadership* is a groundbreaking work at the forefront of current research into the ethical challenges inherent to leadership. Patrick Duignan combines a new perspective on leadership as an influence relationship, with a collective ethic of responsibility. This combination is intended to promote a new paradigm of learning based on the creation of ethical, engaging and technologically smart learning environments suited to the learning styles of contemporary students.

Educational Leadership draws together cutting-edge research, theory and best practice on learning, teaching and leadership to assist leaders and teachers to better understand contemporary educational challenges and respond to them wisely, creatively and effectively. This book is indispensible for all system and educational professionals engaged in policy-making, leadership development, leading learning in schools, and those in academe responsible for programs aimed at the improvement of learning, teaching and leadership.

About the author

Patrick Duignan BA, H Dip ED (NUI), B.Ed, M.Ed. Admin, Ph.D. (ALTA) was Foundation Chair in Educational Leadership and Director of the Flagship for Creative & Authentic Leadership at ACU National, where he championed ethical and moral leadership, especially in not-for-profit organisations. He currently works as a consultant in the area of Educational Leadership and travels the world as an international speaker and consultant on leadership for not-for-profit organisations.

Educational Leadership

Second edition

Together creating ethical
learning environments

Patrick Duignan

CAMBRIDGE
UNIVERSITY PRESS

CAMBRIDGE UNIVERSITY PRESS
Cambridge, New York, Melbourne, Madrid, Cape Town,
Singapore, São Paulo, Delhi, Mexico City

Cambridge University Press
477 Williamstown Road, Port Melbourne, VIC 3207, Australia

Published in the United States of America by Cambridge University Press, New York

www.cambridge.org
Information on this title: www.cambridge.org/9781107637894

First published 2007
Reprinted 2008, 2009, 2011
Second edition 2012
Reprinted 2012

Cover design by Anne-Marie Reeves
Typeset by Newgen Publishing and Data
Printed in China by Everbest Printing

A catalogue record for this publication is available from the British Library

National Library of Australia Cataloguing in Publication data
Duignan, P. A. (Patrick Augustine).
  Educational leadership: together creating ethical learning
  environments / Professor Patrick Duignan.
  2nd ed.
  9781107637894 (pbk.)
  Includes index.
  Educational leadership – Australia.
  Educational leadership – Moral and ethical aspects – Australia.
  School administrators – Professional ethics – Australia.
  Decision making – Moral and ethical aspects.
  371.200994

ISBN 978-1-107-63789-4 Paperback

Reproduction and communication for educational purposes
The Australian *Copyright Act 1968* (the Act) allows a maximum of
one chapter or 10% of the pages of this work, whichever is the greater,
to be reproduced and/or communicated by any educational institution
for its educational purposes provided that the educational institution
(or the body that administers it) has given a remuneration notice to
Copyright Agency Limited (CAL) under the Act.

For details of the CAL licence for educational institutions contact:

Copyright Agency Limited
Level 15, 233 Castlereagh Street
Sydney NSW 2000
Telephone: (02) 9394 7600
Facsimile: (02) 9394 7601
E-mail: info@copyright.com.au

To Nuala, our children, and grandchildren

Foreword

Patrick Duignan has studied and practised leadership for over four decades. In the second edition of *Educational Leadership* he captures all this wisdom in one concise, powerful place. I know the field pretty well, and as I was reading I wondered from time to time whether Duignan would address this or that aspect of what is prominent in education leadership. Every time I thought of a dimension of leadership, it would be addressed seemingly in the next chapter. It is all there: moral purpose, macro challenges, micro challenges, tensions and dilemmas, individual and collective ethics, innovation and more.

Whether it is about *being* a leader or *becoming* a leader, Duignan gets to the bottom of what it means to foster and hone one's leadership. He not only addresses the key aspects of educational leadership, but he uncovers the deeper issues, and then helps the reader think it through with just the right amount of complexity. He doesn't spoonfeed the reader but he does sharply clarify each major aspect of leadership. He furnishes his own insights, but he also pushes the reader to grapple with the underlying issues. His reflective questions at the end of each chapter are a course in leadership itself.

I recently reviewed the broader literature in order to get insights into what it means to practise highly effective leadership, whatever sector one is in. When I compare my conclusions all of them are addressed by Duignan: how to become a resolute leader, motivate others, collaborate, learn confidently, know one's impact – and above all, how to learn from practice, your own and others (Fullan, 2011).

Read this book with the express purpose of how you can become a deeper, highly effective authentic leader. You will be drawn in to examine every aspect of your stance and practice. You will have the opportunity to review and build your leadership systematically, as Duignan says, around your personal, relational, professional, and organisational attributes and capabilities.

Duignan will not only help you to become more effective, he will push you to be a leader who develops others. He shows the ways in which leaders can develop leadership in others, how to assist teachers to become more capable, and how to transform the collective capacity of their schools and communities. These are wrenching times in societal and global development. Duignan challenges us to create 'a future of our own making'. He takes us a long way down that path. It is up to the reader to make it happen.

Michael Fullan
Professor Emeritus
OISE, University of Toronto

Contents

Contents

Contents

Contents

Acknowledgements

Parts of this book are based on a three-year research project funded by the Australian Research Council (ARC). As Chief Investigator of this research, I recognise and appreciate their support.

I owe a big thank you to the university team and the partner organisations that helped develop and conduct this research. A special thanks to Michael Walsh who gave permission to adapt his material on values and ethics from the research report. Also to Michael Bezzina who was a great adviser and support to me in writing this edition.

Of course, without the love and support of my spouse, Nuala, over our forty-four years together, this book, as well as many other adventures, would not have been possible. Thank you for your insightful advice, careful reading of the manuscript, and your encouragement to keep at it when distractions beckoned.

I continue to learn every day from our three children, Siobhan, Patrick and Finola and, of course, from their spouses Christopher, Fiona and Michael. Our grandchildren, Matthew, Benjamin, Joe, Conor, Cormac and Molly Kate are wise beyond their years and I learn to be young again in their company.

Thanks to Cambridge University Press for believing in the book, and a special thanks to my extraordinarily supportive, wise and expert editors, Gemma Tiernan, Nina Sharpe and Averil Lewis. A special thanks to Nina for all she did to ensure that the integrity of the book is preserved.

Introduction and overview

Purpose of the book

In 2006 the first edition of this book was published. The context and challenges for educators have changed considerably during this time period. While some challenges identified in that edition are still relevant, they often present themselves in different clothes. As well, new challenges have emerged and some of the earlier ones have morphed into more complicated forms. For these reasons, and the fact that the book had a strong national and international audience, the decision was made with my publishers to issue a renewed and substantially changed edition.

The primary purpose of this book is to provide educational leaders, including teachers, with skills of identifying, analysing and responding to the complex challenges they face each day, including the ethical tensions inherent in many of these challenges. These are important skills for educational leaders if they are to meet the expectations of a cynical public. It is no longer a defence for leaders to say they didn't understand the significance of their behaviours or that they are too busy to pay close attention to moral principles and ethical standards in their decision making. A values- and ethics-based approach for making decisions in situations fraught with paradox and ambiguity is a central focus of this book.

There are also clear and precise recommendations provided on the need for all those educators in formal leadership positions to share leadership responsibilities with others by building a sustainable collective ethic of responsibility for leadership in their schools. Great emphasis is given to the importance of educational leaders building rich, engaging, interactive, technologically-smart, and productive learning environments in order to enhance the quality of teaching, learning and student outcomes in their schools. Calls for adherence to high ethical standards and the need for educational leaders to be authentic in everything they do underpin these recommendations. Important research-based advice is provided to encourage educational leaders to become much more influential in their fields or spheres of influence, especially with regard to enhancing the quality of teaching, learning environments, and student outcomes.

All in all, this is a substantially different book from the first edition. It builds on the best of the earlier edition but also introduces and explains many new leadership concepts and explores their implications for educational leaders. This book also contains valuable insights for system policy makers and those responsible for system and school leadership formation, as well as for the practice of leadership at all levels in education systems and schools.

Overview

In chapter 1, key elements of the changing context for education are identified, together with their possible impact on schools and educational leaders. The conclusion is reached that there is widespread cynicism about the quality and integrity of many leaders across a variety of organisations and there are increasing calls for greater honesty and authenticity in leadership.

In chapters 2 and 3 key contemporary challenges facing educational systems and school leaders are identified, described and discussed. Those challenges that are of a more global and general nature are referred to as *macro challenges* and are discussed in chapter 2. In chapter 3, the challenges described are more specific to the everyday work of school leaders and are called *micro challenges*. The challenges in both chapters feature some of those from the 2006 edition that continue to be relevant while others have morphed into new forms, thereby presenting school leaders with different and, in some cases, more intense challenges. There are also new challenges presented (primarily in chapter 2) that may have been implied by the findings of the research that underpinned the earlier version of the book, but have now more clearly emerged as key challenges from the author's and others' research. Since 2008, the author has conducted research on key relevant leadership challenges with over 1500 school leaders in Australia, New Zealand, Canada and South Africa, using interactive technologies.

In chapter 4, challenges are described and analysed as *tensions* involving values and ethics; a framework for analysing these tensions is presented in chapter 5. These two chapters contain material from the earlier version of the book, but it is updated and modified to reflect the changing context and challenges presented in chapters 1 and 2. While specific cases have changed somewhat, the challenges and key ethical tensions remain very similar. This fact has been constantly verified by the author when discussing the ethical issues raised in the first edition with a large number of school leaders in a number of countries.

Since the first edition, ethical awareness and sensitivity has intensified, essentially because of the ethically and morally corrupt behaviour of bankers, financiers and politicians during the global financial crisis. Recent activities in countries like Greece, Ireland, Italy, Portugal, Spain, the US and the UK have highlighted these ethical problems. The collapse, or near collapse, of banks such as Lehman Brothers, Northern Rock, Anglo Irish and the Royal Bank of Scotland has stimulated degrees of cynicism and disgust in public opinion not seen in many decades, if ever. The more recent scandalous practices of reporters and executives of the *News of the World* (and perhaps other news media), as well as the constant scandals surrounding many politicians (with expense accounts, collusion with business leaders, developers and planning authorities) have, one could say, put the icing on the scandal-ridden cake.

Chapter 6 deals with issues related to values and ethics in decision-making and presents a practical approach to, including a method for, ethical decision-making. These ideas are connected to the material in the earlier chapters and have a special leadership focus.

In chapter 7 the focus is on a major challenge for contemporary educational leaders, that of encouraging and sustaining a collective ethic of responsibility for leadership in schools. As professional educators and educational leaders, with a special calling (a vocation) to shape the lives of young people, we are bound by a collective ethic to work together to ensure all our students experience the type of quality learning environments that will maximise their life chances. Issues of distributed leadership, talent development, and leadership succession are discussed and critiqued from this collective perspective. Advice is provided on how schools can embrace new commitments to a collective ethic of responsibility for leadership that relies less on one person or position – the principal or the principalship – and engages more productively with a range of expertise and talent from different areas and levels within and outside the school.

The importance for leaders of authentic presence, relationships, and influence fields is discussed in chapter 8. Practical implications are drawn to assist educational leaders become more influential in their spheres of influence. Much new material and new thinking on leadership as an influence relationship is introduced in this chapter.

A key challenge of an emerging paradigm of learning and teaching is discussed and analysed in chapter 9. This is a challenge that must be met head-on by educators and educational leaders if the new education paradigm discussed in chapter 2 is to be realised. It is the challenge of getting all key educational stakeholders working collectively to build and sustain rich, engaging, interactive, technologically-smart, and productive learning environments in order to enhance a broader range of student outcomes. Research-based practical advice is provided for those educational leaders who wish to take on this challenge.

The need to go beyond leadership training and development and focus more on the formation of leaders is a focus of the final chapter (chapter 10). The argument presented is that authentic capable leadership requires, above all, capable human beings with specific attributes, qualities and capabilities. Key capabilities required for leaders to respond influentially to the types of challenges discussed in chapters 2 and 3 are best formed in learning conditions that are described as 'crucibles of learning', involving a *case-in-point* transformational formation methodology.

Overall, practical advice is provided throughout the book on ways educational leaders and teachers can be more authentic, influential, and capable of generating sustainable collective leadership capacities in schools in order to create rich, engaging and technologically-smart learning environments.

'Key ideas for reflection' are presented for readers at the end of each chapter for self-reflective analysis, as well as for further consideration by leaders in relation to leading their schools. Key questions are included to structure these reflections.

Chapter 1

The changing and challenging context for educational leaders

Educational leaders are subjected to external and internal pressures, challenges and expectations that make demands on their time, expertise, energies and emotional wellbeing. Increasingly, they are being held accountable for their own performance and for that of the teachers and students under their care. They are also expected to comply with the highest ethical and moral standards in their relationships and practices.

While some leaders may experience confusion, even frustration, in attempting to respond productively to these challenges, other school members, especially teachers, may feel devalued by the considerable criticism of schools and schooling in the media. The current emphasis on corporate management values, strategies and practices in many educational organisations may seem like an assault on their professionalism.

This book is written within a leadership context that is increasingly sensitive to the need for sound ethical and moral standards in how organisations are led and decisions made. As stated in the introduction, there is greater scrutiny of the behavioural ethics of all our leaders, including those in schools. As many ethical breaches have been exposed in other organisations, the time is now opportune for educational leaders to ensure that they are reviewing and embedding high ethical and moral standards in their policies and practices.

Increasingly educational leaders live and work in a global world that, according to Giddens (1998), influences social processes and institutions and encourages new forms of individualism that contribute to more selfish modes of living. They have, therefore, a particular responsibility to ensure that students in their care receive the type of education and learning experiences that help transform their lives so that they can break the bonds imposed by these forces for intense individualism and better contribute as responsible citizens to the common good (Sommerville, 2000). Educational leaders need to be socially, ethically and educationally responsible, in order to create the conditions within their schools that challenge students to see the bigger picture and to want to make a difference in their own lives and within the larger community.

Unfortunately too many leaders, especially those in politics and the business world, have not lived up to such expectations in recent times. Many in our communities doubt the credibility, especially with regard to ethical and moral behaviour, of leaders of many of our public and private institutions. There is a growing public chorus demanding ethical and authentic leadership. These demands are raising the ethical and moral bar for contemporary leaders.

Influences of globalisation

In his groundbreaking book *The third way*, Giddens (1998) suggests that globalisation is a complex range of processes and events driven, primarily, by '... a mixture of political and economic influences'. It touches all our lives, transforming our social processes and institutions, even the ways in which we relate to one another. It is this latter perspective on globalisation that is of most interest because, as Giddens so clearly points out, it is directly relevant to the rise of the 'new individualism' (p. 33).

In fact, our selfish and self-centred ways are causing us to grasp at more temporary and less fulfilling forms of engagement. This gradual disengagement of self from a sense of the collective can lead to the development of a selective blindness for the plight of others less fortunate than ourselves, to the point where it can become entrenched at many levels of society. While such a development can lead to isolation and disengagement, as humans we need community for our identity, even our survival. Belonging to a community helps give greater meaning and purpose to life.

Some warn of the consequences of this love affair with ourselves. They argue that 'the ethic of individual self-fulfilment and achievement is the most powerful current in modern society', and the choosing, self-driven individual is 'the central character of our time' (Beck & Beck-Gernsheim, 2002, p. 22). They say that individualised modes of living have the potential to spawn a host of addict-making processes or process addictions, which are destructive of collective and communitarian interests. Process addictions – for example working long hours, stressful jobs, winning at all cost, spending beyond our means – are often seen as barometers of success in our societies (Breton & Largent, 1996, p. 2).

Perhaps the most destructive influence of these process addictions is that they are promoted and supported by society at large and by some key institutions. Our schools, churches, media – even our workplaces – can create feelings of dependency in us (Breton & Largent, 1996, p. 4). Many of society's systems, structures and processes may be eroding our sense of worth and wellbeing, creating dependency, and causing us to forget the bigger communitarian picture.

The more serious concern is the possibility that these addictive tendencies may very well start early in life, even during school years. This raises the issue of the potential role of schools in contributing to the development of these tendencies or habits in children.

Influence of schools

How well do our schools prepare students to choose morally, ethically and wisely? This is a very difficult question to answer and any response to it is, necessarily, somewhat speculative. As we will discover in chapter 2, there is much evidence to suggest that many schools are failing our students, especially those who find it difficult to cope with a rigorously prescribed curriculum offered in inflexible and highly structured ways. Much learning in schools is based on regurgitation of facts in tests, without children knowing why their answers are deemed to be correct. Such inauthentic learning does not generally prepare students to live meaningful, compassionate and fulfilling lives (Starratt, 2004). It is much more likely to encourage and reward competitiveness, and push students toward selfish, individualised attitudes and behaviours.

A sobering consequence of such inauthentic learning approaches to teaching and learning is that at least some schools may be preparing students more for addiction than for making worthwhile choices in their lives (Breton & Largent, 1996, p. 4). According to Usher & Pajares (2008), they may give their students very negative messages, primarily through their restrictive control structures and processes, such as tight time schedules regulated by ringing bells, students moving from classroom to classroom, and constant supervision that seems to prevent children from developing independence and, in fact, may coax them into dependent behaviours.

Structures and processes may fail to take into consideration the holistic and integrating nature of knowledge for the lives of learners, and the role of schools in the spiritual and moral development of students. The most destructive part of the hidden curriculum for students is that they may be 'trained to give up a great deal of personal power' and may experience a 'profound sense of disenfranchisement' (Fourre, 2003, p. 77). While recommending a greater commitment to justice, Fourre cautions that a deep sense of moral and social responsibility can only be applied to life by those who possess a sense 'of their own power and their responsibility to use it for good' (p. 77).

This negative view of schools and schooling presents challenges for educational leaders who have a particular responsibility to use learning opportunities to promote the good of students as well as that of the community. They need to regard it as their ethical responsibility to promote and support policies and practices in their schools that better prepare students to be faithful, responsible and contributing citizens who will not just accept the world as it is but help transform their communities into havens of hope, promise and living witnesses of the common good. In a three-year research project entitled *Socially responsible indicators for policy, practice and benchmarking in service organisations*, Duignan et al. (2005) concluded that 'social responsibility is, above all, fostered by the commitment of leaders to the mission of the organisation' (p. 54), and the mission of many service organisations, such as schools, usually focuses on the people side of the organisation and on the capacity of their leaders to be ethically, morally and socially responsible. Providing students with learning environments that engage and challenge them morally, ethically and socially as well as educationally and academically, is a central challenge for educators and educational leaders in contemporary schools. Our students deserve no less!

Leadership for social responsibility

A predominant culture of accountability in today's schools usually means being judged against external standards and benchmarks, but to be socially responsible means to be cognisant of and act on values of justice and equity, as well as on moral principles and ethical standards. By implication, morally and socially responsible leaders need to challenge unethical and immoral policies and practices wherever they find them, especially in relation to justice and equity in their schools and in society.

Of course, taking such action involves risk and daring (Hannah & Avolio, 2010) and ethically responsible educational leaders require great courage. In an address titled, 'The courage to lead', Heft singles out two areas of leadership in which contemporary leaders must do better – *justice* and *diversity* (Heft & Bennett, 2004). In relation to diversity, often referred to as multiculturalism, he cautions that some approaches by leaders '… are based on a false idea of tolerance' (p. 17) that actually avoids commitment to principles and ethical standards. Tolerance and civility shouldn't be characterised as 'moral ambivalence', which can quickly lead to moral indifference (Keane, 2003, p. 199). On the other hand, arrogant adherence to absolute values or inflexible principles can lead to self-righteous behaviours. A basic ethic of tolerance, based on mutual respect for differences enshrined within a global civil society, is one way of striking a balance between bland tolerance and self-righteous behaviours (Keane, 2003). Educational leaders need clearly articulated moral principles and ethical standards for action that will help schools steer a course away from intense individualism, bland tolerance, or self-righteous behaviours, toward more ethical, moral and communitarian processes and actions.

Need for clear moral purpose

A hallmark of authentic leadership is that it is inspired by clear moral purpose (Ryan, 2008). He suggests that all educators need to rediscover and renew their moral purpose and passion (p. 4).

Many contemporary educational leaders are under strong external pressures that tend to drive and control what they do every day and rob them of the meaning, moral purpose, and the passion of their professional work. Ryan argues that teachers join their profession because of deep moral purpose and to make a difference in the lives of their students. Their passion comes from deep inside and is inspired by their personal and professional principles and values.

In recent times a strong emphasis on ethics and moral purpose, as well as recognition that leadership is a values-based activity, has emerged in educational leadership (e.g., Cranston, Ehrich & Kimber, 2006). They suggest that 'communities expect those holding leadership positions to act justly, rightly and promote good …

as well as demonstrate moral and professional accountability' (p. 106). It appears, too, that school principals have the same expectation of themselves. In research with over 550 school principals, Cranston et al. (2006) reported that 'participants emphasised the need not only for ethical organisational cultures but also the importance of having clear personal ethical values and professional ethics' (p. 114). This heightened awareness of ethics may be due to the very nature of their jobs – complex and crises-filled – because Cranston et al. found from their research that leaders may not be fully aware of their values 'until they are confronted with a crisis' (p. 114).

As identified earlier, many leaders do not follow ethical standards or act in socially responsible ways. In fact, there is currently widespread cynicism about the credibility and authenticity of leaders in a number of our public and private institutions.

Growing cynicism for leaders and leadership

Why is there such widespread doubt in the community about the sincerity and credibility of many leaders in our organisations and in public life? Freeman and Stewart (2006) suggest that while 'it is important for leaders to tell a compelling and morally rich story', a problem is that they do not always 'embody and live the story' (p. 3) and this can lead to feelings of cynicism from staff and stakeholders. There may, however, be important reasons why educational leaders fail to give sufficient attention to the moral and ethical dimensions of their work. Moberg (2006) argues that the chief cause of recent corporate scandals is a 'breakdown in moral agency,' which he blames on their reliance on 'patterns of perceptions that undercut the moral capabilities of the actors' (p. 413). People's personal patterns of perceptions or their perspective, which he calls 'a frame', create what he refers to as *'blind spots*, those defects in one's perceptual field that can cloud one's judgment, lead one to erroneous conclusions, or provide insufficient triggers to appropriate action' (p. 414, italics in original). Because of their particular frames, leaders can have both personal and interpersonal blind spots. Interpersonal blind spots occur when they place more emphasis on others' negative characteristics than on their positive traits, thereby making 'positive elements of character less salient than negative ones' (p. 416). Because of this, he suggests that 'whistle-blowing is seen by insiders more as an emblem of betrayal than a sign of virtue' (p. 416). However, he explains that an interpersonal blind spot 'does not appear to represent a serious threat to moral agency' because, while it might 'diminish virtue,' it 'does not undermine the identification of moral qualities altogether' (p. 417).

A more serious threat to moral agency in an organisation is when 'individuals act on an incomplete assessment of their own personal qualities – *their personal blind spots*' (p. 417, author's italics for emphasis). Part of the problem is that leaders (like many others) tend to define themselves predominantly by the content of their lives; for example their position, possessions, achievements, people they know (Tolle, 2005), and by their competencies; that is, their skills, capabilities, creativeness, and efficiency (Moberg, 2006). They do not, according to Moberg, define themselves in terms of their character or moral traits (honesty, generosity, altruism). An implication for leaders is that the more they construct their identity around the content and competencies of their lives, the more distanced they may become from 'the process of becoming moral' (p. 417). As well, leaders tend to be rewarded (promoted) for their competencies, cleverness, and win-at-all-cost attitudes and not, necessarily, for their moral or character traits. One can imagine that in the recent *News of the World* scandals involving grossly unethical conduct, a major part of the problem was that editors and journalists were encouraged and supported in the pursuit of 'competence-based reward systems that ignore morality' (Moberg, p. 418).

A challenge for educational leaders, therefore, is to ensure they do not grow blind spots to their professed core values, moral principles, and their moral purposes of education. Educational leaders need to have clear insights into their own and others' value sets in order to develop their moral compass as a guide for their actions. They need this moral compass to help them in resolving ethical dilemmas, in facilitating 'appropriate action' (Bezzina & Tuana, 2011, p. 2) and in order to provide insightful advice on how leaders 'can intentionally operate in the moral sphere in order to influence behaviour … create commitment to shared moral purpose' (p. 3) and 'promote moral agency in the community' (p. 8).

It is not sufficient, however, for educators and educational leaders simply to be aware of and have a rhetoric of moral purpose in their school; there must be 'a commitment to and ownership of it and, ultimately, it must be enshrined as the norm within a shared sense of community' (p. 3). To do this, Bezzina and Tuana argue that leaders and teachers need to be morally literate, which they define (p. 4, based on Herman, 2007) as 'a basic learned capacity to acquire and use moral knowledge in judgment and action' (p. 4) and also have 'the capacity to use ethical reasoning skills' (p. 5), both of which will be discussed in upcoming chapters. Leaders should also mobilise a shared sense of moral purpose for quality learning by encouraging a culture of ownership, commitment, hope and courage. These challenges are not exclusive to educational leaders in their workplaces (Bezzina, 2012).

Practical challenges in the workplace

Recently, in research and consultancies focusing on authentic leadership practices and ethical tensions in the health workplace, the author has observed leaders in health organisations agonising over the ethics of their leadership and management practices. As a trustee of a large private health care organisation in Australia (with 13 hospitals, pathology, imaging, and community outreach services), the author is acutely aware of the degree to which health and hospital leaders face complex ethical challenges and dilemmas. It is no longer just situations of malpractice that cause headaches for leaders and health professionals but tensions also arise from areas such as occupational health and safety, staff relations, patient dissatisfaction, lack of attention to infection control, and breaches of confidentiality. Mostly, the legal and ethical dimensions of these tensions are inextricably intertwined, making it essential that leaders are very familiar with both the legal and ethical imperatives that can impact on their work.

Leaders in educational organisations face similar tensions and dilemmas. In recent years, legal frameworks related to areas such as workplace health and safety, sexual harassment, child protection, industrial and staff relations, bullying, issues of equity and justice, and regulatory compliance have become more complex and demanding. The penalties for legal non-compliance can be severe, just as those for ethical and moral laxity can be devastating for an individual's integrity, a leader's character and his/her professional reputation.

There is reason to be more optimistic about the future – a gleam of hope. In recent times, the demands in education for increased efficiency and vertical accountability within an economic rationalist framework are being counter-balanced by calls for an uncompromising commitment to real (not just rhetorical) ethical, moral and authentic leadership principles and practices, especially in relation to the leadership of learning (Bezzina & Tuana, 2011; Hannah & Avolio, 2010; Bezzina & Burford, 2010; Lindholm, 2008; Ryan, 2008; Begley & Stefkovich, 2007; Duignan, 2006; Moberg, 2006; Greenfield, 2004; George, 2003).

The call for authenticity in leadership

Leaders are increasingly expected to comply with ethical and moral standards in their relationships and practices. Many educational leaders face increasingly demanding and discerning clientele who challenge decisions and the ethical foundations on which they are based. The danger is that many leaders respond by adopting knee-jerk responses to confusing and ethically charged crises because they have no operational frameworks for dealing with such complex ethical issues (Duignan, 2006).

In recent years there is a growing call in the relevant literature, to reclaim the moral, ethical and spiritual domains of leadership (Degenhardt & Duignan, 2010; Flintham, 2010; Strike, 2007; Duignan, 2006; Freeman & Stewart, 2006; Conger & Associates, 1994; Fullan, 2003). Havel (2007), arguing the urgent need to reclaim and renew our moral footprint for the twenty-first century, suggests that 'the moral order, our conscience and human rights … are the most important issues at the beginning of the third millennium' (p. A33).

Sergiovanni (2007) champions the idea that leadership and administration are essentially moral activities and advocates the need for educational leaders to bring together head, heart and hands in their practice because leadership is, essentially a moral craft. Fullan (2003) too, has strongly promoted the idea that both teaching and educational leadership are moral enterprises. As far back as 1993, he suggested that the key building block for education 'is the moral purpose of the *individual* teacher' (p. 10) and in 2003, he claimed that 'moral purpose of the highest order' provided the environment where all students learn, the gap between high and low performance is minimised, and students go forth from their schools enabled as successful citizens 'in a morally based knowledge society' (p. 29). He points out, however, that this will not be achieved without 'deep cultural change that mobilizes the passion and commitment of teachers, parents, and others' to promote and support authentic behaviours for leaders and teachers and authentic learning experiences for their students (p. 41).

In a passionate and insightful argument for ethical leadership in education and schools, Starratt (2004) argues that leadership involves 'the cultivation of virtues' that generate authentic approaches to leadership and to learning (p. 8). His major message is that the true test of leadership is the degree to which it becomes moral. He also states that educational leaders have to take responsibility for changing those things over which they have some control in order to 'promote the deeply human fulfilment of young people' (p. 144). He suggests that moral leadership '… invites others to transform each day into something special, something wonderful, something unforgettable, something that enables their human spirit to soar and, giddy with the joy of the moment, know who they are' (p. 145). How exciting schools will be for their students if they succeed in achieving these outcomes!

In an important work on authentic leadership, George (2003) claims that leadership 'is authenticity, not style' and that after years of studying leaders and their traits, he concludes that 'leadership begins and ends with authenticity' (p. 11). This view is shared by this author, but always with an appropriate grounding in the changing contemporary context of education and schooling, as well as the needs of an emerging paradigm of teaching and learning. The discussion, analysis and recommendations in the remainder of this book take up Starratt's earlier challenge for educational leaders to transform students each day into something special, something that enables their human spirit to soar.

Initial research and follow-up studies

The author and a team of researchers conducted a three-year research study in a variety of organisations (police service, health care, religious institutions and in

State and Catholic schools). The research was supported by the Federal Government in Australia (2000–2005) and focused on the challenges facing contemporary leaders in service organisations.

A combination of quantitative and qualitative data collection and analysis techniques was employed in a complementary fashion in the study. The study incorporated four data collection stages: questionnaires, interviews, critical leadership incidents, and electronic dialogue on an interactive website.

Questionnaire data were analysed using a variety of quantitative analysis techniques. NVivo (Bazeley & Richards, 2000), a computer analysis software package for qualitative data, was used to help analyse the large volume of data generated by interviews, critical incident technique, and the interactive website. It proved to be a powerful integrating tool that greatly assisted in the generation of concepts and theoretical propositions from the data across the different organisations involved in the study.

Data generated through the website were continually processed, analysed and presented back electronically to participants in the form of a dialogue on emerging themes and concepts. This iterative process helped ensure that the emerging concepts fitted with the real world, were relevant to the people (especially the practitioners) involved in the research, and made sense across the range of organisational contexts. From the analysis of both the quantitative and the qualitative data a number of key leadership challenges and ethical tensions were identified. A number of these challenges are discussed in chapter 3.

Since 2008, the author has actively engaged with approximately 1500 principals in interactive research workshops, using Turning Point Keypad Interactive hardware and software in Australia, New Zealand, Canada and South Africa. The focus of these workshops was on the key challenges and ethical tensions facing principals, their desired learning environments and the obstacles preventing them from achieving them, and their views of the importance of their presence, authentic relationships and influence fields in their leadership.

The findings from both these sources have been integrated to generate the key discussions, findings, conclusions and recommendations in this book.

Key ideas for reflection

Educational leaders live and work in a global world that shapes social processes, institutions and individuals and may encourage forms of individualism that can contribute to more selfish modes of living, often eschewing ethical and moral considerations. The pursuit of intense individualism can lead to a disengaged approach to life and living, to more selfish and competitive choices, and practices that may be very destructive of collegial and collaborative relationships in schools and school communities.

In parallel with these developments, many schools have embraced corporate management practices which are based on efficiency, standards, targets, productivity and accountability. These characteristics have tended to displace professional dimensions of service, collegiality, compassion, and a sense of justice and equity.

It has been emphasised in this chapter that ethical and moral standards need to be promoted and sustained in all forms of leadership. The idea that teaching and leadership must have ethical and moral purposes should be a key consideration for educational leaders and they need to challenge unethical and immoral policies and practices wherever they find them. Courageous, ethical and authentic leadership action is called for.

Questions for reflection

1 What global pressures are impacting on you as an educational leader and what strategies are you using to respond to them?

2 In what ways might schools and schooling contribute to the development of self-serving individualistic and competitive habits in their students? How can you as an educational leader counteract these forces?

3 How can schools better prepare students to make choices that will equip them to live a more fulfilled life and be a valuable contributing citizen in their community and society?

4 What could you do as a leader to assist your school better prepare students to choose a healthy life–work balance in the future?

5 What could you do as a leader to assist your students develop ethical and moral frameworks for life and work?

Chapter 2

Key macro challenges for educational leaders

The challenges in chapters 2 and 3 are derived from the author's research with educational leaders over a ten-year period as well as from a detailed scan of relevant contemporary literature. The challenges are presented in two 'orders of magnitude'.

In this chapter, *macro* challenges are identified, emerging from the continually and rapidly changing context for education and schools. These have been identified by the author from his research and from a wide range of recent relevant literature.

In chapter 3, *micro* challenges are identified which focus on specific challenges for educational leaders when leading their schools. Many of these were discussed in the first edition of this book and have subsequently been tested and confirmed in research with approximately 1500 school leaders in Australia, New Zealand, Canada (Ontario) and South Africa, using interactive keypad technologies.

In recent times, numerous internal and external pressures and changes have challenged schools and their leaders. There have been seismic shifts in the expectations placed on schools by politicians, policy makers, communities, education bureaucracies, and by more discerning and demanding parents. Many system and school educators are now struggling to respond positively and creatively to these challenges.

This is understandable because adapting to new challenges involves learning and the development of leadership capacities that prepare us for changed circumstances. Ironically, over time there is a tendency for such capacities to become 'hardwired' into both individuals and the organisation in an attempt to restore some sense of equilibrium, but this is not necessarily an effective response in a rapidly changing environment (Heifetz, 1994, p. 35). When we discuss the challenges facing contemporary and future schools in the coming sections, we need to be alert to the types of responses – adaptive or attempting to restore equilibrium – that policy makers, educators, educational leaders and schools are making and how appropriate and effective these responses are.

Drawing inspiration from the influential leadership work of Ronald Heifetz of Harvard University, Parks (2005) sees leadership in a turbulent, uncertain, and rapidly changing world as 'a call to adaptive work' (p. 1). She says that a critical challenge for today's leaders is to be capable of responding 'adaptively to the depth, scope, and pace of *change* that combined with complexity creates unprecedented conditions, [and] this new landscape creates a new moral moment in history' (p. 2, italics in original).

In the following sections, a number of macro challenges and accompanying critical choices and responses for educational leaders are discussed and analysed. Leaders will require considerable moral imagination and moral courage, as well as a number of key adaptive capabilities, in order to respond effectively to these challenges.

Educating everyone to higher and higher standards

During more than a decade of attempts to reform education systems in many countries (e.g., US, UK, Canada, Australia), emphasis has focused on ideas such as education for all, no child left behind, and raising the bar and closing the gap in student achievement. The drive for education for all has been paralleled in most Western countries by demands for higher standards of teaching (and for teachers), international benchmarking, and an emphasis on high stakes testing, all leading to a strong culture of accountability for teachers and educational leaders.

These policies have their protagonists and antagonists, with the latter being very passionate and outspoken. While Barber (2011) supports the need for education system reform that includes clear standards, testing, and accountability for teachers and educational leaders, he is – at the same time – critical of the ways in which many of these developments have been implemented. Zhao (2009) also criticises the policies of accountability, standards and testing in educational reform efforts, especially in the US. He concludes that the defining characteristics of educational reform in that country in the early part of this century are that, '(1) excellence equals good test scores in math and science; and (2) standards – and test-based accountability – is the tool to achieve such excellence' (p. 2). While he refutes the ideas that high performance on test scores are predictors of national success in the future (if true, the US should be top, given its students' performances twenty to thirty years ago), he is not sanguine that the current educational paradigm will deliver a brighter future for US students.

Many education policies related to standards, testing, and accountability are driven by educators who seem convinced that education must, primarily, be the servant of economic and industrial development. They proclaim that employers want school graduates to have very specific skills that are best developed by concentrating on a narrow range of subjects (the basics) and then testing to see how well students have mastered the basic skills in these subjects. When asked directly, however, most employers say they want creative thinkers, problem solvers, potential innovators and entrepreneurs, team players, and graduates who are adaptable and self-confident (Robinson, 2011, p. 69).

Why is there this large disconnect in thinking? Perhaps part of the answer is that educators overall do not necessarily read the emerging signs of the times and, anyway, some claim that education is mostly preoccupied with preserving a dying paradigm and with protecting the status quo. The influential headmaster of Wellington College in England (the biographer for John Major, Tony Blair and Gordon Brown), Anthony Seldon (2010), offers an explanation. He is critical of the current status of state education in England and Wales and states that too many state schools in Britain have become 'factories'. He points out that while on paper results have improved, this achievement comes at a great cost because:

> reluctant students are processed through a system which is closely controlled and monitored by the state. No area of public life is more important than education to prepare people to live meaningful, productive and valuable lives. Yet our schools turn out young people who are often incapable of living full and autonomous lives (p. 1).

Much harsher criticism of contemporary schools and schooling, primarily in Australia, is offered by Higgins (2011), a long-time director of a Catholic education system. He is especially critical of those who push standards, testing and accountability in schools as the simple answer to complex questions and challenges. He believes that these people, whom he calls education rationalists, 'seek to quantify everything that matters and, in the quantification, end up with things which are easy to measure but hard to treasure' (p. 5). He argues that these rationalists, in pushing for high performance schools, 'have, in fact, in many ways trivialised and minimised the aspirations of all concerned.' They have, he states, contracted the curriculum to a few easily measurable subjects and outcomes and attempted to have these outcomes 'enshrined as if they are the purpose of the educational act to such an extent that the worth of the child, the teacher, the principal and the school are supposedly able to be accurately quantified (as to their quality) by these measurements. It is a sham' (p. 6).

Hargreaves and Fink (2006) discuss other negative effects of recent education reform movements and, from their research in Canada, the US and England, conclude that the past decade has seen 'the educational reform and standards movement plummet to the depths of unsustainability' (p. 9). While acknowledging that the standards movement started with good intentions – 'improving all students' achievement and narrowing the gap between the richest and the poorest of them' (p. 10) – instead, it 'has degenerated into a compulsive obsession with standardisation (one literacy or mathematics program for everyone, one size fits all) and the ruthless pursuit of market competition ("our standards are going to be higher than your standards, whatever that takes")' (p. 9).

They recommend that to deliver an education that responds better to the needs of twenty-first century children, there is an urgent need to:

1 reduce the excess of standardised testing;

2 become less punitive toward school underperformance;

3 restore educational diversity (a broader and more diverse curriculum with teachers having greater choice and discretion); and

4 develop policies and practices to attract and retain high-quality teachers (p. 15).

In the US, Dufour and Marzano (2011) point to the magnitude of the challenge facing most educators at all levels; they are 'called upon to raise academic standards to the highest level in history with common core standards that are so rigorous and include such challenging cognitive demands that they align with the highest international benchmarks' (p. 5). They also are required to 'bring every student to these dramatically higher standards of academic achievement. No generation of educators in the history of the United States has ever been asked to do so much for so many' (p. 5). Making this challenge even more difficult is the fact that 'the resources available to support their efforts are being slashed' (p. 6).

This theme is continued by City et al. (2009), who are especially critical of contemporary educational delivery systems, especially those characterised by didactic teaching, slavish coverage of content in an overcrowded curriculum, and children in rows of desks in closed classrooms. They recommend an antidote to these, which involves:

> *an organisational learning process* in which educators work systematically together … to build the knowledge and skills necessary for instructional improvement … [a] *culture-building process* in which educators explicitly challenge the norms of privacy of practice, [and a] *political process* that is designed to strengthen and deepen the role that educators play in the broader school reform debate (p. 187, italics in original).

They also recommend that, contrary to current practice, people with a deep knowledge of teaching, learning and the developmental learning stages of children must be consulted (and listened to) about 'the details of the policies and the institutional arrangements that affect their work' (p. 187).

As we will discuss later in this chapter, and also in chapter 9, there are an increasing number of examples of educational reform at system and school levels that include these considerations while still respecting the need for standards, benchmarks, accountability, and smart testing used to inform evidence-based improvement (e.g., Fullan et al., 2006; Sharratt & Fullan, 2009; Delorenzo et al., 2009). Many influential writers on educational improvement and transformation agree that any emerging paradigm for education must include standards, accountability, and improvement-oriented evidence, all informed by authentic assessment. Even those educators who are strong advocates of personalised learning approaches within technologically rich, open and agile learning spaces support standards and evidence-driven improvement (e.g., Whitby, 2011).

A key challenge is that all this debate and differences of opinion (while healthy in itself) places educators and educational leaders between a rock and a hard place. They are torn between the demands of national curricula, standards for teachers and students, national testing and accountability regimes, and growing evidence that such external drivers do not produce the type of graduates that will best serve the emerging needs of our communities and societies. What are they to do? Possible answers are provided throughout this book, starting with the need for educational leaders to better understand the nature of schools as complex and dynamic organisations.

Schools are complex and dynamic organisations

Educators and educational leaders need to address another significant issue if their schools are to offer the type of education recommended by the protagonists for change (Jansen et al., 2011). They need to recognise that schools are living, complex, dynamic, mostly non-linear organisations, and respond accordingly. Many attempts to change schools and the education they provide tend to use traditional hierarchical, bureaucratic and linear structures and processes, with divided functional specialties and a focus on individuals, not the collective or the community. Contemporary educators are familiar with and use the language of schools as communities of learning but, too frequently, they think and act in linear ways which is 'often extremely narrow and rigid' (Hames, 2007, p. 110). While such thinking is appropriate for analysing, categorising and labelling, it does not easily 'facilitate a thorough grasp of relationships, transformations over time and other dynamic variables' (p. 110). The application of linear models of thinking to problem solving may, Hames says, 'perpetuate the illusion that we are solving complex structural issues when, in reality, all we are doing is resolving a few, discrete, easily detected, symptoms' (p. 110).

There is strong evidence to support the view that schools as organisations are essentially networks of non-linear fields of relationships and that leadership influence is not simply a linear process to be effected through managerial, supervisory or hierarchical processes (Duignan, 2010). In other words, human behaviour and human interaction in schools should not (and cannot) be broken down into discrete building blocks (e.g., direct instruction, assessment tasks, provision of feedback, separate subject content) in order for student outcomes to be dissected and analysed, with the premise that when we put the pieces back together we will have a better understanding of the whole. Most educators know this from the vast amount of literature, starting from seminal work of Senge (1992) and Wenger (1998) on learning organisations and learning communities. Educators consistently refer to their schools in language similar to 'learning community' or 'community of learners', yet many of them behave as if they were educating in factories and leading hierarchical, bureaucratic organisations (Seldon, 2010).

Sergiovanni (2007) agrees, and urges that community, not formal organisation, become the metaphor for schools because they are not and should not be defined by 'instrumental purposes, rationally conceived work systems, evaluation schemes designed to monitor compliance, or skilfully contrived positive interpersonal climates'. On the contrary, he believes communities are defined by their centres which are 'repositories of values, sentiments, and beliefs that provide the needed cement for uniting people in a common cause … and give meaning to school community life' (pp. 88–9).

If education reform in schools is to respond to the curricular, pedagogical and leadership policies and practices that are being mooted for the future of schools and schooling, then the metaphor of schools as communities of learning needs to be front and centre. When educators focus primarily on the separate functions of the system parts or on individual human behaviour (e.g., the functioning of mathematics departments, classroom teachers, assessment of students), they may miss out on the rich complexity of connections and patterns of relationships, as well as on new possibilities that emerge when humans interconnect and engage with each other in morally purposeful and mutually influential relationships (Walker, 2011).

An important implication for educators who believe in the metaphor of community is that they shouldn't attempt to solve large and complex challenges on their own. They should reach outwards for assistance. Weber (2010) cautions that the 'era of schools and educators talking only to themselves must come to an end' (p. 7). He suggests that no education system, no matter how innovative, 'will survive in the modern world by closing itself off to good ideas from a wide array of sources ... Failed schools fail in part due to their inability, or unwillingness to seek help on behalf of their students, while successful schools are constantly looking and reaching out' (p. 79).

Schools need to become powerful interconnected learning networks to 'support the lateral transfer of knowledge' (Caldwell, 2006) in order to transform themselves into authentic learning communities. This development will be facilitated, Caldwell suggests, by:

> tailoring to the needs of the school an advanced capacity for knowledge management, building a powerful learning community to ensure that staff are at the forefront of knowledge, participating in and sharing the leadership of networked learning communities and in other ways serving as a system leader ... (p. 193).

He concludes that students, teachers and others at the coal-face are empowered by such a transformation, which he calls a 'new enterprise logic' (p. 80) based on the need to 'respond to the needs of ... students and parents' by radically changing pedagogies for learning (p. 81).

The characteristics of these new 'radical pedagogies' (Degenhardt & Duignan, 2010) include a capacity in schools to: 'work in teams ... operate in networks to share knowledge, address problems and share resources ... [and develop] a sense of community and the building of strong social capital' (Caldwell, 2006, p. 81). While it will take time for the new enterprise logic to become embedded in the educational profession and in schools, the effort will be both a 'challenging adventure,' an 'exhilarating journey,' and it will require a 'readiness to engage in daring action' (p. 116).

It can be argued that this is exactly what Finland did as a high-achieving country in education when it began to engage in daring action over thirty years ago. Darling-Hammond (2010), in her very comprehensive analysis and critique of education systems in a number of countries, notes that starting back in the 1980s, Finland got rid of its 'rigid tracking system that had allocated differential access to knowledge to its young people and eliminated the state-mandated testing system that was used for this purpose' (p. 5). These were replaced with high-quality teachers and 'curriculum and assessments focused on problem solving, creativity, independent learning, and student reflection' (p. 5). These changes propelled student achievement in Finland to the top of the international rankings and helped close a once very large achievement gap.

All this was achieved without unnecessarily prescribing or restricting the curriculum. Students in Finnish schools are encouraged and supported to engage in active learning in order to 'develop metacognitive skills that help them to frame, tackle, and solve problems; evaluate and improve their own work; and guide their learning processes in productive ways' (Darling-Hammond, 2010, p. 170). While some may point out that the culture of Finland is quite different from other countries, it can be argued that all of the educational initiatives Finland has taken are compatible with what many policy makers and educators say they want in their own education systems (e.g., see the *Melbourne Declaration on Educational Goals for Young Australians*, 2008). A key obstacle to achieving such goals is that many education systems and schools don't seem to be capable or willing to break loose from traditional paradigms of education.

To achieve such an outcome, there is a need for a paradigm shift in education, especially in the areas of learning, teaching and leadership. We all can do it just as well as Finland. Yes, we can!

Need for a paradigm shift in education

There is an influential emerging language for the leadership of change in education and in schools that reflects a more enlightened, perhaps radical view of learning, pedagogy, teaching and leadership. The language of 'reform' with its emphasis on testing and accountability is being supplanted by one that focuses more on students and the quality of their learning, teachers as leaders of curriculum and pedagogy, and principals and leadership teams in schools as leaders of learning (Duignan & Cannon, 2011).

Two parallel developments – one on testing/accountability and another on learning/pedagogy – appear to coexist within many education systems, creating tensions for educators and challenging them to find a dynamic balance between them. In the meantime, educational policy makers and practitioners are being pushed and pulled by forces which appear to some to be incompatible, if not contradictory. These forces may very well characterise a transition period between a traditional and an emerging paradigm of education.

In an important contribution to this debate, an OECD Report (2008), titled *Innovating to learn, learning to innovate*, seems to despair of recent (over the past decade) educational reform movements and concludes that:

> *reforms have ultimately come up against a wall, or rather a ceiling, beyond which further progress seems impossible, leading increasing numbers of school administrators and educators to wonder whether schools do not need to be reformed but to be reinvented* (p. 22, italics in original).

Darling-Hammond (2010) is uncompromising in her view that many schools, especially secondary ones in the US, have dysfunctional learning environments because, like manufacturing industries that have failed recently, contemporary schools were designed in the last century 'as highly bureaucratic organisations – divided into grade levels and subject-matter departments, separate tracks, programs, and auxiliary services – each managed separately and run by carefully specified procedures engineered to yield standard products' (p. 62). She sees them as disempowering and, sometimes, dehumanising their teachers and students, with many of their students experiencing them as 'noncaring, even adversarial environments' (p. 63).

She decries the relentless pursuit of greater accountability in schools through high-stakes testing (a consistent criticism of contemporary schooling in a number of countries). She argues that the creation of state standards to guide student learning has had some positive impact by clarifying goals and, in cases where standards and assessments are well designed, has usefully upgraded expectations for knowledge and skills, as well as delivering some improvements for many students. A crucial problem, however, is that where 'low-quality tests have driven a narrow curriculum disconnected from the higher-order skills needed in today's world, educational quality has languished, especially for the least affluent students whose education has come increasingly to resemble multiple-choice test prep, instead of the skills students desperately need' (p. 67; also see Bezzina et al., 2009). Such developments, she argues, have been found to exert strong pressures 'to reduce the curriculum to subjects and modes of performance that are tested, and to encourage less focus on complex reasoning and performance' (p. 71). Poorly designed tests seem to have impacted negatively on both the nature of the curriculum offered to students and on the ways in which teachers teach, including some teachers cheating in order to get higher test results (Levitt & Dubner, 2006). In too many instances, testing tends to dictate the form and content of instruction.

The consequences of the general failure of state education in England to fully embrace rich engaging pedagogies supported by new technologies, as well as their obsession with narrow curriculum and relentless testing and accountability in 'factory schools', include the 'de-professionalisation of teachers, the dumbing down of teaching, the artificial separating of subjects, the development of superficial content, the destruction of creativity and originality, and the narrowing of the vision for education' (Seldon, 2010, pp. 28–33). These are hardly developments to encourage and support creativity and ingenuity in our educational leaders, teachers and students in preparing them for emerging knowledge societies.

It would seem that principals and other educators, generally, are challenged by the many tensions generated from numerous rapid contextual and educational changes and from living in a dynamic, complex transitionary phase between a fading and an emerging paradigm of schooling. Many of their long-accepted assumptions and ways of thinking with regard to learning, teaching and leadership are being challenged and questioned. Calls for the redesign, reinvention, reimagining, even a revolution of education and schooling, are creating challenges, confusion, even deep ideological uncertainty for many educational leaders (Degenhardt & Duignan, 2010; Delorenzo et al., 2009; OECD, 2008; Caldwell, 2006).

An emerging paradigm for educating our students

In recommending a new paradigm for education, Darling-Hammond (2010) reports that research on successful schools identifies a number of different characteristics, including, 'strong teaching faculties who work in organisational structures that create more coherence and a "communal" orientation, in which staff see themselves as part of a family and work together to create a caring environment' (p. 65). These schools are also characterised by 'stronger relationships [and] greater student involvement,' with staff and structures supporting student learning so that students can 'reconceptualise their possibilities and responsibilities, so that they can commit to themselves and their learning' (p. 65).

There is emerging evidence that some movement is occurring in education and schools toward adopting essential elements of a new paradigm while preserving the best characteristics of the older, more traditional one. While Sir Michael Barber (2011) – a senior adviser to Tony Blair and the Labour Party's policy agenda to improve English schools – supports the need for clear standards, accountability, smart testing and evidence-based reform, he believes that we should follow those education systems achieving sustainable improvement in student outcomes. He reports that these more successful systems deliberately set out to attract great teachers and educational leaders and provide them with timely, appropriate and continuing professional support. They also encourage and support their leaders to deliberately intervene to influence the quality of teachers, teaching and student outcomes. They are especially aware that everything they do in curriculum, pedagogy and leadership must have a clear moral purpose and high ethical standards. Given Sir Michael's standing internationally as an expert on education reform, his recommendations will be valued and heeded in other countries.

Despite some promising recent news on how the world's most improved school systems keep getting better (Mourshed et al., 2010, McKinsey Report), a continuing problem is that in too many education systems in too many countries an old paradigm of learning and teaching is still alive and well. While Barber (2011) recommends the need for sustained whole-system improvement, Delorenzo et al. (2009) note that, for many years, education systems in many countries have been trying to 'change, adjust, and tweak the existing traditional education system' (p. 2), but in order to radically change education they need fundamentally different educational philosophies and initiatives characterised by:

1 twenty-first century content – global awareness, financial, economic, business, entrepreneurial literacy, civil literacy, and health and wellness awareness;

2 learning and thinking skills – skills in critical thinking and problem solving, creativity, innovation, collaboration and media literacy;

3 information and communications technology literacy; and

4 life skills – skills in leadership, ethics, personal productivity and responsibility, self-direction, and social responsibility (p. 9).

To achieve such desirable learning processes and outcomes requires no less than a paradigm shift but a key challenge is that defenders of traditional paradigms of learning and teaching (of isolated, independent classrooms; didactic teaching; students fed an overcrowded curriculum) continually attempt to 'fix' and redesign the old ways of doing things, hoping that they will discover new ways of transforming the old. Even with the best of policies and intentions for curriculum and pedagogical innovation, as was the case in a recent state initiative in Australia, forces for regression to old ways and the old paradigm are very powerful (Bezzina et al., 2009). When evidence mounts that traditional ways of teaching are not adequately serving today's children (Robinson, 2011; Duignan & Cannon, 2011; Darling-Hammond, 2010; Hattie, 2009; Delorenzo et al., 2009; Caldwell, 2006), too many system leaders and school educators continue ploughing the same familiar furrow. They seem to confuse the rim of the rut with the horizon.

Breton and Largent (1996) provide an incisive explanation for why this may be happening. They say that working within a prevailing paradigm is an accepted, secure, and often well-rewarded place to be and even when 'anomalies – things that the paradigm cannot explain – start accumulating' (p. 7), most people hope that these will just go away. Changing paradigms, according to Breton and Largent, is very difficult and 'the more the paradigm fails to do its job, the more old-paradigm [apologists] try to make it work … We don't need a new paradigm, they believe, we just need to make the one we have work better' (p. 7).

A favourite ploy is to blame and demonise those who criticise the prevailing paradigm. 'Blame certain people and label them as troublemakers. We need more discipline, more restraints … more tests and tougher grading systems, more hard-nosed business management practices … more laws with stricter enforcement' (Breton & Largent, 1996, p, 8). After numerous, often discrete, failed attempts to fix the existing paradigm and in order to keep people in line, 'the solution is to take away more rights, stifle more creativity, intimidate more people' (p. 8). It could be argued that Breton and Largent's very perceptive analysis seems to explain why a number of our reform movements in education are judged to have failed to deliver on their promises and why we haven't yet moved far enough to embrace a new paradigm of education delivery, one that has been clearly articulated by a number of the key international experts in education discussed earlier.

In Australia, the state of Tasmania intentionally adopted an ethical and socially responsible curriculum focus but, ultimately, failed to implement it successfully. Bezzina et al. (2009) report that while the new curriculum innovations:

> acknowledged the fairly universal opinion that the values and purposes contained within the curriculum were morally responsible, and at face value met the future needs of society, they failed because they challenged the traditional paradigm of what a curriculum should look like and how to measure its outcomes (p. 15).

Educational leaders at every level need to question traditional paradigms and there are some promising examples to assist them coming from the business environment. Senge et al., (2004) claim that business leaders such as Bill Gates, Steve Jobs and Sam Walton have succeeded because they have developed the capacity 'to avoid imposing old frameworks on new realities'. They suggest that their secret is that they take action based on a 'different way of knowing,' (p. 84), one that has a different set of rules for decision-making. They 'feel out' what to do and 'hang back, [and] observe … like a surfer or a really good race car driver … making sense as [they] go' (p. 85). Senge et al. use the examples of Chinese and Japanese artists who may sit observing a landscape for a whole week, drinking it all in, and then they move quickly to paint the scene. This approach represents a different and 'deeper level of knowing' (p. 85) that informs and shapes quick action.

Relating these examples and ways of knowing to leaders facing difficult decisions with teaching and learning, the advice is for leaders to slow down, avoid knee-jerk responses, observe carefully, and position themselves to act fast 'with a natural flow that comes from the inner knowing' (p. 86). Faced with difficult decision situations, similar to those discussed in chapter 3, the advice to leaders is to slow down long enough 'to really see what's needed' and then 'with a freshness of vision [they] have the possibility of a freshness of action, and the overall response on a collective level can be much quicker than trying to implement hasty decisions that aren't compelling to people' (p. 86).

In an insightful argument, Senge et al. (2004) recommend a type of decision-making that is not only informed by past experiences but also from an interrogation of an emerging future and 'from continually discovering our part in bringing that future to pass' (p. 86). This is essential for educational leaders involved in leading a paradigm shift in education, because learning based primarily on the past 'suffices when the past is a good guide to the future. But it leaves us blind to profound shifts when whole new forces shaping change arise' (p. 86). This is exactly the position in which many educational leaders now find themselves. What should they do? Senge et al. seem to provide a wise and realisable answer.

They argue that 'when you're facing very difficult issues or dilemmas, when very different people need to align in very complex settings, and when the future might really be very different from the past, a different process [of decision-making] is required' (p. 87). This new process involves 'sensing and actualizing new realities prior to their emerging' by distinguishing 'different depths of perceiving reality and different levels of action that follow from that' (p. 87). They conceptualise this as a 'U movement' involving: *sensing* (observe, observe, observe, and become one with the situation) *presencing* (retreat and reflect, allow inner knowing to emerge); and *realising* (act swiftly with a natural flow) (p. 88, author's italics).

In contrasting this approach with what they call standard leadership processes of change, they point out that often in the standard model:

> leaders are separate from what they're seeking to change. For example, executives seek to 'change their organisation,' as if it were an entity separate from themselves. They then find themselves frustrated when others resist the planned changes (p. 92).

They suggest that the concept of the U movement poses an important question: 'What does it mean to act in the world and not on the world?' (p. 92). Many educational leaders could benefit from asking themselves this question but, too frequently, they continue to be stifled in their knowing and acting by externally imposed imperatives and internally developed frames that take their shape from traditional ways of knowing and acting. These frames can have disastrous consequences for themselves, their colleagues, as well as the culture and outcomes of their system or organisation.

Jackson (2004), critiquing education delivery in the UK, points to a current malaise in education and educational leadership because of a decade of what he calls externally imposed stifling reform, characterised by 'testing at every stage throughout the system, with elite tables of key stage results; parental choice; funding linked to pupil numbers; schools challenged to achieve publicly stated targets; and performance management for staff with linked pay' (p. 3). School leaders have, simply, been swamped and grossly distracted by external pressures, expectations and demands that have turned out not to meet goals and expectations. In the meantime, in defence of principals and other school leaders, it is somewhat understandable that they opt for what they know best, the 'tried and true.' Jackson seems to hit the nail on the head when he concludes about what the reform movement, especially in England, has or has not achieved:

> At this point, we could have a debate about what this reform has or has not achieved. I could tell you that our teachers are tired, morale is low, we have difficulties with recruitment and not all children are putting their hands up and saying this school is the most exciting place they've ever been (p. 3).

If this is even partly true it suggests that the culture in UK schools may be in need of a paradigm change. I accept that Jackson's words were penned in 2004 and that Barber (2011) and others, like Sharratt and Fullan (2009), would ague that we have learned much about how education systems and schools have improved themselves, but, according to some influential and respected international educational commentators, too many education systems and schools may still be guilty of outmoded thinking and practices that are not working for today's children (e.g., Beare, 2010; Darling-Hammond, 2010; Seldon, 2010; Weber, 2010; Delorenzo et al., 2009; Hargreaves, 2009; Reeves, 2008). In other words, the jury is still out and the verdict could still be 'guilty as charged.'

We need to ask, however, what does this new paradigm involve for educational leaders? The practicalities of the new paradigm will include 'building professional communities of learners and learning' with a focus on 'learning-centred leadership' (Duignan & Cannon, 2011, p. 27). They recommend that the emphasis has to be on leadership that reflects a 'collective, collegial endeavour and [is] not seen as the sole responsibility of any individual, such as the principal' (p. 27). A new enterprise logic requires a collective and sustainable ethic of responsibility for leadership where all key stakeholders have appropriate involvement in key decisions that affect them and, thereby, develop a sense of ownership of interventions as members of their learning community.

In an influential OECD Report on improving school leadership policy and practices, Pont et al. (2008) provide strong support for the reinvention of leadership when they argue that school leadership responsibilities should be (re)defined 'through an understanding of the practices most likely to improve teaching and learning' (p. 9). Hargreaves (2009) argues that in the near future policy makers in education will have to 'concede that innovation and creativity require different, more flexible conditions of teaching, learning and leadership than those that have prevailed in the era of test-driven and data-obsessed educational reform' (pp. 29–30). Such developments will require schools to banish isolationist attitudes and enhance relationships; increase professional collegiality, especially among teachers; generate a greater commitment to openness, networking and learning in order to become professional learning communities.

He charts a challenging but exciting future when he predicts that his fourth way of reform 'lies in less bureaucracy, and more democracy; in collaboration more than competition; in innovation and inspiration, more than data-driven intervention; in the fear factor giving way to the peer factor as the driver of school reform' (p. 32). I'm with Hargreaves in his statement about education: 'This can be its future. Now is our moment of choice' (p. 32). We need to choose wisely.

There is no apparent reason why we cannot develop a judicious balance of the best of the old and new paradigms. It is not a matter of old wine in new bottles but a much more mature wine in a variety of bottles of different shapes and sizes. There are a number of examples in the literature on school improvement and learning transformation of how to produce such mature wine (LTLL, 2006–2011; Darling-Hammond, 2010; City et al., 2009; Sharratt & Fullan, 2009; Fullan et al., 2006). Detailed consideration of these examples will be included in the discussions on how educational leaders can build rich, engaging, evidence-based and technologically-inspired learning environments in chapter 9.

An increasingly important element in choosing a new paradigm is how technology can help us implement it. Most authors and researchers who support the need for such a paradigm change see the use of smart technologies as integral to its success.

Technology for learning now and in the future

In order for technology to effectively serve the transition to a transformed paradigm, it is important to see it as seamlessly part of the pedagogy of learning and not as a tool to assist in and facilitate learning. We have moved through a number of phases in using technology in the pedagogy of teaching and learning, from being what Prensky (2001) referred to as *digital immigrants* (generation X) and *digital natives* (generation Y) to what I call *digital naturals*, also named iGeneration (Rosen, 2011) or 'Screenagers' (Scherer, 2011). My grandchildren do not see tablet computers, smartphones or laptops as objects or tools to be used; they take them for granted as essential personal, social and cultural ways of living a full life in these digital times. They think of technology as enabling them in their personal and social connectivity in an increasingly networked world. Most schools need to appreciate their perspectives better.

There is little doubt that the exponential growth of social media such as Twitter, Facebook, Flickr and YouTube have changed the social landscape for young people and given new meaning to the concept of the global village. These social media have extended, perhaps permanently redrawn, the boundaries of the 'self' in relationships, and catapulted them into a plethora of interconnected social global networks. Most young people's sense of community is boundaryless with one social network of relationships morphing into others. The medium is no longer just the message, as Marshall McLuhan so eloquently phrased it in the 1970s, but it also helps create a global context and mediated social meaning for the message. In a connected world, meaning is constantly discussed, negotiated and redefined to make it relevant to the realities of our lives and contemporary modes of living.

While some of our schools operate as if social dynamics and networks of relationships are still the same as those of the mid-twentieth century, Zhao (2009) argues that they must refocus on new and emerging digital competencies for their students. He recommends that these competencies must be broad, rich and diverse, and urges that we have to get beyond the idea that technology can assist teachers in raising test scores and embrace the view that it creates the potential 'for students … to be creative in art and music, to develop social skills in virtual worlds, and to stay engaged with school' (p. 196). New technologies can 'present new possibilities for creative work' (Robinson, 2011, p. 205) but when they are still new to us and we are learning their potential, they 'tend to be used for the same old thing' (p. 204).

The same old thing simply isn't good enough any more. The rapid advances in high-speed interactive technologies and the continuing emergence of new ones, according to Ackerman and Maslin-Ostrowski (2002), 'poses even more adaptive challenges to educators who place a high value on natural, open, and honest communication' (pp. 132–3). They advise educators and educational leaders not to be suffocated as individuals by the deluge of new technologies but to keep their 'own human voices unmistakably real in the so-called information age so that [they] can enable and nurture human organisational structures, forms, and, especially, leadership that remains passionately committed to human learning in all its infinite variety' (p. 133). What an exciting challenge they present for educators and educational leaders!

In an insightful book about the need for rethinking education for the age of technology, Collins and Halverson (2009) argue for the consideration of educational needs, 'not in isolation, but … the interplay of society, education, and learning' (p. 129). They recommend that thinking about learning also has to change because 'if schools cannot change fast enough to keep pace with advances in learning technologies, learning will leave schools behind' (p. 131). They caution that if exponents of traditional pedagogies continue to impose established methods of learning in schools, 'technologies will leech critical learning resources, such as student motivation, attention, and resources, out of the education system. Trying to reassert the identification of schooling and learning will be a losing battle' (p. 131). While this caution seems somewhat alarmist, perhaps even fanciful, there is little doubt that the continually advancing capabilities of technology will help drive an education paradigm change that will require qualitative leaps in teachers' and leaders' mindsets on pedagogy and technology-enhanced learning.

In a specific example of how teachers' learning mindsets can change with their use of technology for learning, Bower (2011), in a 'technology enhanced assessment for learning' project which involved this author, set out to enhance teachers' ability to differentiate the curriculum using Web 2.0 technologies and student response systems in a cluster of schools – three primary and one secondary – over a two-year period. In a differentiated learning environment, students learn at different paces and in different ways, so teachers present lessons in a form that suits every type of learner.

This is a challenge for many teachers because learning how to differentiate effectively involves a process of discovery, concept affiliation, and pursuit of additional knowledge, and the persistence to follow through involves capabilities that many traditional teachers do not possess (Bower, 2011). One key to making this form of learning possible is an appropriate use of social networking technologies that are becoming more common in the classroom. Encouraging a participatory student culture using student response systems and Web 2.0 tools enables teachers to differentiate lessons and allows them to monitor each student individually (Burley, 2011).

In the differentiated learning project, the teachers were provided with intensive training in the use of the interactive technologies and were also supported in their use in classrooms. Bower (2011) reports that 'the program was able to significantly improve teachers' perceptions of their ability to provide differentiated learning pathways, sharpen their conceptions of what is meant by alternative learning pathways, and increase the extent to which they used differentiated learning approaches in their classes' (pp. 29–30). This surely involves a mindset change about learning. There is also evidence to suggest that it helps teachers find their voice on issues related to learning and teaching and develops a pride and confidence in them as professionals. A future challenge is for the schools and the teachers involved to sustain these newly developed capabilities.

There are also concrete signs that such new technologies will be further used to enhance the value of tests and other assessments. In a report titled, 'Beyond the bubble test: how will we measure learning in the future?', Barseghian (2011a) comments on an announcement by the US Secretary of Education in September 2010, in which he claimed to be excited by a new way of testing students, one that goes beyond the 'bubble test'. He criticises the standardised assessments students in the US take every year as not only useless in measuring any kind of real learning, but as being detrimental to the entire education system. He commends an initiative to create tests that focus on 'performance-based tasks, designed to mirror complex real-world situations' (in Barseghian, 2011a, p. 1). The Secretary of Education also reported that these new tests, which will replace standardised bubble tests, could help transform the nation's education system and provide a platform for new approaches to learning and schooling.

There are, however, some obstacles that must be overcome for technology use to be successful in US schools. Barseghian (2011b) comments on a presentation by Catalano, Principal of Intrinsic Strategy, at the AEP Content on Context Conference

(2010) held in Washington DC and organised by the Association of Educational Publishers. Catalano reports that while there is a plethora of technology initiatives in education across the US, there is need for a more planned, consistent and coherent national approach. He also identified web filtering/blocking software in schools and department approval policies as significant obstacles to broader and more creative use of digital resources and technology. While positive steps in the uses of technology-informed and supported learning are increasing in US schools, a consensus from the conference presentations is that there is still a considerable way to go. Similar obstacles are evident in other countries.

For example, Seldon (2010) critiques the use of technologies in English schools and argues that while information and communication technology has revolutionised school administration capabilities with regard to the management of information, it has not yet revolutionised teaching and learning. He suggests that too many teachers today 'are still using it merely as a sophisticated version of chalk and blackboard … We have yet to get fully to grip … with young people's intimacy with digital technologies, and the influence it has on their intellectual development and cognitive skills' (pp. 3–4).

Perhaps we are still at an early phase of technology use in education. If so, we need to address this problem as a matter of urgency, else we will fail to prepare our students for the knowledge society within which they will have to survive and, hopefully, thrive. The constant changes in the potential and possibilities of communication technologies has led to the creation of what is generally referred to as 'the knowledge society', which is 'stimulated and driven by creativity and ingenuity' (Hargreaves, 2003, p. 1; see also Hargreaves & Shirley, 2009). A knowledge society, according to Hargreaves, is essentially a learning society that helps people 'process information and knowledge in ways that maximise learning, stimulate ingenuity and invention, and develop the capacity to initiate and cope with change' (p. 3).

Whitby (2007) describes the knowledge society as characterised by its speed, innovation, interactivity and constant openness to new learning. Our schools, therefore, should be at the forefront of efforts to create the learning conditions and environments that will enable students not just to cope with, but to help create and flourish in a knowledge society. Undoubtedly, creative use of cutting-edge technology must be at the core of efforts to serve the core values and moral purpose of education in every school. Authentic leaders will know that the ethical thing to do in order to properly serve the needs of children is to provide them with technologically-charged, rich and engaging (interactive) learning environments. For leaders not to do so would be both inauthentic and unethical (Starratt, 2004).

One way to proceed is to give highly skilled teachers and schools the necessary degrees of professional autonomy and responsibility in their practices and enable them to be more creative and flexible with their students (Hargreaves, 2003;

Hargreaves & Shirley, 2009). We have little hope, however, of achieving the status of a knowledge society if teachers continue to believe that they are strait-jacketed by tightly controlled external drivers of standards, curriculum structures and content, and assessment processes.

It will be very difficult to achieve the best of Hargreaves and Shirley's (2009) 'fourth way' reform if we do not have effective and authentic leadership in our schools. We also need to strengthen the collective leadership capacities of education systems and schools and make them more sustainable than they are currently. Robinson (2011) reminds us that creativity is usually 'driven more by collaboration than by solo efforts' (p. 211), and is inspired by positive, can-do cultures that create team synergies and a sense that together we can meet and overcome any challenges.

Building sustainable collective leadership

While the issue of building sustainable collective leadership capacities will be discussed in more detail in chapter 7, it is introduced here because it presents a key challenge for educational leaders if the essentials of the new education paradigm are to be realised. This challenge is well recognised in the literature on educational leadership, as well as by many influential educational policy makers and practitioners (e.g., Duignan & Cannon, 2011; Walker, 2011; Sharratt & Fullan, 2009; Hargreaves & Fink, 2006; Caldwell, 2006). Yet many of the attempts to deepen and strengthen the leadership of schools has focused on traditional conceptualisations of leadership, especially of the principal, or those selected or designated by the principal. As we will see in chapter 7, attempts at developing leadership succession policies and practices – as well as generating shared and distributed approaches to leadership in school systems and schools – tend to focus on traditional, individual-based, linear and hierarchical views of principalship, and on the role of the principal (Duignan & Cannon, 2011). This is a very limited view of the influence possibilities of leaders and leadership in schools.

The many pressures and tumultuous changes of an emerging knowledge society exert strong pressures on school leaders who are often frustrated and confused, prompting them to respond as individuals. The potential impact of these pressures is well described by Hames (2007):

> The sun is setting on the fossil-fuelled age of industrial economism. Meanwhile, another revolution dawns, heralding the first global knowledge age. An age likely to be characterised by tumultuous changes to who we are, what is important to us, and how we live our lives. On this helter-skelter journey, nothing is the same today as it was yesterday. All we can know for sure is that it will be different again tomorrow. No wonder we're all feeling confused and powerless! (p. 109).

While such confusion and uncertainty for leaders can be sourced to the pressures highlighted by Hames, Walker (2011) reminds us that there is another important source of frustration in schools and that is the challenge of putting together all the jigsaw pieces that are part of the complexity of the school. He suggests that 'we know more than ever about a wide array of elements that work in a school, but not much about how they fit together, or how leaders pull them together' (p. 9). School leaders, he suggests, possess 'more of the pieces of the puzzle but don't understand about how they come together to form a coherent curricular, pedagogical and organisational whole, one that resonates positively throughout the school' (p. 9). As discussed earlier in this chapter, schools are more complex and dynamic than many school leaders seem to appreciate or understand and when they feel confused by relentless changes and constant challenges they tend to resort to individualised responses and the use of well-known, traditional hierarchical structures and processes. But traditional approaches will not necessarily help them make meaning of the complex dynamic connectivity and the overlapping networks of relationships that characterise contemporary schools. They need help to do this.

One of the best ways to come to such a deeper understanding of their schools' complexity is through courageous conversation and dialogue, where the varied perspectives of students, parents, teachers and other key stakeholders are shared, carefully considered and, where appropriate, acted upon. Constructive engagement, dialogue and consultation are essential in today's organisations if their leaders are to be influential (Duignan & Cannon, 2011). Jackson (2004) of the National College for School Leadership in the UK, previously a school principal for fifteen years, states that 'leading schools and developing systems is a complex, chaotic and intuitive business. There isn't much clarity on a day-to-day basis, and you don't often drive home after work thinking that you've been running a successful business' (p. 1). This is much more likely to happen if you think that the challenges of school leadership revolve around, or have to be solved by, *you* as principal. Such an approach can have harmful results leading to severe, even devastating life–work tensions.

To counter this problem, school environments need to be constructed within which curiosity and the natural desire to openness in leadership can be nourished and enhanced by all members of an educational community, aimed toward 'helping leaders value themselves, and toward uncovering the spirit in emotional discovery that leads the leader to become a life-long learner' (Ackerman & Maslin-Ostrowski, 2002, p. 133). Above all, it aims toward an awareness that 'genuine leadership is not something dependent on outside sources but [is] instead within all of us' (p. 133). Part of this perspective is that influential school leadership not only comes from within the self, but also from within others and from within the school. There are many talented and expert people in a variety of positions and at different levels in schools. Surely it is a sensible leadership decision to involve them more as a collective in making key decisions on curriculum structures and content, relevant learning pedagogies for diverse learning styles, and other educational issues that impact directly on their lives and the lives of their students. Maximising leadership influence in schools demands a collective ethic of responsibility (discussed in chapter 7).

Concluding comments

In this chapter a number of macro challenges have been discussed and their implications for educators and educational leaders considered. These macro challenges form a framework that can help educators and educational leaders better appreciate and understand the forces and pressures on contemporary education and on schools. To more deeply understand these pressures is to be better prepared to respond to them.

While these macro challenges continue to change in response to emerging global and societal developments, the micro challenges presented in the next chapter seem to be perennials for educational leaders, even though responses to them will change in emphasis depending on the evolving nature of the macro challenges.

Key ideas for reflection

The following questions focus on the key ideas in this chapter. You are encouraged to take some time to reflect on them and generate some practical leadership strategies in response to the major macro challenges.

1 In what ways would your understanding of a school as a complex and dynamic network of relationships impact on your philosophy and approach to leadership?

2 It would appear that we are in transition from a traditional paradigm of education to a new one. What are the leadership challenges for you in leading this transition?

3 There is strong evidence to suggest that the lone-ranger approach to educational leadership has passed its use-by date. The way forward involves building sustainable leadership capacities in schools. What adjustments, if any, will you need to make in your leadership in order to build these capacities?

4 Much is written about the importance of integrating interactive technologies in teaching and learning in the future. In your opinion, what are the challenges for educational leaders in supporting this development?

Chapter 3

Key micro challenges for educational leaders

The micro challenges in this chapter are accompanied by illustrative real-life cases generated by school leaders. Some of the details of these cases have been changed to help protect anonymity without affecting their key messages. The following cases appeared in the earlier version of this book but are still relevant to and valid in today's schools. The author has continued to interact with school leaders around the content of these cases, and they confirm the reality they represent for them in leading schools.

Personal and professional relationships

Most educational leaders will say that leadership is, essentially, relational. Those who have been apprenticed in a hierarchical, control-type model of leadership are, however, often unsure of how close they should relate to others, especially with those who are accountable to them. It is important to distinguish here between personal and professional relationships in organisations. Professional relationships will, of course, have a personal dimension, but it is equally important to develop personal relationships within a professional framework. The issue is not how friendly formal leaders should be with those who work with them, but how all organisational members can work together professionally as a team to achieve the goals and objectives of the organisation.

Professional relationships must always be predicated on the core values espoused in the organisation. Being honest, trusting and trustworthy, respectful, tolerant, empathetic, open to critique, and willing to be a team person are as essential to professional relationships as they are to the development and maintenance of personal relationships. In a school setting, core values also include valuing students and the educational processes that best serve their needs. The bottom line in a school community setting is how well relationships serve the needs of students and their parents.

Often, however, educational leaders face the problem of dealing with unprofessional behaviour while balancing their professional responsibility for ensuring the smooth operation of their organisation, with their personal feelings for those staff acting unprofessionally. Time and again the practical difficulties related to this issue were noted in interviews and cases in the study. A typical example was provided by a school principal:

> My clerical assistant has been very unprofessional and, at times, rude and unhelpful to all of her colleagues. I have had interviews with her regarding her attitude and interpersonal skills. The incidents are repeated almost daily and occur in the workplace. They impinge upon others' personal lives as well.

Many educational leaders find it difficult to face up to finding a resolution to such problems. They prefer to think that if they ignore the situation it will go away. Some such challenges are potentially very serious issues and are often the source of much concern and stress for leaders. A principal of a school described a lengthy tension-filled event that he found very difficult to manage:

> I can give you an example of one [tension] that we've just had recently which is: we've got a young boy who has been here for three years and he's diagnosed as having [medical] problems and is on medication and he is a big lad and his home life isn't so wonderful. He takes out his aggression here at school. What happened last year is that we had another lad here who is physically handicapped and for whatever reason this other boy decided that he wanted to attack him and he did; he actually kicked him and bruised him. The parents of the injured boy were very upset but they were prepared to forgive.
>
> The staff here thought that this was an outrage and regardless of the parents they wanted the boy [who'd attacked the other] removed. It was an interesting situation, in that the dilemma I had was all about: where does this boy go if we remove him from the school? The parents were forgiving and understanding and were prepared to just set up structures so it wouldn't happen again and also to guarantee that this boy would never go near their son again. That was a major tension because it took a little while to realise that we couldn't guarantee to this other family that we could be everywhere all the time with this boy … What it meant for me was an awful lot of sleepless nights worrying about all the different avenues.

These issues are illustrative of the range and difficulty of the challenges involved when dealing with tension situations involving leading people in educational organisations. Educational leaders often avoid confronting such problems if they can, because they believe that solutions are hard to find and the legal environment of the employment contract often ensures that the poor performer or difficult person will not be dealt with promptly, if ever. So a response often is: 'Why put yourself in an unwinnable position that may also undermine your future effectiveness as a leader?'

Managing staff relationships

Many educational leaders find it surprising how building and managing relationship in their schools can be such a challenge and yet they know that effective relationships are the energy source of leadership. A principal shared his views on how leaders can build authentic relationships:

> The promotion of staff morale, keeping staff motivated, cultivating teamwork and providing opportunities for staff development are some of the greatest challenges for leaders of educational organisations. It could be said that valuing others is a common thread in these elements and provides an authentic bond between the leader and those in the group.

Empowering others by simply trusting people to get on with their tasks underpins effective leader–staff relationships in ways that link strategic purpose to everyday practices. When trust is breached there is a tendency to retreat to the classical organisational model, with remote personal exchanges, reliance on quasi-legal rules, and withdrawal to a hierarchical and bureaucratic form of control. A principal of a school commented on what happens when trust is betrayed:

> What happens to the leadership relationship when there is a massive breach of trust? This is not an uncommon occurrence. The leader retreats to a position of power and control. The aggrieved staff members feel excluded and do not give of their best. Morale is affected adversely.

Some leaders believe that developing relationships requires too much with regard to time and resources. This is an inappropriate way to think about relationship building. Developing relationships for their own sake, or conversely for instrumental purposes, is not what authentic leaders do. They regard relationship building as one of the core ways that leaders value all those who work in and for them. It is the way a school, as a community, actively and fully engages its talented key stakeholders, giving them a sense of belonging and encouraging and supporting their commitment to the vision and moral purpose of the organisation. Building relationships is not just a matter of managing people but of providing the leadership necessary to build a culture of trust (Tschannen-Moran, 2004) within which everyone feels responsible and accountable for the overall performance of their school community.

Managing accountability and individual performance

The high public pressure for accountability in schools discussed in chapter 2, means that there is a constant challenge to improve performance outcomes for students. The economic rationalist philosophy and management practices that have influenced governments since the mid-1980s are continuing to drive many educational systems and schools. Many people in the education sector see this rationalist approach as dominated by an expectation of 'doing more with less'. A principal claimed that the prevailing management expectations have led directly to a change in culture in schools from a former collegial approach to one that is less open and collaborative:

> I think [there is a] complete change in culture and the way in which the organisation now operates. It's quite different from what we experienced [in the past], for example, it used to be a much more open and collaborative style but it has become quite different to that now ... there is much less openness, much less collaboration.

Both scarcity of and constraints on resources are apparent in many educational systems. However, it is not always clear whether this situation is driven by increased expectations of what can be achieved or by constant cuts in the resources available. Whatever the case, contemporary leaders perceive themselves as having to juggle their strategic objectives against the reality of reducing resources.

It appears that a balance needs to be struck between 'hard' and 'soft' approaches to leadership so that leaders accept their responsibilities and accountabilities without feeling overwhelmed and resorting to heartless and soulless practices and relationships. A balance between personal responsibility and teamwork is also desirable, where the burdens are shared to make the pressures more bearable. We need to develop a more formative and developmental approach to accountability because current approaches often appear summative and punitive. Accountability processes must be just and equitable and should clearly reflect the core values espoused by the organisation. Where values are ignored or violated, accountability processes will be seen to be, and most likely will be, antithetical to the real moral purposes of an educational system or school.

Apart from external pressures, the issue of dealing with poor performance in a responsible and professional manner that considers the interests of all concerned emerged as one of the most significant accountability challenges for educational leaders. Many leaders feel frustrated by the general reluctance of system personnel and others to deal with poor performance, often due to the perceived difficulty of the legal and industrial issues involved. For example, a principal considered it virtually impossible to improve the performance of poorly performing teachers because, in his view, the union mostly supports the teacher without seeking to find out the facts.

While governments and education departments often take a strong line on this issue in the media, it is the principal who usually has to deal with the direct tensions and trauma involved (Degenhardt & Duignan, 2010). Apart from the uncertainty of knowing if they have made good decisions, principals have the stress of dealing with the emotional issues as well as the facts of each situation. A principal provided an insightful example of the difficulties associated with many issues of poor performance:

> At our school we have a teacher in his early fifties who has difficulty with consistency, leading to poor classroom management structures with some children in his class every year. The teacher is a nice person, well-liked by his peers. Most of the children in his class continue to perform at a reasonable level. However, this year three boys regularly disrupt the class. One of these boys, an extremely difficult child, is a challenge for any teacher.

The teacher in this example had taught at the school for over twenty years and during that time many staff worked with him to help with preparation and management strategies; however, similar problems seemed to appear nearly every year. The stress affected the teacher's wellbeing but he could not see any alternatives to teaching.

The principal in this situation had not instigated formal procedures for dismissal because he regarded teaching as a caring occupation and the role of educational leader as one of helping and supporting people in a difficult profession where it is almost impossible to influence all thirty children in a class to the same level. The principal stressed that dealing with poor-performing staff is not as clear-cut as is often portrayed by the media or by political leaders.

The following example further illustrates this challenge for principals. A principal of a small K–12 school appointed a new teacher, about fifty years old, who had already converted a nursing degree into a qualification to teach biology and health education. In a very short space of time it became obvious, however, that she was going to struggle to get teacher registration. The principal had to decide whether to look after the teacher's personal welfare and provide her with far more support than would be normal, knowing that otherwise the educational outcomes for her students could be disastrous.

Eventually, district office personnel were alerted to the problem and accepted a recommendation that the teacher's probation be extended and that she be moved to another, larger, school with more resources to assist her. Mostly, the principal suggested that this was not a very satisfactory solution to such a problem; in fact, it merely shifted the problem sideways. Reflecting on this experience, the principal pointed out that the first responsibility for an educational leader is to ensure the best possible outcomes for the students and suggested that in future he would:

> 'Bite the bullet': tackle the performance issue head-on and early. Any personal issues arising from this course of action will need to be dealt with, but I can no longer support or overlook inefficient teaching practices because of personal problems.

Another case illustrated that a failure to act quickly and appropriately may have a negative impact on the individual teacher, the students, or both. It also illustrates how a leadership challenge often presents dilemmas and tensions to those trying to resolve it. The principal of a probationary teacher whose substandard performance led to complaints from students and parents reported this case. This teacher, who had also retrained from a previous career, grabbed or hit students on two occasions. Although he had been on a program of improvement, he showed little sign of progress and the principal did not believe he would ever achieve an acceptable level of performance. The principal, however, had concerns about the teacher's mental state, and had to weigh up this concern for the welfare of the teacher with his potentially disastrous impact on the students. The principal felt that he had no real choice, and decided to protect the welfare of the students by advising the teacher to seek an alternative career, or else he would initiate formal proceedings for dismissal. The teacher appreciated the principal's concern for the students, revealing that he had similar concerns himself, and resigned his position.

In another example, a principal made the decision to dismiss a teacher who had been placed on a support and development program that extended over two years. The teacher's ability to interact appropriately and effectively with staff was an issue. The principal involved the industrial relations personnel, a supervisor at the school, the teacher concerned, and a support person for the teacher, as well as the union. He considered that not only was there no evidence to indicate that the teacher was able to complete the required tasks, but also that any further assistance would require the input of huge resources from other staff, which would impact on their workload and stress levels, without an appreciable outcome. Reflecting on the incident, the principal concluded that, in spite of what policies state, when you are dealing with human beings, you are dealing with complexity. He decided that one must be pragmatic but must act for the good of the many.

The majority opinion of educational leaders in this study was that teacher performance problems can and should be identified by leaders early in a teacher's career. Support and programs of development should be given to those so identified. If a teacher shows no evidence of improvement as a result of such development opportunities, then those in leadership positions must protect the children under their care and set in train processes for the teacher to resign or be dismissed.

Communicate! Communicate! Communicate!

If effective leadership is relational, then a key to relationship building is effective communication. Good communication requires, first, that one has something purposeful to communicate; second, that one chooses appropriate times and means to deliver the message; and third, that one actively engages with others beyond a simple one-way communication to clarify the intended message and dispel misunderstandings. Respectful listening and meaningful dialogue with staff in their day-to-day working lives facilitates effective communication.

Large systems are sometimes slow to process issues and problems, so gaps in communication may occur between those who make the decisions and those who implement them. Leaders may assume that everyone in the organisation knows where they are going and why, but these are not safe assumptions. Many staff are often heard to say: 'Why doesn't anyone tell me anything around here?' or, 'Why am I the last to know what is happening around here?'

No matter how much communication is used, no matter how accessible it is, down the line or at the local level, messages will be subject to different interpretations. One of the responsibilities that leaders have is to correct misinterpretations and put to rest certain myths. Without this, sometimes the myths develop a life of their own and rumour can become accepted as fact.

There is no guaranteed process for ensuring that people in an organisation are optimally informed about new policies and changes. Often people will hear what they want to hear and reject or distort what they perceive not to be in their interests. The size of the organisation, of course, influences the degree to which formal leaders can engage in one-to-one conversations, which is the most effective form of communication. The CEO of a large bank in Australia made an art form of regularly communicating live online with all staff members on key topic areas or current issues. Staff generally appreciated his attempt to personalise his communication. A director of a school system in Australia uses blogs and wikis (as many now do) to get key messages to all stakeholders and to encourage them to engage in dialogue with him through their replies. From a time perspective this is a very difficult challenge for a leader but given the current sophistication of the technology infrastructure and software in most education systems, it is possible for leaders to periodically generate short visual messages on key issues of interest and beam them live into schools (or in a package sent to schools for a five-minute replay at staff meetings).

No matter how large the school community, educational leaders need to devise creative ways of engaging directly with key stakeholders. Every means, formal and informal, must be used to keep all stakeholders informed and up to date. If nature abhors a vacuum, then so do organisations: if communication isn't regular and meaningful, then someone (or some group) will invent a version of events, and rumours will spread to fill the void. This is especially true when leaders are attempting to bring about change in their organisations. Change usually threatens some stakeholders and fears can be exacerbated if the facts of the change are distorted or manipulated by those who are resistant to the change.

If key educational leaders are clear about the core values and vision for their school, understand how these values and vision can inspire others, and they have created a culture of trust, then communication is likely to flow much more easily. If leaders' personal values are explicit and well understood by key stakeholders this will assist them to interpret communications 'in the right spirit' on first reading or listening. Effective educational leaders use both formal and informal communication to build relationships, partnerships, teams and networks.

Connectivity, teamwork and networking

Walker (2011) argues that school leadership involves connective activity. A central message for school leaders, he states, is that leadership is 'essentially about designing, managing and energising the right connections ... in order to make schools successful, equitable, happier places' (p. 3). A well-connected school is one in which there is 'a high degree of harmony between the structures, values and relationships which guide student learning and lives' (p. 3). He concludes from his research on building and leading learning cultures in schools that there are three core sets of connective pathways in a school: namely, cultural connectors (based on values, beliefs, assumptions); structural connectors (the ways in which a school organises itself); and relational connectors (how people relate to and work with each other) (p. 9).

Responses to the challenges facing leaders in education that are discussed in this chapter demonstrate, overall, a preference for connected activity, teamwork and net-'working' with others. The importance of the cultural elements of values, ethics, and trust are consistently raised as important. Structures, values and relationships that are not aligned are changed and rational approaches are usually adopted to resolve difficult issues. A regional educational leader saw his preferred responses as involving both teamwork and networking within a sensible and rational framework:

> We don't try to make a huge change overnight, which overcomes a lot of the cultural resistance, negotiating with people and using persuasion and consultation to find a better course. In terms of getting that better course, it really is a team-driven approach as much as possible. You like to have teams that are functioning well. In some cases it works and in some cases it doesn't, but using the team involvement in the change helps with a lot of information dissemination so that rather than throwing out a heap of information and getting information overload, it is better to provide information that does focus on the issue, keeps the community briefed as to where we are going and [makes them aware] of the types of pressure that we face.

Another educational leader reported that he had communication strategies whereby:

> people are drawn together once a month with the prime goal of information exchange; disseminating the type of information that we think is critical from the management level and the feedback and the questions asked from campus levels. Those people then go back and are asked, as part of their role, to disseminate the information so each person talks to another five, like the pyramid-type process, and a form goes with each group so that the information stays the same. It is about people having the information to discuss rather than just having another piece of paper handed out.

A principal stressed the possible informal characteristics of teaming and networking when he suggested that 'sharing some of those things [real issues and challenges] with parents in conversation, informally not just always appearing as if you are preaching' is effective. He suggested that it was important for him:

> to stop sometimes and speak and say what can I do to delegate organisationally, out to other people, to the deputy or things that can easily be done by the secretaries. I don't mean just secretarial things. I have two very generous, confident secretaries here; they are always up there, they are just wonderful.

Perhaps the most important connections for educational leaders is those that help connect students with their learning and we will address these in some detail in chapter 8.

Leading an ageing workforce

The workforce in education is ageing. Educational leaders in this research project considered it essential to professionally challenge people who have stagnated in the same role for years. A principal observed that it is rare to meet a person who has not become complacent after a number of years, unless they have had a change of responsibilities. She suggested that it was difficult to find a person who could maintain enthusiasm over the long haul: 'I don't think any of us can afford in an organisation, like a huge educational institution as we are, to settle into anything.'

A challenge for any individual school and for a system of schools is to encourage an ageing teacher population to continue to meet the contemporary challenges of teaching and learning. Early retirement may lead to a great loss of organisational memory, wisdom and know-how; losses that cannot easily be replaced even if financial resources were more plentiful. Some educators merely tolerate change while they serve their last few years. Such a response is especially serious at both teacher and leadership levels where it is essential to respond to change if the school is going to grow and flourish. There is a danger that teachers and other educational leaders who are nearing the end of their careers will act as one principal suggested: 'There are people who have reached pretty well the end of their careers or have gone as far as they want to go in their career [and] are satisfied to sit on their hands.'

As the average age of educators, including educational leaders, continues to rise, education systems and schools need to devote more resources and generate creative solutions to ensure that they continue to be professionally challenged. Teachers with many years' experience should be more intimately involved in leadership and decision-making at their school, a challenge that is discussed in greater depth in chapter 7. Formal leaders need to tap into their talents and expertise and challenge them to continue making a contribution to the core activities of their school.

It is also wise for leaders to celebrate the wisdom of experience and recognise and reward those professional teachers who are in the twilight of their careers by encouraging and supporting them to 'share their wisdom' on teaching and learning, and to engage with younger teachers in a two-way dialogue on how to enrich the learning experiences of students in the school. Both they and the younger teachers will gain much from such dialogue. A major challenge for school principals and other formal educational leaders in schools is to help build a culture of sharing, open dialogue, and courageous conversations on what really matters in schools – improving learning and teaching.

In an era when more and more professionals are searching for a healthier life–work balance, many are opting for part-time employment or retirement, when they can afford it. There is a need for '… a variety of options for flexible work solutions to help keep life and work in balance' (Birch & Paul, 2003, p. 68). Such options could include part-time employment, flexible working hours, shorter working hours, job sharing, and other family-friendly practices. Those responsible for policy and leadership in educational systems and schools must wake up to the reality of an ageing workforce. There are also many achievable options for sharing leadership in schools, thereby building a collective ethic of responsibility for the quality of learning and teaching. Creative leadership succession policies and development programs and practices will need to be encouraged and supported to help build such leadership capacity in educational systems and schools (Duignan & Cannon, 2011; Mulford et al., 2009; Chapman, 2005; Davis et al., 2005).

It would appear, however, that much more is said than done about these challenges. Some will be difficult to resolve, but more leaders and organisations need to face the contemporary realities of their workplaces and dramatically change their ways of thinking and acting about these leadership challenges (Duignan & Cannon, 2011; Birch & Paul, 2003, p. 80).

Issues of life–work balance

Maintaining a proper balance between personal needs and professional responsibilities is problematic for many contemporary educational leaders. In attempting to maintain this balance, as well as coping with the pressure of heavy workloads, educational leaders speak of feeling 'inundated' and of having to do more and more without adequate support. Resource pressures in educational organisations are contributing significantly to this problem. This sense of inundation implies that the pressures to achieve the same or greater outcomes with fewer resources generally overwhelm educational leaders. The impact of technology is promoted as improving the input–output ratio of the flow of work processes; however, it may also be contributing to this feeling of inundation. Indeed, many educational leaders perceive that more advanced technology is not redressing the balance. A principal put it quite succinctly:

> We are doing an awful lot, with a lot less. Our time is really precious, we are inundated not just at my level … but all levels of the organisation … we are inundated by this technology which is supposed to be so helpful.

The following extract from an interview with a school principal indicates the heavy time demands of the job and the added pressures coming from the use of communication technology, especially ubiquitous emails. He states:

> Well, it's pretty much a seven-day working week. I think I'm usually in the office for about nine or ten hours [each day]. When I get home at night I might do a bit of reading but I'm not the sort of person who goes home and gets back on the computer. On the weekend I would. All of us email each other about this, that and the other on Sundays and it is becoming an expectation.
>
> *Question*: Is it becoming a game?
>
> *Response*: Yes, I think so. One of the standing jokes is about how late the emails get sent and about how you can set your computer to send emails at 2.02 am. You can get emails being sent at 9 or 10 pm … I get emails from my boss at 5.30 am. Of course, what I think it has done is increase the

pressure enormously. Initially, it sounds like a really good and efficient time-saver. You don't have to worry about long telephone conversations when you do relationship building, you can just dash off this email but it has compressed the timeframe, so instead of having more time the benchmark's gone up so you are supposed to deliver more work.

This principal is really describing a power game being played. There would appear to be a lack of thought, even respect, for the person on the receiving end of the email messages; the implication being that the person is at the beck and call of the one in control, the one with the greater organisational power. Time for reflection and mature consideration for problem-solving purposes is clearly limited by the pressures to respond quickly to emails, to be seen to be 'on the ball', as it were.

An implication is that many leaders feel that they are being thrown 'off balance' or 'out of balance', with their work lives dominating their personal and private lives. This life–work balance problem is also blamed for why many eligible people in schools do not apply for the principalship (Chapman, 2005; d'Arbon, Duignan & Duncan, 2002). There is also a tension or inner conflict for some leaders as they wrestle with the conflicts between personal and organisational goals. This conflict can eventually lead them to question whether the commitment to remain with the organisation is worth the personal sacrifice. The question of continuing to commit can consume the person's thoughts and have a negative impact on attitude and performance. If work and relationships no longer inject meaning into daily life, then quitting, or at least disengaging, becomes a possibility. A principal stated:

> I must say that, at times, I can become quite philosophically disengaged because I think it is not … an organisation that I came into and was committed to … So, I have, at times, felt that my overall personal challenge was to maintain my engagement and maintain my commitment … and get on with it, as opposed to saying 'I don't think I can work in this organisation,' or, 'I don't believe the policy framework is going to be suited to my philosophical, educational background'. So that sort of sums up the issues that I am facing at the moment.

The element that seems to be absent here is the identification of methodologies or processes to systematically determine priorities. Clear priorities could alleviate some of the stress and conflict that arise when pressures become too great for the individual to withstand. This challenge was highlighted by a principal as part of the balancing act:

> Just on a day-to-day level the biggest challenge is dealing with the competing priorities and the volume of work and the volume of issues you've got to stay on top of, professionally and managerially.

However, too few educational leaders seem to have developed specific strategies and methodologies for dealing with the complexity of their jobs, for establishing priorities in their work, or for targeting specific professional development to assist them (Duignan, 2006). Often educational leaders do not seem to use the job or the workplace as a basis for experiential growth and learning. In fact, the opposite seems to be more the case: the job and the workplace are often seen to be inimical to personal and professional learning and growth. It would appear that the feeling of being inundated and overwhelmed by the job causes many educational leaders to withdraw within themselves, to become defensive, and to rely more on formal methods of communication (e.g., email or memos). Instead of building relationships, such communication habits can inhibit relationship development.

Added to these pressures are the macro global and social challenges discussed in the previous chapter. Responding to the pressures generated by rapidly changing environments places increasing demands on educational leaders.

Leading change

We live in times of rapid change and transition and, in such periods, it is necessary to realise that there may be casualties in any change process. Part of the leadership of change is recognising that not everyone is going to come on board immediately, or even in the short term. Leaders need to be sensitive to the fears and anxieties of those involved in a change process (Degenhardt & Duignan, 2010) and as one principal wisely suggested, 'you have to have a set plan on how you are going to deal with that [anxiety]. You have to be caring and have a plan that maintains their self-esteem. You cannot dump people. I think that is an important aspect of leadership'.

Leading change involves a sensitive balancing act. In developing a framework for change in schools, it is important for leaders of this change to:

> anticipate the struggle to maintain sufficient stability and equilibrium for [the] people to function on a daily basis without excessive psychological and organisational stress, while taking account of the need for the school to be constantly destabilised in acknowledging and responding to new needs' (Degenhardt & Duignan, 2010).

If leaders want teachers to respond constructively to the destabilisation involved in the improvement in their practice, 'they need to model the courage it takes to face the emotional discomfort associated with such an imperative [because] making emotional meaning together is a powerful and transformational endeavour'. They claim that a 'world of possibilities awaits schools whose leaders develop such cultures of care and connectedness' (Leithwood & Beatty, 2008, p. 148; Beatty, 2007).

An emerging culture of transformational learning does not just respond or adapt to change, 'rather, it *thrives* on change, integrating it into its process as one of its environmental variables and creating further change' (Thomas & Brown, 2011, p. 37). They say that 'it makes no sense to think of people adapting to what they are already doing. But it does make sense to see them as functioning within a broader culture and creating it, rather than merely responding to it' (p. 37). Long-term transformation of learning can only be achieved when all involved in it are architects of the cultural change required to sustain it.

Sensible and sensitive leaders will ensure that they involve those affected by change in the key change decisions impacting on their personal and professional lives. If there is no involvement it is difficult to see how there can be buy-in and the development of a sense of authorship and ownership among them. Part of this sensitivity is accepting and acknowledging that 'every person is a change agent' (Fullan, 1999, p. 18). He reminds leaders that conflict, controversy and diversity can have positive generative powers if wisely managed. He suggests that 'you often learn more from people who disagree with you than you do from people who agree' (p. 23), and that 'working through the discomfort of each other's presence, learning from dissonance, and forging new more complex agreements and capabilities is a new requirement for working on the edge of chaos' (p. 23). Degenhardt, as principal and key leader of a reinvention of educational delivery in her secondary school, strongly attests to Fullan's insights, wisdom and accuracy on this issue (Degenhardt & Duignan, 2010).

In the research that underpins this book, a clear example includes that of a principal who found, when attempting to introduce a mechanised system of reporting, that while the change better reflected the school's (Thomas & Brown, 2011) value system, it was not necessarily appreciated by a number of staff members. She learned that during the process some staff feared they would not be able to cope with the new system of reporting. The principal used different approaches, including one-to-one discussions and public announcements, to help allay these fears, but also to make it clear that the change would bring great benefits to teachers, students and parents and that it was in their interests to be part of it. She was pleased, however, when a number of teachers actually suggested better and more beneficial ways of doing it.

Some leaders may, in fact, perceive others to be overreacting to change when they seem to be reacting more than they are themselves (Bridges, 1995, p. 22). Leaders of change need to remind themselves that 'changes cause transitions, which cause losses – and it's the losses, not the changes, that they're reacting to' and 'it's a piece of *their* world that is being lost, not ours' (p. 22, italics in original). Leaders who are trying to manage a top-down change may be reluctant, according to Bridges, to talk openly about the change, '... arguing that it will "stir up trouble" [or fail] to acknowledge people's feelings' (p. 23). But leaders of change *must* engage openly with those who will be affected by the change, and they must acknowledge and address positively the losses and psychological transitions being experienced by these people. Research about what helps people recover from loss concludes that 'they recover more quickly if the losses can be openly discussed' (Bridges, 1995, pp. 23–4).

One way to help overcome fear of loss in change situations is for leaders to devise change strategies that strike a balance between top-down and bottom-up change. Those affected by the change must not only be consulted about it but also must be actively engaged in its genesis. A principal cautioned that:

> The processes used for the implementation of change can, as a matter of course, alienate members. This is especially true if the change and the change processes are mandated from the top down without adequate, if any, consultation with those who are most affected by the change.

Most people do, of course, have the capacity to change; it is a part of life and this capacity for change is inherent in us all. Those affected by change need to know that the comfort zone they leave will not be replaced by a situation that creates unnecessary conflict, tension, even chaos for them. Some who initially resist change may finally become excited by it and transformed when given the opportunity to experience the change in a practical situation, especially if they are encouraged and supported by those in leadership positions. A principal emphasised the need for a supportive leadership approach that is sensitive to the level of readiness of those who are expected to change and/or to implement change:

> You have got to be there for them when that [change resistance] happens. Yes you know how they feel and you can say *'God I feel the same way'* and, in fact, there is a lot of commonality to be shared. People want to know that you appreciate where they are; if they are not ready for this they may be ready in six months' time.

A number of strategies for dealing with conflict situations are well dealt with in books or chapters on conflict management. What has become very apparent from this author's readings, observations and experiences is the need for honest and transparent dialogue with staff at all levels so that they are constantly kept up to date on what and how changes are occurring. Communicate! Communicate! Communicate! If leaders feel that at a particular stage they have nothing substantial to communicate, then they should communicate this.

There is also a need for decisive leadership in constantly changing environments. It is important to collaboratively look at the available information, analyse it, make a decision, develop and implement new strategies, and consistently evaluate their effects. These processes should be based on collective discussions. A system educational leader in this study highlighted the need for increased dialogue among the senior managers and leaders of an organisation. She favours open, honest, collaborative, and transparent processes for doing things and recommended that:

> You've got to have people by your side who are professional and who can give you quick advice based on a really quick and honest analysis of the system. There is a tension between being ethical and introducing notions of ethical leadership and doing the right thing by the right people and, at the same time, being political and playing the political game to survive in the organisation. I think, in summary, it is a question of the river of life syndrome, recognising where you are at a particular time and taking appropriate strategies to deal with that. I also think that if I need help, either professional

help or other advice, then I'm quite happy to seek help from anyone who can provide it. You just simply can't do everything on your own.

Some leaders meet the challenge of change by accepting the need to be up to date on educational developments and engage through professional associations and networks with other members of staff across the system and the wider educational community. Networking outside one's school is one way to break out of group thinking and be exposed to national and international thinking. This means taking time to reflect on professional literature, since the effects of change can often be predicted, because it is happening in other countries. Degenhardt and Duignan (2010, p. 119) report that Fullan's prediction of an *implementation gap* occurred in their school reinvention initiative, and was reassuring for them to know it was not just happening to them. Networking can provide similar checks because it is reassuring to share with colleagues who are struggling with the same issues and coming to similar conclusions. Also, as one principal stated, 'on a personal level, it is good to have kindred spirits'.

The challenge to lead in a time of change is a difficult one, because it often requires a shift from a hierarchical world model to an inclusive and collective leadership model. Some educational leaders in this study acknowledged that they still used a control model more than an inclusive model because they have not shifted their mindset to the new paradigm in which many of them now live. The new paradigm has different assumptions and a different context from the old paradigm within which many leaders were trained and developed. An educational leader in the study summed it up well:

> The old, put simply, is born of mechanism and clocks and enlightenment and the new is born of complex living systems. Once you appreciate how that works you operate from a different metaphor and often the metaphor carries more significance than the facts. Once you work from a different metaphor it is more difficult, but I have a sense that, in terms of making decisions for the future, you'll actually be more in tune [with what's likely to happen]. Today will be a preparation for the future, to get the right direction, but what we tend to do is go back to the old framework to make our decision because we are more comfortable there and more secure and we can often put a better argument. It's the whole cult of rationalism we get caught in, whereas in the new [paradigm] it's much more to do with the whole and the whole person, the creative imagination.

Some stakeholders are willing to be engaged in a process that is unfolding, and accept that change is automatically built into an organisation's life, because there has to be constant reviewing and making of key decisions that are part of the new way of looking at reality. How change is actually introduced can also have an important bearing on how such new ideas and new ways of thinking are accepted.

Another challenge for educational leaders is to ensure that while they are frantically attempting to deal with everyday urgent issues, they keep one eye firmly on a vision for the future, a vision that is driven by core values and moral purpose.

Sustaining a values-driven vision in times of rapid change

Values and mission imperatives are usually the drivers of vision and strategic planning for a school. The notion that authentic leaders base their vision for their organisation on their moral principles and shared core values is well accepted in relevant literature (e.g., Jansen et al., 2011; Flintham, 2010; Mendonca & Kanungo, 2007; Davies, 2006). Indeed, one of the distinguishing characteristics of successful authentic educational leaders is their capacity to provide a vision for the future and inspire hope in those with whom they work (Flintham, 2010). It is their 'belief in the capacity to make a difference and the vision of a preferred future that it predicates' that, according to Flintham, 'provides the reservoir of hope on which headteachers draw to sustain their own self belief and from which they energise, empower and enable others' (p. 176). By living the vision to the full, authentic leaders lift the spirits of their people and help them to transform the vision into meaningful daily work practices. In this way they help to inject meaning into the daily grind of getting the work done, thereby providing a sense of purpose, direction and excitement in their organisation.

In their book on reculturing schools to become professional learning communities, Eaker et al. (2002) recommend that through collaborative processes the first key activity involves developing and being clear about a shared and meaningful 'mission, vision, values and goals' (p. 10). The vision statement then 'forms the basis for school-improvement planning' and all discussions on improvement should then focus on the question, 'How will this help us move the school toward the vision we have for our schools?' (p. 15).

The vision for a school must be clearly connected to the expectations of the school for student learning and there needs to be an appreciation of how this connection can be translated into action. Vision statements do not represent wish lists but help focus on the moral purpose of the school expressed in terms of learning and teaching outcomes. It should not be an abstract set of statements of a desired future but a practical set of specific statements of key expectations, especially for students' learning. Degenhardt and Duignan (2010) recommend that the first step in any reinvention process for a school is to focus on the moral purpose of education and schooling, and then identify and articulate 'the school communities' core values' (p. 43). With clear moral purpose and associated core values, the next important step is to develop a vision using inclusive processes 'into a shared paradigm of student learning and growth' (p. 45). Without such a shared vision and paradigm, any change or improvement process will wither and die.

A similar concern is expressed by Sharratt and Fullan (2009). They argue that 'early improvement gains, while critically important, cannot be overvalued as it only represents the beginning of a much deeper journey that leads to sustainable achievement levels' (p. 24). They recommend that it is necessary for a school district and its schools to have 'a strong, consistent, and very explicit vision' and they quote a principal who states, 'Being able to say that literacy is the top priority [for the system] provides me with lots of strength and power in what I say and what the school priority is, and how teachers follow it' (p. 25).

The articulation of such a vision necessarily involves leaders consulting with and sharing the hopes, desires and expectations enshrined in the vision with the members of their school community, and establishing the foundations of an organisational culture that supports the aspirations of all stakeholders. The intent and content of the vision helps motivate all the members of the school community. Reflection on and the communication of this vision is essential if it is to become part of everyday practice.

Linking vision to practice seems to be a vital component in the relationship of the leader and those led. Drawing people beyond their daily tasks and routines, and engaging them in helping to shape a desired future, facilitates the creation of a more meaningful and inspiring workplace. The formative nature of this process also seems to be important in bringing people to a fuller understanding of their moral purpose and direction, and to a strategic sense of their work. To effectively connect vision with strategies and actions, leaders need to be clear about their values, morally literate, and act intentionally as moral agents (Bezzina & Tuana, 2011; Mendonca & Kanungo, 2007).

Educational leaders undertaking vision-inspired improvement are challenged to engage with their staff in ways that take the whole group forward, rather than plugging gaps and responding primarily to perceived emergencies. It is wasteful of time, energy and talent to simply fill gaps as they appear, without reflecting on and working through what is really needed to position the school to meet future challenges. Communicating the strategic purpose to everyone is vital in drawing together staff at all levels. Clear purpose, inspirational communication, and an appeal to shared values and belief systems, will point clearly to the journey forward.

A major problem identified by a number of leaders in this study was finding the time to reflect on and communicate a vision in the face of busy schedules. A principal of a school summed up this issue very well: 'I see a very important part of the leadership role as having time to reflect on direction, to have a sense of vision and to lead others who share that vision, but I find that a great challenge to that is finding the time within the daily routines to ensure that you structure that in'.

Leaders cannot do it all by themselves. They have to work with and through others to achieve their organisation's vision and goals (Duignan & Cannon, 2011). There is simply not enough time in the workday for one person to provide the scope and depth of leadership required in contemporary school communities. A principal encapsulated this challenge when he said that, 'you have got to be a strong communicator and relationship builder. You have got to have the capacity to build relationships, to make connections, to build partnerships, and strong alliances with others'. The principal is referring here mainly to relationships internal to the school, but of course leaders also have to develop and maintain strong external relationships and networks. They have to be effective public advocates and represent their change initiatives in various public arenas. This is especially important in an era when education is seen to be everyone's business and is continually under scrutiny and critique by a sometimes sceptical public. It will be much easier to fulfil this role effectively if they are crystal clear about their moral purpose, values and vision.

Achieving a dynamic balance between coping with current realities and keeping a strategic eye on the vision for the future is difficult for most educational leaders. A principal suggested that one way to help maintain this balance is to involve key stakeholders in generating moral purpose and a strategic vision while, at the same time, ensuring that day-to-day concerns are not neglected. He suggested that there is no better way of serving this purpose than by communicating directly with organisational members so that they are aware of the nature of their psychological contract as members of that organisation. The legal contract of employment, of course, is only one aspect of the contract necessary to become and remain an effective member. Active membership requires engagement at a deeper, affective level where there is a close relationship between personal and organisational vision and values. Knowing the values that motivate organisational members and articulating these values clearly can assist in developing a shared vision and mission for the school. Clarity of purpose based on a shared set of values and expectations would seem to be fundamental to effective educational leadership.

The discussion on macro and micro leadership challenges in this and the previous chapter indicates that contemporary educational leaders face complex, dynamic and varied challenges in their daily work. These can be stressful but it is how educational leaders respond that determines whether they will be stressed or not. In fact, many educational leaders relish these challenges and see them as opportunities for collective initiatives for school improvement. They regard the challenges as part of the drama of leadership and they simply take the positive attitude that they need creative approaches and practices in dealing with them.

It is important to note, however, that many educational leaders do not feel comfortable or confident when dealing with challenges involving personal and professional conflict or when values are contested and ethical tensions arise. Part of the reason for this is that most educational leaders are not formally prepared for leadership in situations where conflict and contested values and ethics arise. What they require are ways of identifying, analysing and framing such situations with a view to making them more amenable to wise and creative resolution. These issues will be the focus of chapters 4 and 5.

Key ideas for reflection

A major contemporary challenge for educational leaders is to lead people who are experiencing fear and psychological loss in a context of rapid and continuous change. They must engage openly with them to help them cope with their fears and anxieties. Top-down mandated changes often create great consternation and fear among those who have to implement them. Leaders need to be sensitive to the levels of readiness of those involved in a change initiative and leading in conditions of continuous change requires a shift from hierarchical approaches to more inclusive transformational models that deal with the whole person.

One of the most demanding challenges for educational leaders is dealing with poorly performing staff where there is deep concern for students under their care. Such situations are complex and multidimensional, however, the consensus among principals in this study seems to be that it is better for the principal to 'bite the bullet' and deal with the problem early and head-on.

Educational leaders in the twenty-first century need to devise new and creative ways of ensuring that teachers and other educators with many years of experience are continuously challenged and actively engaged in their own personal and professional development. Many with long years of experience can become stale and complacent if they are not constantly encouraged and supported to be reflective and creative practitioners.

Leaders also need to collaboratively develop and communicate a value-driven vision for the future in order to give a sense of purpose, meaning and hope to their school community. This envisioning process requires them to engage meaningfully with people, building authentic relationships in order to serve the needs of students and their parents. Another challenge is to translate the vision into everyday practices. A good start is to create more purposeful and inspiring workplaces built on trust, transparency and open communications.

Questions for reflection

1 What are some of the most difficult challenges you have encountered when dealing with poorly performing teachers? How did you overcome these challenges? After reading this chapter, how might you deal differently with them in future?

2 In what ways do you, as a leader, try to ensure that teachers are personally and professionally engaged and committed to the values and vision of your school?

3 What strategies do you use to help ensure that you communicate meaningfully and authentically with teachers, students and other key stakeholders in your school community?

4 What leadership style or approach(es) do you prefer when leading significant change in your school community?

5 What strategies and processes do you use to develop a collaborative vision and then translate the vision into everyday practices?

Chapter 4

Leadership challenges as tensions

Many of the major challenges facing educational leaders involve situations where values and ethics are contested. Some of these challenges constitute what may be called 'contestable values dualities', or 'ethical dilemmas' (Dempster & Berry, 2003; Dempster, 2001; Wildy et al., 2001)). There seems to be agreement that 'the whole field of ethics is a contested terrain' (Cranston et al., 2006, p. 108) and for educational leaders it may often feel like they are 'blindfolded in a minefield' (Dempster & Berry, 2003, p. 457).

Frequently, we tend to think of dilemmas as 'ethical dilemmas' because they identify difficult and challenging situations 'in which a choice has to be made between two equally undesirable alternatives' (*Australian Pocket Oxford Dictionary*, 2007, p. 294); hence the saying, 'on the horns of a dilemma'. However, the majority of the challenges discussed in this chapter represent situations where there are more than two alternative possibilities; in fact most of the challenges are multidimensional in nature. In this book, the word 'tension' is preferred to 'dilemma' to describe these situations, because it denotes that relationships exist between a number of contestable values dualities (a dilemma with multiple horns) and that different possible solutions for each situation will reflect how these relationships are mediated.

This perspective has profound implications for how educational leaders respond to difficult and challenging situations. The 'real challenges' of educational leadership – the ones that keep educational leaders awake at night, cause them to take stress leave or retire before their time – usually involve tensions between and among people based on differences in philosophies, values, interests and preferences. While managerial issues – such as strategic planning, resource allocation, or organising and scheduling educational processes and tasks – demand the application of sound management processes, it soon becomes apparent that the devil is in the details of the relationship issues between and among the people involved. Rarely can issues involving complex human behaviour be reduced to, or resolved only by, logical and linear management processes, no matter how systematic or thorough these may appear. There is also a need for leaders to have a large measure of emotional intelligence if they are to succeed in such contested situations (Goleman et al., 2003; Cooper & Sawaf, 1997). No amount of logical and rational analysis and explanation alone will convince emotionally involved 'contestants' in a tension situation. Leadership based on a sound understanding of psychological and emotional states is also required.

Many of the tension situations discussed in this chapter involve issues related to student discipline, staff relationships, and teacher competence (Duignan, 2006). Dempster and Berry (2003), in their exploration of ethical decision-making with 552 school principals in Australia, categorised ethical dilemmas in four ways; 'those related to students, staff, finance and resources' (p. 109). By far the most difficult ones to resolve are those involving student misbehaviour and staff performance.

Similar findings are highlighted by Cranston et al. (2006) from their study of independent school heads in Australia; they report that 'all participants commented that ethical dilemmas emerge in the course of their work as leaders' (p. 112).

The examples that follow provide a clearer picture of the nature of the challenges and dilemmas faced by educational leaders. What may appear on the surface to be simple can often escalate into something more complex and difficult. The molehill truly becomes a mountain! While many of these tensions were identified in the study underpinning the 2006 version of this book, these and others emerging since have been tested and verified by a large number of school leaders in research workshops with the author and by postgraduate students in leadership programs at two universities where the author is involved.

A typical complex tension was recounted by a principal in an incident about possible student involvement in drugs that typifies the complexity, multidimensionality, and tensions in staff, student and parent relationships that characterise many leadership challenges in schools:

> There are the expectations of staff who don't generally, and didn't in this case, know the full details of what had gone on. You had enough information to have certain expectations of how students would be dealt with and there were a number of competing needs in that. One is that some parents felt that any girl in any kind of drug activity in the school was creating an unhealthy environment for the students and should be asked to leave. There were other parents who actually contacted us and said that they were familiar with these girls and felt that they deserved a second chance … Some people thought the girls should be admitted back to the school. The girls were at different stages of their academic careers and the implications for some would have been far more serious than for others. So all of those things came into the decision-making. There were some competing values. Valuing the need to create a safe environment for the remainder of the student body; wanting to also deal with these girls justly and to enable them to move on from their mistake; protecting the interests of the parents and also creating an environment in which staff felt that there was still a level of discipline within the student body and that we weren't going to give the wrong messages about that.

On the surface, the resolution to an issue of students being involved in drugs might appear to be rather clear-cut. After all, use of illegal drugs is against the law and is certainly against school rules. A clinical application of rules would leave little room for any consideration of personal issues or extenuating circumstances in deciding the fate of the students. Surely, suspension, at the very least, or more likely expulsion, would be the expected outcome! Yet a close scrutiny of the case demonstrates that expectations and perspectives may differ when the human elements of a dilemma or tension situation are considered.

Usually in situations of human drama, *either/or* thinking that adopts a one- or two-dimensional response will not encompass the complexity of the competing issues. *Both/and* responses are more likely to lead to satisfactory outcomes. A more detailed exposition of this particular perspective is presented in the next chapter on analysing tensions.

The key lessons emerging from such complex cases can be regarded as examples with wider implications beyond the particular situation. In fact, a number of categories of tensions consistently emerged from leaders' responses to challenging and complex situations in this study, though they were manifested in a variety of ways. The development of these categories of tensions, as well as the selection of examples for each tension, were guided by the work of Kidder (1995) and form the basis for the discussions in the remainder of this chapter. It is essential to note that in the headings the tension is not couched in the language of a dilemma, *either/or* or *versus* but uses *and* to emphasise that a *both/and* approach to its resolution is usually preferable. There is a philosophical distinction here whose significance and importance will become more evident as each category of tension is discussed.

Common good *and* individual good

This was one of the most frequently discussed tensions. There appears to be a consistent tension between deciding whether to support decisions promoting the good of the group or the rights of the individual. Generally, when talking about the common good, educational leaders referred to a group or the community, especially the wider student body and their parents, while with the individual good they are usually referring to teachers and/or students.

Most decisions in this category tend to favour the group or community over the individual, but, overall, resolutions do not involve either/or positions. While priority may be given to the common good, leaders often agonise over the impact of their decisions on the individuals involved. Principals in the study note the need to consider and protect a student's welfare, safety and educational outcomes, even when this student's behaviour or performance is having some detrimental effects on colleagues and others. However, when these negative effects are perceived to have a significant impact on the student's class or the school community, the principal's decision is normally to suspend or expel the student (or students). While students are not expelled without serious consultation and without a number of attempts to deal with the problems they were having, one principal stated: 'I learnt as well a benchmark for when the price for individual "good" is too high in relation to the "good" of the whole group.'

There are times when the decision favours the individual over the community or group. In every case of a tension in this area, principals express concern and compassion for the welfare of the individual. In cases where principals refuse to expel students, the choice not to expel is governed by concern for the student's welfare and the basic right of every child to receive an education.

In the case of ineffective staff, long and loyal service is acknowledged but is usually outweighed by the concern for the needs of the student body whose education is being affected by their lack of teaching competence. One principal decided that the task of removing a long-serving and loyal teacher was too difficult and opted to 'wait it out'. This decision was, in hindsight, regretted, and the principal concluded that the decision to move the teacher on should have been made earlier:

> I should have put her on an improvement program. Her students deserved better ... Some staff considered my lack of action weak, as she was also undermining my decisions. I sat her out. She's retired. I should have acted earlier before it got to the stage where there was only one or two years to go before retirement. I have learnt that the process of looking at duty and obligations in ethical dilemmas is really important and I let down the people who are my first responsibility, the children.

Another principal decided that it was too difficult to fight an ineffective staff member who was applying for voluntary redundancy for the second time. He considered the opportunity cost of initiating and implementing a dismissal process and decided to spend his time in more productive ways. While the principal, in this case, did not believe that this payout should be approved, he decided to avoid the tension and possible conflict involved in following a dismissal process:

> I would have preferred to terminate his services. In the end, I approved his voluntary redundancy. I weighed up the time and effort involved in trying to bring an unwilling and uncommitted staff member up to speed against the other priorities I had, together with the emerging initiatives and projects which were in the planning stage. I also thought very carefully about where my time would be better spent in terms of staff development, change management, redirecting the organisational culture and repositioning the school for the future. I also know what it is like to prove incompetence in the area I work in. I believe I made the right choice.

Issues like the ones just described are representative of the many difficult, complex challenges faced by educational leaders on a daily basis, which requires them to seek a number of possible resolutions. Often a decision has to be crafted that constitutes a 'best fit' resolution, given the specific circumstances of the case. There is usually no 'one best way' that can be consistently applied, even to similar situations and tensions.

Another example, as highlighted by a principal, further illustrates the complexity and multidimensionality between an individual student's rights or interests and the pursuit of the common good:

> A student came to the school after a fairly troublesome time at another school. She was very bright and had a great deal to offer but her behaviour was extremely difficult and disruptive. Initially she settled in well although, at times, she was challenging to teachers and in particular to myself. She would stand up to me publicly and always seek to challenge me in front of other students. I accepted this because I thought that we would eventually make a difference in this young person's life ... It was really between the individual and the common good. This young person's future could be determined by my decision to ask her to leave the school. She passionately wanted to stay. She wrote at least six letters begging me to let her stay and promising that she would change.

What is the principal to do? How are they to strike a just balance between concern for the individual and the protection of the group (the common good)? We will see that a number of the tension situations discussed in the remainder of this chapter help shed further light on the complexities of this issue and help in the development of a framework for managing such tensions.

Care *and* rules

Educational leaders continually face challenges and decisions that involve tensions between a concern for 'care' *and* 'rules'. Care encompasses compassion, looking at the individual circumstances and making a decision that puts care and concern for the individual or group above policies, rules and procedures. Rules or policies provide frameworks and guidelines for leaders on how to make decisions. Some leaders argue that by complying with rules they are also fulfilling their duty of care to the community and they, therefore, do not recognise any real tensions in this area. This is a legalist view of care and caring.

In schools there are instances where educational leaders feel that they must follow the 'letter of the law' to protect their own careers and reputations. This is understandable but the approach can have negative consequences for some individuals. An example was where a teacher disciplined a student for breach of rules on a school camp but, in order to placate certain parents, the teacher was disciplined. Staff, and indeed the principal, agreed that the teacher had an impeccable reputation and acted appropriately. Another teacher was falsely accused of sexually assaulting an infant student. The teacher was a valued member of staff and the accusation was later found to be baseless. However, the strict procedures related to sexual assault were implemented and, as a result, the teacher suffered loss of reputation and trust from the community and system.

There were occasions when those faced with a tension situation used the rules, primarily, to determine the outcome. When rules were rigidly adhered to, leaders reported that they felt that they had no alternative but to follow them because the law demanded it. Examples from this study include:

1   a student with aggressive behaviour was suspended with allegations of drug use at home. The principal noted that for legal reasons a detailed record of all interactions and decisions was kept;

2   in two cases of sexual assault, both principals strictly followed procedural guidelines; and

3   in two cases involving violent parents, principals adhered strictly to system rules and guidelines.

It is important to note that in most cases like these, principals consulted widely with appropriate authorities. These included system personnel, welfare agencies, police and other members of staff. Where students were suspended or expelled, the rules were followed by principals in order to protect the body of students, and it was considered also to be in the best interests of the students who were directly involved; that is, that they would learn from the discipline.

Some principals, however, tended to emphasise care over rules where the decision guidelines were not mandatory. Rules were suspended or 'bent' when leaders considered that a care outcome was a 'better' resolution of the tension. For example, a disadvantaged student was disciplined and because of the type of penalty required he should have missed out on a major sporting event. The senior executive 'overruled' these rules and the student was allowed to compete. This was said to be a once-in-a-lifetime experience for the student. Care for the student was, obviously, the prime concern. The principal gave the following account of the incident:

> Our school has a policy where, if a student has received more than one 'blue slip', that student is not allowed to participate in special activities such as excursions, visits, or play sports until his/ her behaviour has improved. If it is their first 'blue slip', the ban is for one week only. One student, a talented athlete, had reached eligibility to participate at regional level. The student had received no support from home and had been known to run in bare feet! One week prior to the athletic event he earned, fairly, his first 'blue slip'. Technically the full week was up the day after the carnival. The dilemma of allowing this child a chance at the carnival was taken to the Executive who decided he should participate.

The executive, in fact, judged that it was in the long-term interests of this student to be able to participate in an event at which he excelled, and which would, most likely, aid in promoting his self-concept and self-esteem. Of course, they were cognisant of the fact that they were setting a precedent and that other students and their parents could question the fairness of their decision, given that other students had been dealt with in the past 'by the rules'.

These are typical of decisions faced by educational leaders every day. In the end, it often means making a judgement as to whether the benefits outweigh the possible negatives. In the cases just cited the decision-makers typically gave precedence to caring over the rules.

In another interesting case a principal disregarded regulations as he felt that this was in the best interests of the child, and the end result proved his judgement to be correct. He concluded, however, that this would probably not be a course of action that he would repeat again as the risks were high and, with maturity and experience, he would handle the matter differently. This principal told a story of a situation containing a number of tensions and dilemmas. While it is a lengthy example, it is included here because it highlights the complexity of many typical challenges facing educational leaders in the normal course of their work.

The incident took place in a small town. This is the school of which I am principal. There was a child who attends the school; her mother who has a drug problem; and her grandfather who is a prominent citizen. The mother was neglecting her child and her lifestyle was not providing the child with the best opportunity for long-term success at school. As the grandfather lived in another town, my contact with him was limited to twice a year at face-to-face meetings, and fortnightly phone calls.

There were a series of incidents involving the child that started to concern me. She was coming to school having no food, she was not being picked up in the afternoons, and her personal hygiene was being neglected. I contacted the Department of Community Services, as I am required to do, but nothing was done. I called the grandfather and told him about my concerns as well.

A week later, there was a fire at the child's house, due to the drugs that the child's mother had been taking. It could have been fatal. Later that week, the grandfather made a phone call to the school and asked to speak to the child. This is not in line with system policy, but I allowed the child to come to the phone. That afternoon she was taken from the local park by her grandfather and was sent to an aunt in another town. Two days later, the child's mother came to the school looking for her daughter.

This incident presented two ethical choices. The first was to allow the child to speak to her grandfather. This choice had to be made on the spot. I knew it was not within normal operating guidelines, but I felt it would be in the best interest of the child. I personally trusted the grandfather. This made the choice more difficult.

The second choice was after the child had been taken and her mother had come to ask if I knew where she was. I was prepared for this choice. I knew that it would come. I could tell her what had happened, tell her where her child was, or claim that I had no knowledge of the incident.

The choices I made were with the best interests of the child in mind. In the first instance with the phone call, I decided to allow the child to speak with her grandfather, knowing full well that I would be doing so outside the guidelines that were set down. When I was questioned by the child's mother as to her daughter's whereabouts, I decided to deny all knowledge of the incident while knowing that I should have reported it.

The first choice was made for a number of reasons. I was becoming increasingly concerned for the child. I was actually relieved when I got the phone call and he asked to speak to his grandchild. I was hoping that it would result in an improved home situation for the young girl. The second choice, regarding what I would say if I were ever questioned regarding the child's removal, was an easier one, because I had time to think the situation through. I knew that other people in the town had seen the grandfather take the child and that it would only be a matter of time before she found out. I decided that no information that could lead to the child being returned to her mother would be coming from me. This decision was also formed partly due to my breach of guidelines in the first instance with the phone call.

With the benefit of hindsight, I'm not sure that I did make the right choices. The end result could not have been better. The child is now in a warm, safe environment and her mother's visits are short and supervised. No action was taken against anyone, and all parties are happy with the new situation. But I don't think that I can judge my actions purely on the basis of the final outcome. As a leader, I should have been able to work within the guidelines to bring about a favourable result. I think I showed inexperience. I was fortunate that the repercussions of my actions, and inactions, were positive. If I were faced with the same situation in the future, I would hope that I would handle the situation with a much greater sense of professionalism. In fact, I am confident that I would handle the situation differently.

This complex situation brings clearly into focus the tensions that can arise for leaders making decisions in situations where people's lives are involved. A rule approach to making decisions in such situations may appear to be the easy option but there is always the tug of the heartstrings pulling us toward a more caring and compassionate course of action. After all, teaching is a caring profession and educational leaders will always pay close attention to the needs of students as human beings. The author has used this case study for analysis with a large number of educational leaders and it is remarkable the differences of opinion in their responses as to how they would act in a similar situation. Obviously, not all the facts of the case are presented but it is somewhat surprising that most of these leaders would make every effort to find ways to protect the interests of the girl. Very few would opt for simply applying the rules in this situation.

In another example, a staff member was found to be inappropriately using system cars. The person in charge decided to waive the rules because she was informed that the 'accused' person was threatening to commit suicide and the leader concluded that while the rules had been waived in good faith, there was a sense of manipulation by the staff member. She stated:

It was reported to me that a person was suspected of inappropriately using a system car. My initial response was to take disciplinary action. The allegation was significant given that many thousands of kilometres were used privately. The situation arose as the person was fulfilling a role that was difficult to supervise.

At the same time, I was contacted by a counsellor employed by the Employee Assistance Program stating that she believed the officer to be suicidal. I explained the misuse of the car to the counsellor. I was informed that his mental state was fragile.

The ethical choice was whether to comply with system regulations concerning significant misuse or to avoid raising the issue to ensure the welfare of this person. The choice became more difficult as I was also contacted by a number of principals who wished to raise other concerns about this same person.

I met with the person and had the staff welfare officer also in attendance. I highlighted the positive aspects of his work and let him know that his contribution was appreciated. I also let him know that his use of the car was sometimes not appropriate. I also informed him that I was not going to pursue the matter but wanted a commitment that he would comply with guidelines in the future. I did not raise the other issues as I considered they could be dealt with at a later stage. In this case, however, I considered the welfare issue to be more important than the misuse of resources.

In general terms, I believe the right choice was made, as it is my opinion that a leader has to place a high priority on the welfare of employees. Specifically, I am not sure, as subsequently I was informed that this person had threatened suicide on a number of occasions in different settings to have matters disregarded or to get his way.

What are leaders to do? They can never hope to know fully all the facts of any case or situation. They can only do the best they can with the information they can obtain by consulting those who may have important and relevant information on the issue. Often, they have to follow their instincts as well.

These examples from the cases just discussed demonstrate that, in hindsight, leaders believed their care-based choices, while usually having positive outcomes for others involved in the situation, were not always the wisest courses of action for themselves. They seemed to have some regrets about taking the caring approach because doing so left them exposed to possible sanctions consequent upon breaking or bending the rules. And yet, despite their concerns with what they did, it appears that faced with a similar situation again they might opt for a caring outcome. At least, a majority of educational leaders who later analysed these cases in workshop situations also tended to select a caring outcome.

Long-term *and* short-term considerations

Any leadership decision has a range of possible long-term and short-term consequences. For example, a principal may decide not to expel a student, because, while it may bring short-term relief for the teachers who have to deal with this student, the decision may not be in the long-term interests of the student's education.

Leaders, if they are not reflective and strategic, can be overwhelmed by short-term pressures and perceived emergencies. In this way, they may be merely reacting to what they perceive as urgent, rather than to what is important, significant, and worthwhile. While it would be very unwise to neglect or ignore current realities, leaders must ensure that they remain strategic in their thinking and planning and stand apart so that they can bring a 'big-picture perspective' to any challenge or tension situation. This is especially true when the interests of students are involved. Of course, the best result is usually a compromise between short- and long-term interests and between short- *and* long-term outcomes.

Another category of challenges faced by educational leaders reflects tensions between the desire to be *loyal* to people *and* the need to be *honest* and see that justice is done.

Loyalty *and* honesty

Loyalty is defined as being committed to the organisation, the person in charge, or colleagues. Loyalty can constitute allegiance to individuals, groups or to the vision and mission of the organisation. Honesty is speaking truthfully about any person, issue or situation and refraining from intentionally deceiving or misleading.

A number of tensions involving loyalty *and* honesty were identified by educational leaders in this study. The following examples provide insights into the nature of these types of tensions:

1   balancing the recognition of long and loyal service against the need for restructuring and redundancies;

2   making provision for older personnel to retire with dignity even though their current performance is not up to standard; and

3   students balancing ethical issues related to their work for a teacher against their positive feelings and loyalty to the teacher.

An example of this latter type of tension was provided by a principal. Students were asked by a teacher to enter the results of peers' marks into a computer:

> A teacher involved students in entering other students' results into the computer in preparation for writing reports. The incident took place in the teacher's office. She, the teacher, had asked the principal to 'borrow' the students to assist her in preparing for some event. They had finished this work and were kept to do this report work. The teacher had told them to keep an eye out for any Faculty Leader and to alert her if one came by. The students were not discomforted at the time. That evening one of them reflected with her father about the 'oddness' of the situation and how she felt uneasy. Her father suggested she and the others come to see me, as principal. The students did so the next day and were very anxious that they would not be seen to be 'dobbing' but they felt they should not have been asked to participate in a clearly unethical activity.

In another incident, a principal faced a very personal quandary when dealing with an elderly teacher's classroom problems:

> [An elderly member of staff] had been showing increasing signs of dementia for about two years. Several senior staff members expressed their concern about her but, more especially, for her students. I initially spoke with her husband whom I'd known for many years, thinking he would discreetly follow up on the possible onset of dementia. My 'unwise' tactic resulted in her absolute denial of any problem. Nevertheless, I persuaded her to take long-service leave for a term. When she returned she was even more disoriented and students were becoming very distressed at her decreasing ability to teach. I was being deluged with complaints from staff, such as, 'When is she (me) going to do something about it?' and student complaints were naturally escalating … I chose the method of reducing her teaching load in the hope [the teacher] would eventually see that she was no longer able to teach … Her years of service precluded termination, and I knew she would not accept the offer of time out on sick leave … In the final analysis, the needs and rights of the students were the deciding factor in removing her from most of her teaching.

This is an example of a tension situation with numerous ethical dimensions. The tension between the values of loyalty and truth/honesty is very evident, but so also is the concern for the good of the individual and the need for the 'common good' to be protected. The principal's care and compassion for the elderly teacher is in tension with the need to follow rules and procedures on inadequate performance. Clearly, the tensions between these three 'contestable values dualities' make a complex tension situation that is best resolved by *both/and* thinking based on wisdom and good judgement.

A tension that casts a wide shadow over many aspects of contemporary educational leadership is that of the recent emphasis on rationalist economic philosophies, strategies, and practices in leadership *and* the need also for a human service organisation, such as a school, to provide a 'human service'.

Service *and* economic rationalism

Issues related to economic rationalism and managerialist approaches in education were discussed in chapter 2, where it was noted that an excessive emphasis on rationalist approaches to leadership and to education can clash with the desire of leaders to promote and support a new, more caring and engaging paradigm of education with the wellbeing of students at its core. This tension highlights those instances where respondents in this study believed that the imperatives of economic rationalism had a negative impact on their core business. Economic rationalism was considered to include making efficiency a core value, increasing accountability and audits, using redundancy to reduce costs, and restructuring (e.g., merging of organisational structures). The core business of schools, the *raison d'être* for their existence, in contrast, was considered to be providing a responsive, compassionate, high-quality educational service.

Often in such tension situations educational leaders attempt to maintain the core values *and* meet the imperatives of accountability. It appears, however, that the caring service dimensions of the tension are often implied, even when they are not directly discussed when dealing with the situation. There tends to be an awareness and acknowledgement by educational leaders that the increased emphasis on efficiency, generally, has negative implications for the quality and level of educational services that can be provided by their school.

Several examples of these types of tension were reported in the study. The following are examples from school principals:

1 parents pleading questionable financial difficulties and wanting reduced fees, yet were able to afford a new car;

2 an organisation *driven* by performance and accountability with little consideration of the emotional impact on its culture and staff morale;

3 funds allocated to those areas targeted as being high priority by the system, despite alternative priority requests from schools and teachers;

4 funding required for students with special needs but resources being allocated, primarily, to improve academic outcomes; and

5 rational economic corporate management demands clashing with individual leadership philosophies and styles.

A principal of a school gave an example, related to school fees, of a tension in this area:

> I think, most probably, one of the times when I do experience a little bit of tension is in making decisions when you have a parent in about school fees. For me sometimes this can be difficult. You really know that the parents are able to pay something, but they are really spinning you a great story about how they can't really afford to pay and you know that the person has just bought a new car, for example. There is also the justice issue because you know that out there is Mrs So and So, who is already a single parent and you've had several conversations with her and she is determined that she will pay the school fees in the best possible way she can.

Another principal commented on the problems that scarce resources, especially lack of staff, creates:

> I think the other tension is to do with staff. It has been an enormously onerous task, and still is, for staff as we implement new assessment requirements. But most schools don't have the resources to make significant concessions in terms of time, and again that is a conflict in terms of caring for your staff and being driven by external requirements. That is an ongoing difficulty really.

An area of tension recognised by principals in the study was that related to a corporate, hierarchical management approach to leadership in a collegial, collaborative educational context. A principal captured the essence of this tension:

> It [corporate culture] resembles a shift from, say, collaborative professionalism to a rational economic corporate management style. I think that's happening in a lot of organisations as people are consumed and absorbed by this sort of budget-driven approach to management.

A principal explained the challenges imposed by decisions to reduce staff numbers and the human drama involved in responding to these challenges:

> I had the job of handing out to two-thirds of the staff a big white envelope that said 'Would you like a voluntary redundancy? If you want to put your name forward this is what you'll get …' The impact on your support staff … is great … very difficult! Trying to keep the ship going and, at the same time, not always believing in these values. I'm the messenger, I've got to stand up in front of the staff and say that this is what we are doing and this is why we are doing it and, at the same time, not believing that it was the best thing in every aspect.

> So that's very hard to do and it is very hard not to overlay your own perspective and undermine it. So it is difficult for me to get up and say that this is what our bosses have decided and then not say, 'Well, I think it stinks'.

He went on to suggest that passing on orders from 'on high' that he didn't personally agree with was very difficult. His belief in the integrity and worth of the individual made it difficult for him to give orders that treated individuals as expendable:

> Conveying to staff the message from on high is not very palatable for me. My beliefs are in the individual. I think an educational organisation is based on teaching individuals and every person within it should be treasured and valued and cultivated and you just shouldn't be saying to people that we really

don't need your sort any more. We should be saying, perhaps, 'your profile is not what we actually need but we can look around for another position for you, we can retrain you', but we've moved away from that to being a more typical private sector [organisation].

There is a strong view, however, among most principals in the study that, despite budget restrictions and economic imperatives, it is always possible to exercise care and concern for those with whom they work. They recommend the need to be fair in relationships and provide others with the reasons for why you decided the way you did. Honesty, they say, is the best policy when trying to manage complex and tension-filled situations.

The leadership challenges identified by many leaders in this study included another category of tension that was usually described as 'status quo *versus* change and development'. These are situations where various staff members disagree as to whether the 'way they currently do things' (*status quo*) is preferable to suggested new ways of thinking and doing (change and development).

Status quo *and* development

Maintaining the status quo is about avoiding and resisting change. Development or growth implies embracing changes. (A principal)

There were claims by a number of principals that many staff, especially those close to retirement, are marking time, and are content with doing things as they have always been done. This issue was addressed in chapter 3 under the challenge of leading an ageing workforce. A principal reported the challenge this way:

A teacher, in the last years in the service, had been an outstanding practitioner but was now tired and cynical. His room looked like his attitude. All new policies were treated as, 'We've done this before' or 'If I don't change, it will go away'.

Another principal was cynical about the prospect of changing many of the older teachers:

When you look at the demographics of the teaching profession now, it's an ageing profession. There are fewer young people coming in, but yet there are more and more changes put in place. Many of the older members of staff are resistant to change. There is a cynicism; they've seen it all before, right through to the extreme of, 'I won't be here much longer, why put myself through this messy stage of change and learning new skills?'

A number of educational leaders suggest that many older personnel are choosing to retire rather than cope with rapid change. In some cases, the loss of the experience and knowledge of these older members of the organisation is perceived by leaders to be detrimental to the life and effectiveness of the school. When older members retire, vital organisational memory and wisdom can be lost with them.

It is unfair, however, to brand all elderly staff as lacking either the capability or willingness to change or to make valuable contributions to their school community. In fact, some leaders regarded experienced older personnel as valuable members of staff so far as they are able to distil the essence of current practice that need to be changed. A principal argued that:

> working with experienced staff, you get the experience of years. You get a lot of [experienced] staff who are willing to look at change, or look at a program and say, 'OK, let's look at this and let's change it this way. We can do a short cut or we can do something that will make it easier for us.'

Some educational leaders noted that while replacing older personnel is complex, absence of 'new blood' might lead to a lack of creative energy and enthusiasm in the school. A principal put the problem clearly and succinctly:

> I think one of the other things that I find that I'm challenged by, and I'm sure everybody else is too, is the whole issue about the ageing workforce. We've got an ageing workforce and because we've got changing budgets, we've got shrinking recruitment, which doesn't bring in the new staff; we've got, therefore, less injection of enthusiasm, and youth.

A principal warned, however, that all staff need to be prepared to move on from the *status quo* and embrace change, if they are to thrive in contemporary schools:

> I am talking about change in every facet, externally driven change, yes. Change in people's own lives and belief systems … I mean there are changes in people's lives, and this impinges upon their work. So [I refer to] change, in its broader sense, but certainly there are external forces in terms of curriculum, in terms of school … issues where there is a lot of change happening. They are pretty significant [in terms of] their impact.

This tension between opting for the *status quo* instead of change and development generates numerous ethical tensions for leaders. While they must respect the traditions and practices of long-serving staff, they are also ethically responsible for keeping their school and its teaching approaches 'up to date' and constantly improving. This is a real challenge and one that is not going away anytime soon.

Dealing with tensions: lessons from leaders

The educational leaders in this study were asked to reflect on the tension situations in which they had been involved and identify lessons they had learned from them. The following recommendations are paraphrased from some of the most pertinent and insightful responses and should prove to be useful for leadership practitioners and for those responsible for leadership development and formation.

1   There is no 'one best way' for determining which dimension(s) of a tension situation you should choose. You have to examine the facts of the situation carefully, and then use your rational thought, wisdom and good judgement to strike a dynamic balance among sometimes competing values and interests.

2   There are no simple and easy answers when dealing with people and a conflict of values. The pursuit of a rational approach to decision-making is recommended but it must be tempered with care and emotional intelligence.

3   You have to be true to yourself and live your values. You have to live with yourself at the end of the day. Honesty and openness, when attempting to resolve such tensions, is always the best policy. Deceptiveness and playing politics are condemned.

4   It is better to deal with a difficult situation sooner rather than later; putting off the difficult steps in a process of decision-making does not make the difficulties disappear.

5   Sometimes there needs to be a clinical approach to situations; compassionate leadership should be the norm but often a less soft approach must be considered, in the interest of the common good.

6   Always be guided, when making ethical decisions, by what you believe is 'right and good'.

7   When the going gets tough and you know you're right, you need to stick with your decision. It takes moral courage to stand up for what you believe to be right.

8   Decisions will be different depending on the persons involved and on mitigating circumstances. Don't expect that when a similar situation arises again the same decision will be the most effective one.

9   While good does not necessarily come from getting consensus first, those who have to implement decisions must have input into making them.

10   The easy option in difficult situations is to do nothing. Leaders, however, must speak up against injustice. They are duty bound to follow ethical and moral courses of action.

11   It seems easier to arrange for the transfer of ineffective staff or ignore them altogether, than to try to dismiss them. However, leaders should 'bite the bullet' and tackle the problem of inefficient staff members sooner rather than later.

12   Leaders need to 'walk the talk' and do what they say they are going to do. It is not good enough to say all the right things but, in times of stress, practice entirely different principles.

13   It is important to trust the basic 'goodness' of people. Leaders have to give trust to get it in return.

14 At the end of the day, you need to own your decision, be able to give sound reasons for it and defend it in public.

A conclusion from this research is that a *both/and* rather than an *either/or* mindset and approach will be more effective in resolving tension situations. It is usually not a matter of the individual *versus* the group or common good; or loyalty *versus* honesty, but that consideration be given in decision-making to the individual *and* the common good as well as to honesty *and* loyalty.

Leaders need to be able to map complex situations that involve tensions, apply frameworks that help them make sense of this complexity, and find productive pathways through what may appear as a maze. *Both/and* responses that can take into consideration contradictions and opposites are more likely to lead to satisfactory outcomes. The elements of such a framework are identified and discussed in chapter 5.

Key ideas for reflection

The real challenges for educational leaders are usually characterised by tensions between and among people – especially with regard to their philosophies, values, interests and preferences.

Tensions usually reflect the quality of the relationships between and among people. Rarely, however, can issues involving complex human relationships be resolved by neat, logical and linear management processes, no matter how systematically or thoroughly they are applied.

A close scrutiny of many of the cases presented in this chapter demonstrates that expectations, perspectives and opinions may differ when the human elements of a tension situation are considered. Usually, *either/or* thinking that adopts a one- or two-dimensional response will not encompass the complexity of real human dramas.

Questions for reflection

Briefly describe a recent critical incident involving tensions where you had to make difficult ethical choices:

1 What happened in the situation (the facts of the matter)?

2 Who were the people involved and what were their possible intentions/motivations?

3 What were the key dynamics and processes in the incident?

4 What tensions were experienced, and by whom?

5 What choices did you and others make, and with what consequences?

6 What lessons did you learn from the incident?

Reflect on and analyse the incident from a *both/and* perspective

When identifying the tensions involved, refer especially to those related to: common good *and* individual rights; care *and* rules; long-term *and* short-term; loyalty *and* honesty; service *and* rationalism; status quo *and* change and development. Not all these tensions will apply to every critical incident so choose those that are relevant and useful in understanding and resolving your critical incident.

Alternatively, you may wish to use one of the cases reported in this chapter that is similar to a situation you had to deal with. Feel free to embellish the case by including elements of the situation you had to resolve.

Remember, the more complex and multidimensional the case the more challenging it will be to apply *both/and* approaches to resolving it, What has become clear in relevant research is that these cases approximate real-life tensions faced by educational leaders in schools every day.

Chapter 5

A framework for analysing ethical tensions

The challenges and tensions faced by educational leaders in this study and discussed, primarily, in chapters 3 and 4, are complex and difficult to resolve. They created ambiguities and uncertainty for those trying to decide which response is likely to be the most successful. An important finding to emerge was that most of the leaders in the study had no rigorous and systematic method for analysing and responding to the tensions. In other words, in such situations they were often flying blind or trusting their intuition.

It seems clear that educational leaders require frames of reference and decision guidelines for making choices in situations that seem to present opposing values and ethical positions. This need is not well accepted, never mind understood or appreciated, by a majority of those who study and practice educational leadership and management. The traditional perspective of a world of certainty and precision that can be controlled through tried-and-true management processes and techniques, still tends to dominate educational leadership thinking and practice.

Frameworks are needed, particularly, to help educational leaders appreciate that just because the forces operating in a situation appear to be contradictory, even irreconcilable, the situation is not intractable or irresolvable. Handy, in his 1994 influential commentary on leadership dilemmas, provides valuable insights into the nature of a tension or dilemma and on how to respond to them. He argues that in life and work 'opposites are necessary to each other' (p. 48) and leaders must learn to frame the perceived ambiguity and confusion and 'find pathways through the paradoxes' (p. 3) by understanding what is actually happening in a particular situation. They must break the bonds imposed on their thinking by dualistic *either/or* mindsets and try to cultivate *both/and* thinking and decision-making approaches.

As discussed in chapter 1, leaders must become morally literate, develop their moral compass, and intentionally operate in the moral sphere in order to transform their values into guides for appropriate actions. They must underpin their leadership platform with well-articulated ethical and moral support pillars, and work collaboratively to generate a culture that doesn't tolerate ethical blind spots and that encourages all key stakeholders to have clear moral compasses and to commit to moral agency.

Analysing tensions using *both/and* thinking

In a significant research study entitled 'The double-headed arrow', English (1995) suggested that while managers and leaders usually approach a paradox or tension situation as a contested duality, it is more productive to first look for relationship and complementarity rather than polar opposites. He defined tension as '*two contrasting phenomena in a relationship that embodies both competition and complementarity*' (p. 58, italics in original). A challenge for educational leaders is that tensions often represent 'phenomena separated at an arbitrary point on a continuum. Sensitivity ◄────────► insensitivity is such a tension – there is no unequivocal division between sensitivity and insensitivity' (pp. 58–9). The resolution of tensions, English concluded, is a matter of good judgement that is '… heavily influenced by the nature of the judge' (p. 60). He continues by arguing that, in the context of managerial work, the analysis and interpretation of tensions ' … is grounded in experience and the perceptual frameworks that actors take to that experience'.

The world and situations within it are not so easily dissected and divided as many might believe. Leaders and managers must be careful not to impose their own built-in dualistic mindsets to resolve tension situations. Many in Western cultures have been conditioned to think in dualistic ways as we have inherited from the Greeks down through Thomas Aquinas and Christianity generally, an understanding of the world and life as essentially dualistic. While Aquinas is often associated with supporting the idea of duality between body and soul, he built on Aristotle's concept of 'form' to argue that 'soul' reflects 'the unity, identity and activity of a living being' and both body and soul 'are the two *principles* of created human nature. They are not to be thought of as separate parts or components of a person, but as *principles* that together explain what we are as human beings' (Gleeson, 2005, p. 20).

The strength of the Aquinas approach is that 'while it affirms a limited dualism – the relative independence of the soul – it also preserves the unity of the human person as a both bodily and spiritual being, not one or the other' (p. 23). Perhaps Aquinas has been unfairly blamed for his role in promoting a belief in duality in Christianity and, especially, within Catholicism! However, it is fair to say that over the years, neat categories have been invented to describe a perceived divided world – body and soul, heaven and hell, good and evil, right and wrong, masculine and feminine, and many more.

Many Eastern philosophies and cultures do not think like this. For those of us brought up in Western philosophies and beliefs, it is difficult to appreciate, let alone understand, the Buddhist perspective of 'emptiness' (see Senge et al., 2004, p. 190) or the Chinese perspective of 'yin and yang'. Having been brought up believing in the 'law of excluded middle,' that is, that something is either true or false, it is difficult to comprehend the view that all things, being in a state of flux, are interrelated, mutually dependent and never in irreconcilable conflict. The concepts of yin and yang maintain that opposites only exist in relation to each other and seemingly contrary forces are interconnected, interdependent and constitute an 'unbroken wholeness' (Senge et al., 2004, p. 199).

A similar view is promulgated by Aristotle in *Rhetoric*, (McAdon, 2004; Roberts, 1954) when he claimed in his contingency view that multiple possibilities are present in every situation and the complex nature of decisions creates and invites possibilities, even opportunities for discourse, dialogue and, thereby, promote harmony. In a recent commentary on leadership, Walker (2011), from experiences for over twenty years in different countries of Asia, particularly in Hong Kong, sees a leader's key challenge with regard to relationships and collective decision-making as 'connecting, disconnecting and reconnecting pathways' (p. 3). To illustrate, he uses the metaphor of 'reflexology' within the Chinese context, as holding that 'the health of each part of the body – the being – is dependent on what happens in others. The state of one element resonates in the others' (p. 7). The Chinese, he states, generally see the world and life 'not as collections of discrete objectives but as an interwoven mass of substances in search of harmony' (p. 5) – key thinking underpinning *yin* and *yang*. At times (even at the same time), in dynamic and changing environments, leaders will be busy connecting (e.g., activities with vision; individual colleagues into teams), while disconnecting from restrictive and harmful structures (perhaps even from some people), with the clear intention of reconnecting key elements (e.g., new collaborative forms of decision-making; new processes and patterns of pedagogy, teaching and leadership). In many ways, there is nothing new in such approaches for many contemporary leaders because this is what they actually do on a daily basis. The key emphasis, however, has to be on intentionality driven by moral purpose and not on allowing such dynamic elements (connecting, disconnecting, reconnecting) to emerge because of chaotic conditions and then cause confusion and dysfunction.

English (1995) appreciates the importance of interdependence and connectivity in the work of leaders and managers and understands that every yin needs its yang for wholeness. In research on challenges facing managers in an Asian context, he recommends that leaders should see dilemmas and tension situations, not in terms of polarity and *opposites* but in terms of *relationships* that encompasses both competition and complementarity. They should, he says, determine as best they can, the qualities and conditions of relationships in each situation by asking how the issues and seeming contradictions are connected. Using this approach leaders can better understand and manage a change situation (usually characterised by uncertainty and confusion) by building a profile of the positive dimensions, especially in people's relationships, within the tensions. In Handy's (1994) terms they are framing the confusion.

Based on seminal research by English (1995), a tension situation can be characterised by a *double-headed arrow* (p. 276) as shown in figure 5.1. Seeming polar opposites are seen as in complex and mutually interdependent relationships, and influences are rarely one-way. Instead of being mutually exclusive, most opposites are in tension, characterised partly by both competition and by complementarity (English, 1995). In tension situations, leaders should start their decision–resolution processes by searching for and focusing on the positives and the complementarities. Sometimes these may not be evident but they are there and, when found, you build upon them.

Figure 5.1: *Double-headed arrow*
(Adapted from English, 1995)

A similar and complementary message can be found in Seligman's (2003 & 2011) propositions for a positive psychology where he argues that 'psychology has badly neglected the positive side of life' (2003, p. 6) but when our 'well-being comes from engaging our strengths and virtues, our lives are imbued with authenticity' (p. 9). He points out that:

> there is an astonishing convergence across the millennia and across cultures about virtue and strength. Confucius, Aristotle, Aquinas, the Bushido samurai code … and other venerable traditions disagree on the details, but all of these codes include six core virtues:
>
> • Wisdom and knowledge
> • Courage
> • Love and humanity
> • Justice
> • Temperance
> • Spirituality and transcendence (Seligman, 2003 p. 11).

In building his case for positive psychology from his research and experiences, Seligman concluded that in order to motivate and get the best from others, it is unproductive to focus on correcting their shortcomings. Instead it is much better to 'see into their soul' and nurture their strengths (p. 28). Identifying and amplifying the strengths and virtues of others and 'helping them find the niche where they can live these positive traits to the fullest,' is the best pathway for leaders (p. 28). A key challenge for leaders within their lives and work is 'exploring what makes life worth living and building the enabling conditions of a life worth living' (Seligman, 2011, pp. 1–2) in order to 'increase the amount of *flourishing* in your own life and on the planet' (p. 26, italics in original).

The purpose of this discussion on positive psychology is to remind leaders that their preparation and training has, most likely, neglected the positive side of human relationships and conditioned them to look for perceived pathologies and negative instances. Seligman is encouraging them to develop positive frames that help them focus on positives, strengths, mutually beneficial relationships, and positive habits of mind when confronted with contentious and potentially volatile situations. These positive habits, together with such Eastern philosophical positions on 'emptiness' and 'yin and yang', help to develop frames for thinking and action that will assist leaders when attempting to resolve complex, challenging and potentially divisive dilemmas and tension situations.

By emphasising positives, strengths, connections, relationship and complementarities, instead of the seeming contradictions and opposites, leaders have a better chance of influencing the direction and intensity of the positive elements of a tension situation (English, 1995). It is not productive to opt for the *either/or* approach, perhaps believing that the opposing forces are mutually exclusive and incompatible, thereby creating a win–lose situation.

Let us take an example in which a teacher has contributed quality service for over twenty-five years but is currently performing at a much lower level. A number of tensions, identified earlier in the cases related to teacher performance, are inherent in such a situation. Decision-makers require frameworks for dealing with these tensions. Tensions in this situation can be analysed using the concept of the double-headed arrow, in ways that will help leaders frame and analyse the tensions. All six of the major tensions discussed in chapter 3 may be seen in this single situation:

1 considerations for the **individual** (the teacher) *and* the **common good** (the clients/students);

2 **care** (showing compassion and a caring attitude to the teacher) *and* **rules** (following the 'letter of the law' with regard to the rules on performance appraisal);

3 **long-term** (interests of teacher and students) *and* **short-term** (the quick but not necessarily easy way would be to dismiss the staff member);

4 **loyalty** (to the teacher for long service) *and* **honesty** (about current performance in the interests of justice);

5 **service** (providing the best possible support for the teacher and teaching for the students) *and* **economic rationalism** (making most thrifty use of resources, including other staff's time); and

6 **status quo** *and* **change and development** (it is often easier to leave things as they are but this will not usually solve the problem) (an obvious option is to provide the staff member with professional development opportunities).

These tensions and their possible relationships are presented in diagrammatic form in figure 5.2.

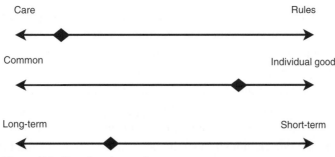

Figure 5.2: *Framing the tension*

If leaders approach this situation with an *either/or* mindset, they may see the issues in terms of only one of the polarities, for instance in terms of the common good, without due consideration for the individual rights of the staff member, or they may decide that 'rules are rules' and therefore compassion isn't really an option. However, if they adopt a *both/and* mindset they will look for the positives and the complementarities in these tensions and try to choose options that reflect a dynamic balance between considerations for both rules and caring. In this way they can better frame a difficult, multidimensional tension situation and make a more enlightened decision. In the end, however, judgements have to be made to resolve the tensions.

While the framework suggested by English proves to be very useful for educational leaders when confronted with resolving tension situations, it can be improved. The approach, in fact, reflects a modified linear approach to decision-making. Most organisations react ineffectively to rapid change and uncertain situations because, as Senge (1992) argues, they tend to be 'dominated by linear thinking, not systems thinking' (p. 231). What is needed in organisations is systems thinking which he defines as 'a discipline for seeing wholes. It is a framework for seeing interrelationships rather than things, for seeing patterns of change rather than static snapshots' (p. 68).

Senge calls systems thinking the 'fifth discipline' because it 'offers a language for structuring how we think' (p. 69) and shifts our mind from '… seeing parts to seeing wholes, from seeing people as helpless reactors to seeing them as active participants in shaping their reality, from reacting to the present to creating the future' (p. 69). He provides leaders with very insightful advice on how they can positively influence relationships and outcomes in real-life situations. He says:

> The key to seeing reality systematically is seeing circles of influence rather than straight lines. This is the first step to breaking out of the reactive mindset that comes inevitably from 'linear' thinking. Every circle tells a story. By tracing the flows of influence, you can see patterns that repeat themselves, time after time, making situations better or worse. From any element in a situation [e.g., feedback, direct instruction], you can trace arrows that represent influence on another element (Senge, 1992, p. 75).

A problem is that while many educational leaders use the language of learning community, spheres of influence, and systems forms of thinking frequently, they think and act in narrow, restrictive and restricting linear ways and, as reported by Hames (2007), encourage an illusion that they are actually solving complex dilemmas and tensions when all they are really doing is 'resolving a few, discrete, easily detected, symptoms' (p. 110). What is required is that leaders use the new language for restructuring their thinking and for generating mindset changes.

For example, there is strong evidence to support the view that schools as communities of learners are essentially non-linear fields of relationships and that leadership influence is not simply a linear process to be effected through managerial, supervisory or hierarchical processes (Duignan, 2010). In order to appreciate this position, educational leaders must have a greater appreciation of what non-linear processes mean and how they actually operate in leadership practice.

Viewing relationships in non-linear ways instead of linear ones allows for a wider range of possible independencies and interdependencies. Often when leaders are faced with a situation where the facts are few or information is scarce, they may assume a simpler, linear relationships – a cause and effect approach. This is understandable because, as Senge (1992) argues, we are 'steeped in a linear language for describing our experience. We find simple statements about causality and responsibility familiar and comfortable' (p. 79).

However, when a tension situation is 'opened up' to dialogue and collaborative analysis multiple, mutually interdependent relationships emerge. Such relationships are, typically, represented by a curve and not a straight line. When using statistical analysis of relationships (e.g., relationship of independent and dependent variables), the representative curve is one whose slope changes as the value of one of the variables changes, but in figures 5.3 and 5.4 we use a constant curve because the intention is simply to highlight for leaders that complex tension relationships can be multidimensional and multidirectional. This point will be explained in the discussion that follows.

The relationships depicted in figures 5.1 and 5.2 are represented by straight lines and are essentially linear, but by using double-headed curves instead to represent relationships, leaders are reminded that when faced with complexity and tensions, non-linear, systems thinking is more appropriate (see figure 5.3). Also, with the use of double curves, leaders should be alert to the possibility of numerous interrelationships and multiple interdependent connections in a tension situation.

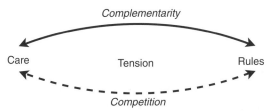

Figure 5.3: *A non-linear view*

By applying non-linear curved double-headed arrows to tension situations a profile of relationships emerges which is more likely to result in informed choices that are responsive to the complexity of the problem. Taking again the case of the teacher who gave loyal service for over twenty-five years (as depicted in figure 5.2), an analysis using non-linear and systems thinking can be depicted as in figure 5.4.

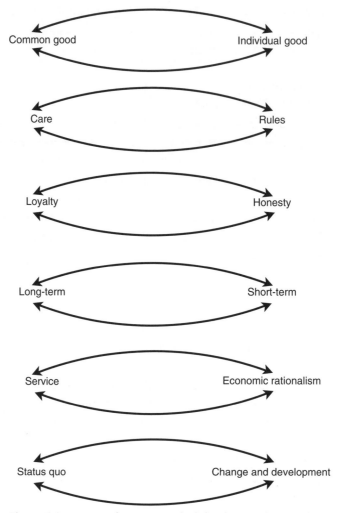

Figure 5.4: *Framing the tension 1: look for the complementarity*

Generating a profile of the tensions involved in this case helps a leader avoid responding to complexity in simplistic and linear ways (e.g., cause and effect). The profile simplifies the complex, by illuminating the key interconnected relationships of a particular situation. The curved arrows remind decision-makers to look for multiple perspectives, contested value positions, and differences in experiences so typical of individuals and groups involved in contentious situations. However, these curved, double-headed arrows also indicate that tension situations involve the possibility of complementarities and positive relationships as well as competition and negativity.

It doesn't mean that leaders will need to formally graph the tensions in particular situations (with significant problems and tensions they may do so) but it encourages them to apply this form of systems thinking so that it becomes 'a habit of mind' (Costa & Kallick, 2008). Habits of mind, according to Costa and Kallick, are key characteristics of 'what intelligent people do when they are confronted with problems, the resolutions to which are not immediately apparent' (p. 15). The processes engaged by habits of mind include 'habits of thinking flexibly, thinking about thinking (meta cognition), thinking and communicating with clarity and precision, and perhaps even questioning and posing problems' (p. 15). They claim that a 'critical attribute of intelligent human beings is not only having information but also knowing how to act on it' (p. 16) and this challenge appears to be a crucial one for leaders faced with resolving complex tensions.

While it is essential to understand that the application of a particular form of thinking (systems thinking) or a frame of reference will not deliver a 'cut-and-dried' answer, it will assist educational leaders to make better decisions in difficult situations by encouraging them to consider relationships and complementarity, rather than conflict and disagreement, thereby enabling them to balance the tensions for a positive outcome. Equally important, the framework will support leaders to clearly communicate the reasons for their decisions, so that even if stakeholders are unhappy with the outcome, they know that most aspects are considered.

It is also important to note that not all the dimensions identified in figures 5.2 and 5.4 will apply to every tension situation. Educational leaders will need to judge which ones are relevant and useful in analysing a particular situation and this wisdom comes from reflecting on experiences and practices, seeking honest feedback, and developing intelligent habits of mind. In the case of the student who received a blue slip as a penalty for misbehaviour within one week of a major regional athletics carnival (in chapter 3), only three of the dimensions were addressed directly by the principal and these are depicted in figure 5.5.

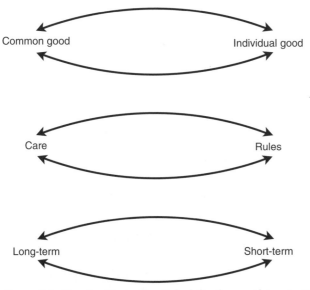

Figure 5.5: *Framing the tension 2: look for the complementarity*

The decision was made to allow the student to compete even though it was against the school rules, thereby emphasising the care side of the care–rules continuum. However, through discussion and dialogue among staff members, serious consideration was given to the dynamic balance between care issues and relevant rules. The rules were discussed and considered. This is as it should be. The ultimate decision gave greater weight to the individual good of the student over the common good of the other students, because by 'bending' the rules a precedent was established which could have been criticised as other students who committed similar offences in the past were excluded from athletic competition. As well, the decision considered the long-term consequences for the student whose self-concept was so dependent on athletic performance, over the short-term implications of excluding him from the competition, even though it was setting a precedent. No doubt, short-term consequences for all parties in the situation were also canvassed.

Often in cases like this, decision-makers have no frameworks to help them identify the multidimensionality of challenging situations, or the type of tensions involved. The application of a framework like the ones in figures 5.4 and 5.5 helps make sense of complex situations and highlights *both/and* approaches to decision-making. In the end, judgement is still called for in reaching a resolution to the tensions involved, but the framework helps clarify what exactly is under consideration.

The framework in action

In many of the complex cases already cited, it might be tempting for decision-makers to quickly jump to conclusions, to blame one side or another, or to opt for one set of values over another simply because they more closely reflect or support their own assumptions, mindsets and values. It is often easier to adopt an *either/ or* approach because this may seem to reduce the confusion and frustration of dealing with competing value positions or unpopular alternatives. Many leaders tend to think in terms of cause and effect in such situations or simply opt to select from our own preferred set of solutions. The philosophical approaches (seeing interconnectedness and wholes), approach to thinking (systems thinking), and framework (for profiling tensions using non-linear relationships), should remind decision-makers that '… *the inclusion of competing value perspectives may be essential to adaptive success'* (Heifetz, 1994, p. 23, italics in original). Finding the simple solution, or the one *right* answer, is often neither judicious nor effective.

In the incident about possible student involvement in drugs described and discussed in chapter 3, there were some, including teachers and parents, who did not know all of the facts of the situation. There were also sharp differences of opinion between and among groups (teachers and parents) as to how the girls should be dealt with, especially considering that some were nearing the completion of their academic careers. The principal who reported the case indicated that at first the simple option would have been to apply the rules strictly and suspend or expel the students. Through discussion of other relevant information and with a consideration of a diversity of viewpoints with different value positions and the canvassing of a possible range of consequences, an alternative resolution was decided on. He elaborated on some of these considerations:

> Valuing the need to create a safe environment for the remainder of the student body; wanting to also deal with these girls justly and to enable them to move on from their mistake; protecting the interests of the parents; and also creating an environment in which staff felt that there was still a level of discipline within the student body and that we weren't going to give the wrong messages about that.

The framework of double-headed arrows can be usefully applied to this case. It is important for the principal to start by trying to establish the key significant facts in the situation. Often this is best achieved through open dialogue, though privacy issues must be dealt with as necessary. The idea is to start with the facts that are not in dispute (finding a touchstone) and then build from there. There may also be values, ideas and opinions that are not in dispute, and these are important positive touchstones. Finding touchstone(s) is the key. As most people who have had to deal with such situations know, it may be impossible to determine the full truth of the matter. This usually means that informed (but not necessarily fully informed) judgement will be called for at some stage.

Clearly there are individual and common good considerations in the case of the girls. What is in the best interests of individual students? What about the effects on the school population if the sanctions for these girls are regarded as inadequate or unfair? How can both dimensions be considered and what should be the dynamic balance between them? There are short- and long-term considerations to be decided. There are care and compassion considerations as well as the need to carefully consider the rules and the possible consequences of not following them. A decision that is in the short-term interests of the school or of particular classes in which the girls are taught may not be in the long-term interests of the girls and their parents. And perhaps more importantly, rules are rules and drugs are strictly prohibited. It is usually well-known to students that being in possession of drugs in school, or being involved with them outside school, attracts severe sanctions.

How then can the decision maker (or decision makers in this case) apply a degree of care and compassion to the resolution of this situation when the rules are so clear? Not all of the dimensions of a tension situation will always involve contestable values dualities. In this case the girls were dealt with on a case-by-case basis. This raises a concern over the principle of justice (discussed in chapter 6) if some are treated more leniently than others. However, the details of each girl's involvement differed, so the manner of dealing with them should also differ. This is why the proposed method for ethical decision-making in chapter 6 emphasises collecting and understanding, as far as possible, the facts of the situation. A decision based on false or unsubstantiated information is not going to be a wise one.

The framework can help the decision maker focus on and analyse the numerous dimensions inherent in the situation. The concepts of relationship and complementarity help to remind the decision maker that in a situation where facts, values, ideas and opinions are all in tension, it is essential to look for and build on the common ground or touchstone.

This discussion on the use of the framework in the case of the girls with drugs has focused, primarily, on a single decision maker, for example an educational leader such as a school principal, applying it to a difficult situation involving tensions. However, groups can use this framework successfully. In the case just discussed, it is clear that different teachers had different points of view on the facts and on the possible alternative solutions. Parents, too, had divergent views on the seriousness of the situation and on possible alternative solutions.

Using the framework to build group understanding

The concepts of positive relationship and complementarity should be emphasised in any group analysis of a tension situation. The author has used the double-headed arrows with groups to build a profile of the numerous possible tensions inherent in a particular challenging situation and, mostly, these groups are surprised to see the complexity and multidimensionality of the situation spread out before them. It is emphasised in such discussions that what often appears to be polar opposites, or equally unwelcome possibilities as with a dilemma (e.g., with regard to values, perspectives or opinions), usually lend themselves to a more positive analysis using the concept of the touchstone, and to a greater appreciation of the usefulness of *both/and* thinking as opposed to *either/or* thinking.

The use of systems and non-linear thinking as well as an analysis framework not only helps make sense of confusion but it can also help a group approach tension situations with a positive mindset, helping them discover and concentrate on common ground instead of differences. As with any group analysis approach, good judgement should be exercised in its use with parent groups and other sensitive stakeholders. Issues related to drugs, as well as other serious student discipline issues as discussed in chapter 3, can generate much heated debate and an unwillingness to compromise. When using this framework with such groups, a focus on a group search for the touchstone(s), relationship(s) and complementarity in tension situations should be the primary agenda item, and this should be reinforced by pointing out the usefulness of systems or *both/and* thinking. While there are no guarantees of general agreement, never mind consensus, on such occasions, it seems sensible to identify common ground, no matter how small, and build from there.

A constraint in all group decision situations, especially when dealing with sensitive information or when issues of privacy are a concern, is that it may not be advisable or wise to share all the known facts of the situation. Obviously, then, it will be difficult, if not impossible, for the group to come up with a well-informed decision.

Another consideration is that identification and analysis of tensions, and their subsequent resolution, involves the use of good judgement, and that can be greatly influenced by the background experiences of those making that judgement. Educational leaders can temper their possible biases and prejudices by entering into open discussion and dialogue with key stakeholders, by developing sympathetic listening skills, by learning to suspend their own judgements until all, or most, of the significant facts of the situation are known, and until key perspectives and opinions are canvassed. The wisdom of groups should never be underestimated (Surowiecki, 2005).

Even in situations that appear to be intractable, where opinions seem to be diametrically opposed, there is usually some degree of touchstone or common ground. Considering the tensions methodically in this way will assist educational leaders to discover these touchstones. Once they have identified them, they can build on them, accepting of course that there will continue to be differences of perspective and opinion. Usually, there is no one solution in such challenging situations; resolution based on collaborative dialogue and good judgement is likely to be the most productive outcome.

With practice, this approach can become 'habit of mind' (Costa & Kallick, 2008), which can be applied with the speed of thought. Although some people may always prefer to sketch a rough diagram as an *aide-mémoire*, once familiar with systems and *both/and* modes of thinking there will be no need to apply elaborate diagrams or engage in slavishly step-by-step processes. It is important for educational leaders to take the concepts and the framework discussed in this chapter and apply them in ways that work for them. A slightly more formal approach may be necessary with groups.

An important added consideration when analysing the type of challenges discussed in chapters 2 and 3 is that complex situations involving people in disagreement or tension usually have ethical and value-based dimensions that have to be factored in when making decisions to resolve the situations. An ethics and values approach to, as well as a method for, decision-making in such situations is discussed in the next chapter.

Key ideas for reflection

A tension situation can best be characterised by a *double-headed arrow* showing the relationship between seeming opposites. Many of the tensions identified in chapter 3 represent values, perspectives and opinions separated at an arbitrary point on a continuum or on a non-linear curve; for example, individual good ⟷ common good is such a tension. Part of the difficulty in making a decision involving this continuum is that there is no unequivocal, indisputable division between what may appear to be polar opposites. Even when a systems thinking and non-linear approach to understanding relationships is adopted, a decision maker still has to make judgements as to which point on the curve will deliver the best solution to the tension. Based on the philosophy, concepts, and frames presented in this chapter, reflect on the following questions.

Questions for reflection

Take the analysis of the critical incident you described at the end of chapter 4 to a new level by focusing on the relationships and complementarities in the tensions (as depicted in figures 5.3 and 5.3). This will help you to better understand and apply systems and non-linear thinking to the concept of the double-headed arrow, as well as develop a habit of mind of *both/and* approaches to resolving tensions in real-life situations.

1 What are the key tensions in the situation?

2 What are the complementarities and interconnections within these tensions?

3 Where are the touchstones, in terms of the facts and values, in each of the tensions?

4 How can you build on these touchstones to influence the intensity and direction of the positive elements of the tension situation?

5 What are several different ways that you might be able to resolve this situation?

6 What is the best possible resolution (your judgement) of this situation at this time?

Chapter 6

Vision-inspired leadership and ethical decision-making

The tensions identified in earlier chapters are part of the fabric of life and work in service organisations, such as schools. They can be very challenging, even frustrating, but cannot be ignored or wished away. Part of the responsibility of working in service environments is to engage in positive, productive and ethical ways with these tensions. Decisions have to be made based on informed judgement and educational leaders will benefit from understanding how values and ethics can help them influence outcomes in decision situations. This understanding is the focus of this chapter.

Values and leadership

There is a special need for leaders to call on their core values when leading in complex and dynamic situations. Duignan and Cannon (2011) suggest that 'when all seems to be in constant crisis and when strategic direction seems to be swamped by short-term emergencies, leaders need to focus on core values and moral purpose' (p. 26). It is important, however, that the espoused values of a school are agreed on, shared and form the basis for all decision-making. Core values are usually enduring values and, according to Degenhardt and Duignan (2010), 'constitute the one permanent foundation for the school when everything else within and outside ... seem to be changing' (p. 175). In their research on transforming a traditional secondary school into a twenty-first century learning environment, they reported that in the change process 'significantly, one of the most powerful weapons within the school's culture was to accuse another person or group of not being true to the school's values' (p. 175). In fact, they argue that these values were 'significant in establishing a compelling rationale and inspiration for change, a sense of urgency and a catalyst' for transforming the school's pedagogy and learning environments (p. 175).

The moral principles on which educational leadership stands should be supported by 'a clearly articulated value system which explicitly or implicitly underpins leadership actions by providing the reasons why leaders do what they do' (Flintham, 2010, p. 53). Based on interviews with 150 school principals in the UK and Australia, he claims that all of these principals viewed core values as essential for their leadership and they could 'articulate instantly and often passionately, the value system that inspires and motivates their leadership' (p. 53). He cautioned, however, that value sets might be deeply challenged when leaders are faced with complex and difficult situations but that this is not a bad thing. He quotes from one of his principals who testified that 'the experience [of a critical incident] shook my belief system about what I stand for, but then paradoxically led to a reaffirmation and strengthening of what my core values actually are' (p. 59). Perhaps there is some truth in the old adage, 'what doesn't kill you makes you stronger'.

A set of core values is especially important for effective leadership of change and one of the most effective things leaders of complex and dynamic organisations can do is to create conditions and opportunities for stakeholders to 'explore and articulate their individual and shared values' (Jansen et al., 2011, p. 71). Based on their research on values and belief systems of leaders in twenty-five non-government organisations (NGOs) in New Zealand, they recommend that defining, discussing and getting an agreement on core values is 'vital' as it establishes 'a bedrock on which to base critical decisions' (p. 71, based on a finding of Davies, 2006).

Problems can arise, however, when values and beliefs, even though loudly espoused by leaders, do not drive their actions and behaviours. The numerous examples in recent times of organisational leaders who seem to have forgotten or ignored values and ethics in the choices they make (e.g., *News of the World* and many banks during the global financial crisis) seem to support this view.

In their research on reculturing schools to become professional learning communities, Eaker et al., (2002) report that such reculturing involves a shift in a school's mission, vision and values, and the biggest cultural shift that must occur in the area of values 'is the shift from belief to behaviour' (p. 15). They point out that 'in traditional schools the focus is on beliefs' (p. 15) with many of their learning documents starting with 'We believe …' statements. Instead, they suggest that professional learning communities focus on behaviours that emanate from the core values and these 'values are articulated as behaviours and commitments' (p. 16) that are necessary to achieve the vision for the school.

In discussing values-inspired leadership, Kraemer (2011) claims that 'leadership, simply put, is the ability to influence others. Values-based leadership takes it to the next level. By word, action, and example, values-based leaders seek to inspire and motivate, using their influence to pursue what matters most' (p. 2). He argues that leadership should flow from who you are as a person and from what truly matters most to you and for this to happen, he suggests, you must know and be able to clearly articulate what you stand for – your values – and then do the right thing as best you can. He proposes four principles of values-inspired leadership:

1 *self-reflection* to assist you identify your values and what matters to you most;

2 *balance*, which is the ability to see situations from multiple perspectives and differing viewpoints;

3 *true self-confidence* based on recognising your strengths and weaknesses and striving for improvement; and

4 *genuine humility*, which helps you keep life in perspective, your feet firmly on the ground, and to develop a healthy respect for others.

Educational leaders would do well to embrace these four principles if they wish to authentically influence what really matters in their schools – maximising opportunities and outcomes for all students.

These principles and the call for values-inspired leadership have implications for leadership formation and character development. When discussing the possible effects of character education and development, Hattie (2009) has an important message with implications for educators and educational leaders when he says that 'the major outcome from moral education programs is the facilitation of moral judgement, that is, the way in which people define decisions and actions as morally right or wrong' (p. 149). An important implication of what Hattie suggests is that values must be at the core of decision-making.

Values and decision-making

Values are important for determining our sense of who we are. They develop over time and are influenced by family, education, peers and a whole range of experiences, both good and bad, that help shape identity. Even though we share many of our values with others, there will always be differences; whether in the degree of intensity with which we hold them or the way we prioritise them. These differences can lead to disagreement, dispute, and even outright conflict. X may believe that truth is the most important value to be preserved in a certain situation, such as the one described earlier for the students who were asked by the teacher to enter other students' marks into the computer. On the other hand, Y may believe that loyalty to the teacher ought to predominate. Both of them presumably believe that truth and loyalty are important values, but differ on how they ought to be prioritised in this case.

We might call this type of problem a tension characterised by a 'difference of opinion'. Sometimes the difference may not be over which value is more important, but whether or not an agreed value is best served by a particular line of action. X may believe that justice is best served by doing things this way, while Y may believe it will be better served that way. This sort of problem is described as a choice between *right and right* (Kidder, 1995). In decision-making in tension situations, such choices and differences of opinion occur on a regular basis, thereby giving considerations of values and ethics the reputation of being contentious.

This conundrum of right-versus-right is often faced by leaders who have to make choices in situations where values and ethical considerations are core (Cranston et al. 2006). Kidder (1995) stated: 'Tough choices, typically, are those that pit one right value against another' (p. 16). He pointed out that right-versus-right values are at the heart of most difficult choices in life and work. While there are numerous right-versus-wrong situations, they are, for the most part, more easily discernible and therefore more easily dealt with by honest, well-intentioned people. The most difficult choices faced by leaders are so difficult 'precisely because each side is firmly rooted in … core values' (p. 18).

Such choices usually present tensions between competing value positions (the double-headed arrow) where each can be interpreted as 'right' and justified in a given situation. Many of the tensions faced by leaders discussed in chapter 3 fall into this category of right-and-right and involve such choices as:

1 the rights of the individual *and* those of the group or community;

2 the exercise of compassion *and* following the rules;

3 the provision of a quality service *and* the efficient use of scarce resources; and

4 doing one's duty *and* doing the just thing.

Often there are deep ethical issues embedded within these four choices and judgements must be made as to the most appropriate dynamic balance between and among them.

Ethical decision-making

Decision-making can be painful and difficult. Some decisions are contentious. You may find that some of your staff or parents don't support you. Most decisions have consequences for other people. These consequences can be serious, even devastating to them. Decisions about discipline or employment can be like this (Strike, 2007, p. 113, author's italics added for emphasis).

Strike sets the context well for the challenges involved in ethical decision-making. As we saw in chapter 3, many of the tension situations faced by principals involved considerations of expulsion for students or the possible termination of a teacher's contract. Principals reported that they were acutely aware that any decision they made in such situations had the potential to harm someone. It is very pleasing, Strike suggests, when 'you have win-win choices, but the world often doesn't give them to you' (p.113). Of course, the veracity and legitimacy of your decisions may be, and often are, challenged by others. You may be accused of: not knowing, or ignoring, the 'true facts'; not following due process; not consulting the 'right' people; following flawed logic; or basing your decision on contested values or unwarranted assumptions (Strike, 2007). These accusations are all good reasons why educational leaders must have well-developed models for decision-making, especially those with contested ethical considerations.

In such contested situations, it is very important for leaders to see their leadership 'as a fully ethical task' and they need to deliberately 'frame their actions in ethical terms' (Freeman & Stewart, 2006, p. 7). They can also influence the ethical behaviours of others by creating a culture where sound ethical and moral judgements are encouraged, supported and celebrated. What ethical leaders essentially do is 'speak to us about our identity, what we are and what we can become, how we live and how we could live better' (p. 8). While these seem like lofty expectations, in reality 'ethical leaders are ordinary people who are living their lives as examples of making the world a better place' (p. 8). Put in these terms, the challenge to be (or become) an ethical leader does not appear so daunting but, as we will discuss in chapter 10, there are significant implications for the ways in which we develop and form our leaders.

A key to successful ethical decision-making is for leaders to have clear frameworks for the analysis of ethical situations.

Ethical analysis

There seems to be general agreement that ethics is about what we ought to do when confronted with value tensions, 'thus requiring judgement about a given situation or circumstance' (Cranston, et al., 2006, p. 109). When making such judgements, leaders must include ethical analysis as part of their thinking and reasoning because ethics is 'at the core of a given human enterprise … [it] addresses issues through a disciplined way of thinking' and it helps answer the 'question of why' in relation to complex and contested human dilemmas (Rebore, 2001, pp. 7–8).

The challenge in ethical analysis is that it involves values, choices, dilemmas and grey areas that often pose questions of character. We are constantly challenged in life to make choices about the kinds of people we are going to be and the kinds of actions we will or will not take. Ethical decision-making requires a keen sensitivity to the implications and consequences of particular choices when the facts of the matter may seem unclear, or even contradictory. It also requires knowledge of how to apply different ethical viewpoints in everyday decision-making.

The complexity of ethical issues is evident time and again in the responses of leaders in this book. Ethical considerations and challenges are especially evident in areas where leaders must take responsibility for their actions even though it is not clear to them how best to act in a particular situation. Examples of major challenges, discussed in chapter 3 include, for example: the need to initiate action or to follow through with disciplinary actions, despite personal cost to themselves; and how to prioritise or balance organisational needs and values in restructuring situations with the needs and values of individuals, even their own.

An example of the first type of challenge is the case of the principal who had to deal with an elderly member of staff who was showing increasing signs of dementia. The principal had known the staff member and her husband for many years and his initial approach to her husband backfired when perspectives differed and positions became entrenched. The principal had to overcome his own positive personal regard for the staff member and her husband in the interests of the students under her care. He indicated that 'in the final analysis, the needs and rights of the students were the deciding factor in removing her from most of her teaching'. While care for the students was uppermost in his mind, he also felt a duty of care to a staff member who had served the students and the school very well for a number of years. There was a personal cost to him because of the decision he made.

The case of the educational leader who had to hand out white envelopes inviting staff to accept a redundancy package is an example of the second type of challenge. This leader clearly indicated that he had great difficulty doing this; 'I'm the messenger. I've got to stand up in front of the staff and say that this is what we are doing and this is why we are doing it and, at the same time, not believing that it was the best thing in every aspect'.

The first example seems to be a matter of making a difficult choice to do what is right (e.g., apply the rules fairly to all who are subject to disciplinary action), even though it may be at a cost to the individual being disciplined. This usually concerns a tension between the good of the individual versus the common good. The second example can also be viewed as a choice between two rights. Those who have the responsibility of leading organisations have the right to respond to their organisation's needs, goals and strategic purposes, even though these, at times, may conflict with the needs, goals, desires and strategic intentions of individuals within the organisation. Leaders are challenged to find a balance between these two 'rights' and they need ethical and value-based frameworks for making wise decisions in such situations.

In life and work, we are constantly faced with making choices. Some of these are trivial, such as what outfit to wear or what meal to select in a restaurant. Others are important, such as what shares to buy as a long-term investment or in which house to invest. Still others are core, such as what kind of person I want to be. These latter choices are 'ultimate choices', since they really shape us and help make us who we are. Back in 1979, Singer gave the prophetic example of Ivan Boesky and his decision to get involved in insider trading (p. 4), which clearly involved a choice between right and wrong. Many of the choices made by leaders who later ended up in court (e.g., from Lehman Brothers, Bernie Madoff, *News of the World*) involved issues of moral temptation as well as legal sanction and, given many of the court findings, seem clearly classifiable as both legally and morally 'wrong'.

Sometimes, however, we are faced with the dilemma of making a choice between two 'wrongs' – whatever we do seems to bring unwelcome consequences – hence the expression 'damned if you do, damned if you don't'. In the novel and movie *Sophie's Choice*, the situation in which Sophie had to choose which of her two children should be sent to death in the gas ovens epitomises such a dilemma.

Often the choices we make based on our value system will not be confusing or impossible, like Sophie's. They will be stark and clear but will require real courage if we are to go through with them. These are the ones that demand character on our part. The ethical thing to do may test our courage. Examples include the problems associated with 'whistle blowing' or the refusal to follow unethical instructions from a boss or a valued client. The issue of moral courage can be seen clearly in some of the interview responses of the principals quoted earlier, especially those where they had to 'bite the bullet' and take action against personal friends, those with long loyal service, or when there is an easier way out.

Ethical choices often reflect grey areas in which laws, policies or guidelines may not give clear guidance, leaving leaders unsure how to proceed. In such grey areas they ought to clarify the facts of the matter, but if the situation still remains unclear, or if an urgent decision has to be made, then all they can do is use their best judgement. As long as they do their best, mostly all they can be accused of is making a mistake or an error of judgement. Having a clear sense of what one is facing – value choice, difference in perspectives, dilemma, or grey area – makes the ethical issue a little easier to understand as well as easier to discuss and, ultimately, manage and defend.

Discussing ethical issues with other key stakeholders is usually a wise strategy. Ethical dialogue usually reflects a variety of voices, all of which have a right to be heard and believe they are right. Once we start discussing values, we have to confront the fact that, in pluralistic and multicultural societies, there may not be a consensus on essential values and there may even be a general reluctance to talk about one's own values.

Nevertheless, one of the functions of ethics in society is to enable us to enter into dialogue with others about the appropriateness of human decisions and actions. Ethics is not normally about my belief that X is good/right and Y is bad/wrong. Ethical analysis and justification usually begins when we start giving reasons for our views about X and Y. To explore possible underpinnings for these reasons, we will now examine different approaches to ethics and their possible relevance and application to decision-making in tension situations.

Perspectives on ethics

This discussion attempts to introduce and discuss the essence of major ethical theories and principles for busy practitioners who need a quick reference guide for ethical decision-making in tension-filled situations. All educational leaders, however, should study ethical principles and theories in some depth, and consider the implications for their decision-making processes and for making judgements, especially when their choices are not clear-cut. Numerous books on ethics and ethical leadership provide detailed discussions and analyses of ethical principles and theories for practitioners (e.g., Strike, 2007; Shapiro & Stefkovich, 2005; Beckner, 2004; Rebore, 2001).

Some people approach ethics by means of a theory, which they see as giving them an understanding of ethics and ethical issues. They seek one theory which encompasses all dimensions of ethics and enables people to find a sound answer to any ethical issue. The two major theoretical approaches in ethics are deontology and utilitarianism.

Deontology (rule-based thinking or 'doing one's duty')

This ethical theory derives its name from the Greek word *deon*, meaning 'duty'. The origin of this approach to ethics is found in the writings of the German philosopher Immanuel Kant (1724–1804). Kant insisted that we can know our moral duty by *rational reflection*, and if we are to be ethical then we must fulfil the demands of duty. Rational reflection, then, becomes the focus of the individual's autonomous choice to live in accordance with the demands of moral duty. In fact, doing one's duty becomes the motivation for action. It is sometimes described, therefore, as duty- or rule-based ethics, because the rules clearly indicate your duty in a particular circumstance.

Deontologists also believe that there is something right or wrong in an act itself. For example, lying or stealing is simply wrong, regardless of what good you could accomplish by acting in this way. This rule-based ethical theory has the advantage of offering clear and absolute positions on a range of issues such as euthanasia, truthfulness, honouring of promises and so on. However, these same rules can act as constraints on choice and may be 'bent' as we saw with some of the situations faced by the principals in chapter 3. In many 'grey areas' in tension situations, absolutist positions may prove to be in conflict with ethics of care, compassion and justice.

Utilitarianism (ends-based thinking or consequentialism)

The other great ethical theory derives from the writings of the English philosophers, Jeremy Bentham (1748–1832) and John Stuart Mill (1806–1873). The basic insight of utilitarianism is that the morality of an action is to be evaluated in the light of its consequences. Hence the other name associated with this approach is consequentialism.

Probably the expression that best sums up this ethical theory is one that is quite familiar in the field of economics. It is the demand that one should strive to bring about the greatest good for the greatest number. The ethics of an action then are determined by an estimation of whether or not it has increased or decreased the sum of happiness for the greatest number of people. The focus is on the consequences rather than the action itself. It is also described as ends-based thinking.

A major criticism of this approach is that it fails to pay sufficient account to the needs of individuals. Nor is it particularly concerned with the question of rights. Another problem is whether to focus on immediate or long-term results. It also has the complication that we cannot always foresee the results of all our actions. How can we really know the full potential consequences of our proposed actions or choices? Gleeson (2005) puts this latter criticism forcefully when he states that 'it is highly implausible to suppose we can reliably identify better and worse states of affairs, or even to suppose there is such a thing as "the best state of affairs" overall' p. 34).

In more recent discussions on ethics, there is a move to focus more on care and compassion rather than to simply look at actions and consequences.

Care-based thinking

Some of this change of focus from rules/consequences to care has come from feminist criticism of deontology and consequentialism. It has been particularly developed within the nursing ethics literature, as it seems to harmonise with the fundamental driving force of this profession in terms of *care for patients*. It is, however, equally applicable to other professions of a pastoral orientation, for example teachers, in particular, are aware of their duty of care for students.

There is no doubt that care must be an important guiding principle in ethical decision-making but is it the best principle to resolve difficult issues and complex problems clearly? From the responses of principals in chapter 3, it would seem that it is not always clear how care is best exercised in a complex situation. Trying to decide how to do the right thing or to serve the common good and, at the same time, exercise compassion for individuals can be very challenging. There are times, for example in cases of child abuse or sexual harassment, when rules, regulations and legal imperatives may have to be weighted heavily in the decision-making process. The answer, of course, is usually not found by a simple appeal to one overriding principle.

Principlism

Many practitioners are often not satisfied with the solutions to ethical problems offered by deontology or utilitarianism and they feel that these theories are too abstracted from the challenges and complexities of real-life situations. The sole consideration of actions or consequences does not seem to take sufficient notice of all the factors that might influence a final choice or decision. They suggest that we come down to more practical second-level principles, or *principlism*, to guide us in greater detail (Josephson, 2002).

There is no one agreed set of principles but among the commonly suggested ones are the following:

1 autonomy;

2 common good; and

3 justice.

Autonomy

This broad principle means that in making ethical decisions, especially involving adults, we should respect them as individuals with autonomous rights to make their own decisions and shape their own lives. While children in their early years need to be guided, and often have their decisions made for them by parents, as they come to adulthood parental control should relax, leaving them to be responsible for their own lives. In school life, especially in upper primary and secondary schools, we are often dealing with autonomous young adults and ought to show them the respect that is their due. This principle finds expression in many ways when dealing with people: not interfering with their freedom; telling them the truth; supplying them with all the information they need to be able to make their own decisions; and treating them with respect as equal human beings.

Common good

In practical terms, the common good refers to doing those things that are in the interest or wellbeing of the whole community because these actions will provide a better quality of life for everyone rather than just a few. For example, everyone in the community benefits from having good schools, a clean and safe environment, and effective transport systems.

If we are to be ethical in serving the common good, then as far as possible our aim should be to do good to a maximum number of people and to refrain from doing harm. However, it is not always clear in practice what 'doing good for the greatest number' might involve. It could be, for example, that the ideal of the common good is difficult to attain in a multicultural society. Also, as was discussed in chapter 3, the interests of the common good (e.g., a class of students) may conflict with the interests of individuals (various individual students) and a caring profession, such as teaching, needs to balance all these interests.

The reverse principle of not harming is perhaps clearer. It means that we should refrain from actions that will result in harm to people. Generally speaking, it means that we are not justified in taking actions that directly harm others.

Justice

This is a major principle in ethics, and there is a vast amount of literature on justice, particularly on distributive justice, meaning the distribution of burdens and benefits within society.

The philosophical concerns about justice have been how to define it accurately and how to devise a system of justice that can operate satisfactorily in society. The basic notion of justice is that each person should be given their due, in a way that does not harm society in general. In approaching justice, some will want to emphasise the primacy of the individual and their rights, while others will emphasise the good of the community.

Despite the fact that we may believe that all people are created equal, when we observe society we soon realise that people are, in fact, not equal. There are vast differences in talent, abilities and social situations. This disparity can be explained in terms of the genetic and social lottery. For some, their advantage stems from genetic factors such as basic good health and intelligence. Others owe their advantage to the social situation into which they were born, such as those with wealthy, well-adjusted parents who were able to provide them with a sound education and a good financial start in life. Those less well-off may regard themselves as unfortunate, but no injustice, necessarily, has been done to them. Some will say that is simply the way things are – unfortunate but not unfair. It is, simply, part of the lottery of life. Others will say that while this may be true, justice demands that something be done to offset their disadvantage.

While principlism has much to offer, another, much older, approach to ethics is also very relevant to ethical decision-making.

Rational wisdom (virtue ethics based on Aristotle's thinking)

Many think that the approaches just discussed do not provide an adequate response to the complexity inherent in many ethical tensions. The *theories*, they argue, are too remote from real-life complexity and the *principles* often are in conflict with one another; for instance, doing good to someone in a particular situation may conflict with the demands of justice for someone else. These ways of applying ethics often leave unanswered questions, and this has led to a continued search for a more complete approach to ethics. In this search, many are returning to the ideas of some of the ancient philosophers, particularly those of Aristotle.

Aristotle's first principle of ethics is not an action-guide, but simply the goal we all seek – to live well, to live a good life, to achieve fulfilment, to flourish (see Seligman, 2011), to be happy while we live. Happiness, in the Aristotelian sense, is not, according to Flintham (2010), to 'be construed in a hedonistic sense of present pleasure [but as] the ultimate goal of life being achieved through a lifetime of virtuous action in striving for, and encouraging others so to strive for, the fulfilment of one's full potential' (p. 57). Virtue ethics, as it is also called, 'sees the fundamental task of the moral life as the development of a vision of "who we ought to become", and then striving to attain it' (p. 57).

The emphasis in his approach is on the good of the person performing the action. Behaviour that makes our lives good is considered virtuous, and behaviour making our lives bad is considered worthless. The assumption is that most people want to live well, so this desire for a good life becomes the starting point of ethics. In this view, 'the quality of a person's ethical reasoning will be governed by the quality of a person's moral character. A just person is more likely to know how to act justly than is a habitually unjust person' (Gleeson, 2005, p. 33). Moral development, Gleeson argues, 'is best explained in terms of growth in the key virtues of justice, courage, moderation and prudence (or practical moral wisdom) as the stable excellences of character, emotion and reasoning that constitute and enable the living of a good human life' (p. 34).

While there will always be disagreements about the particularities of what constitutes a good life, there is, usually, a large area of agreement shared among people. The best indicator of this agreement lies in what we teach our children. We want our children to be happy and try to teach them how to achieve happiness (Deveterre, 1995, p. 20). We teach them to be truthful, caring, fair and tolerant because we want them to have a good (virtuous) life.

However, in order to work out what is really good for us as individuals and as members of society, we need to develop our skills of ethical judgement. This requires the virtue of *wisdom*, which Aristotle describes in terms of knowing how to respond appropriately in different sets of circumstances. The work of ethics is to help us clarify what truly constitutes a good life and then deliberate on how to achieve this in whatever set of circumstances we find ourselves. So, for Aristotle, it is not just a matter of having the right overarching theory or having a set of principles or rules to apply, it is a question of choosing to strive for the correct end *and* to find the right means to achieve that end. This requires the development of virtues, or habits, which enable us to act in a consistent fashion. There are two kinds of virtues: moral and intellectual.

The moral virtues include justice, courage and temperance, which Aristotle regarded as 'golden means' between two opposing vices of excess and deficiency. For example, he regarded courage as the golden mean between the excess of 'rashness' and the deficiency of 'cowardice'. He recommended moderation in all things, with the ultimate aim of being a virtuous person or a person of good character, in order to lead a virtuous life.

The intellectual virtues, which Aristotle regarded as of a higher order than the moral virtues, are wisdom and prudence. These are now discussed at some length, as they are more directly relevant to an understanding of the type of ethical tensions discussed in this book.

Wisdom, according to Aristotle, is the kind of knowledge needed for science and an understanding of things. It is the kind of knowledge that is useful to leaders trying to understand and respond, appropriately, to complex challenges. This form of wisdom is referred to by Groome (1998), as a 'reasonable wisdom', which engages the whole person, and 'encourages integrity between knower and knowledge' (p. 288). Wisdom includes, but goes beyond, knowledge and reason, and it constitutes *the realization of knowledge in life-giving ways – for self, others, and the world* (italics in original). A reasonable wisdom constitutes a 'wisdom way of knowing', which, in essence, is 'knowing with an ethic' (p. 288). It also constitutes a quest for truth, which has '*cognitive, relational*, and *moral* aspects' (p. 301, italics in original).

Groome (1998) explains that the cognitive aspect of truth points to what 'rings true to experience', 'makes sense' to one's way of thinking, and 'works for life' (p. 303). The relational aspect of truth refers to loyalty and faithfulness in commitments and relationships. The moral aspect of truth constitutes a commitment to 'living the truth', as truth must be '… one's way of life' (p. 304).

Prudence, on the other hand, is a practical type of reasoning: the kind of knowledge we need for doing things. In Aristotle's way of thinking, it is the kind of knowledge necessary to direct a military operation, lead a school, practice medicine, play a musical instrument, or to live our lives and achieve personal happiness. Prudence is not just shrewdness or keeping an eye on the main chance. It is the deliberation and thinking necessary for one to work out what is the appropriate thing to do in any given set of circumstances. As the circumstances change, so will one's judgement of what is or is not appropriate action. This does not mean that one is cut free of any principles or ethical rules. They still have bearing on the ethics of one's action, but prudence involves knowing which rules or principles to apply in any given set of circumstances, and how to prioritise them.

This is why the Aristotelian approach gives such emphasis to the circumstances or context in trying to judge the morality of an action. The problem it sees with deontology and utilitarianism is that they devote too much attention either to the action itself, considered in the abstract, or to weighing up the likely consequences. Both actions and consequences are essential to any judgement about the ethics of a line of action, but not in isolation. *It is the circumstances that really shape the ethics of an action or decision.* So, as the circumstances change, so might our judgement of the ethics involved.

In today's pluralistic and multicultural society there is not necessarily agreement about fundamental values or ethical positions. The attempt of theorists to establish one overarching value or theory, which ought to guide actions, seems to have failed as an adequate response. Utilitarianism founders when we disagree on what counts as the good to be maximised or when we are called to take due account of the rights of minorities. Kant's deontology fails to satisfy those who are not prepared to accept his view of absolutes. Second-level principles are very useful indicators of essential considerations in resolving problems in ethics, but they do not, of themselves, offer a total solution. In resolving ethical conflict we are left to rely on skills of *wise reasoning*. These are skills which can be learned and 'formed' through experience.

As suggested at the start of this section, in recent decades, some ethicists are returning to aspects of Aristotelian ethics with a focus on practical judgement (Hursthouse, 2010; Gleeson, 2005; Nussbaum, 2001; Nussbaum, 2000; Solomon, 1993; Deveterre, 1995; MacIntyre, 1985). While not prepared to take on the historical and cultural baggage of Aristotle, they hope to be able to work toward a consensus in ethics through a form of wise reasoning and practical judgement that takes account of the particular issues in the complexity of their circumstances.

A virtues approach is unlikely to result in complete agreement, but if the issues are subjected to careful examination and appropriate questions are reflected on with an eye to the line of action proposed and its likely outcome, a wise and practical judgement can be made which can be reasonably defended. A consequence is that we will not achieve black-and-white answers (*either/or*), but wise judgements on what is a reasonable course of action. This will mean that reasonable people may reasonably disagree with the judgements of others, but the ensuing dialogue should help to clarify the issues further and progress the matter.

Many find it difficult to live with this kind of uncertainty when faced with making a decision, but it seems that in ethical matters in a pluralistic society, the most we can hope for is an open dialogue where cases can be argued on their merits.

Thinking about ethical and moral problems

Many business and educational leadership textbooks discuss decision-making and offer a number of different models, which can be extremely useful as a guide to procedures. Sometimes these models, such as the seminal 'Vroom and Yetton decision tree' (1973), take the form of a detailed structure, with arrows showing lines of procedure and alternatives to follow if one line of reasoning does not lead to a satisfactory outcome. Similar decision trees are presented in many texts on ethics. At times, these models can give the impression that if you put the right question in at the top and go through sequential and logical steps, you are almost guaranteed to come up with the best conclusion. Ethics is not, however, that straightforward and there is not always a guaranteed 'right' answer.

There are a number of ways of making decisions, either individually or in a group, that have many features in common with decision-making in ethics, but there are some differences that are worth considering. Some decision trees are organised as a checklist of things to do or steps to follow, with the intention of leading, sequentially, to the 'correct' decision. Some of them are presented almost as an algorithm that can be applied to a problem to come up with the 'right' answer. Some fail to take any account of ethical issues and base the decision solely on economic factors.

A key feature of ethical decision-making approaches is that they focus on helping us with *how* to think about an ethical problem, rather than teaching us *what* to think. Ethical decision-making is a process involving a number of key steps or stages, not necessarily in sequential order, but the application of these steps in resolving an ethical problem requires practical wisdom and good judgement. In other words, the steps help the decision-maker approach and think about the problem in a particular way but cannot determine what the content or outcomes of the decision will be. This can only be done when the facts of the particular problem are considered in context.

Educational leaders need a strategy to aid them in coming to an appropriate decision about how to act in a given tension situation. An understanding of ethics can help leaders apply systematic thinking about values and ethics and their application to real situations (Strike, 2007). They need to ensure that their systematic thinking reflects their core values and ethical standards or viewpoints.

There are, however, two possible barriers to sound ethical judgement. One is in the area of personality development; the other comes from lack of clarity about the nature of ethical inquiry.

A brief historical understanding of developmental psychology is very helpful in understanding how people *actually* respond ethically and morally (Piaget, 1965; Kohlberg & Turiel, 1971; Power et al., 1989; Gilligan, 1982; Turiel, 1983; Seligman, 2003, 2011). Developmental psychology has demonstrated that it takes time to grow, flourish and show 'maturity' when making choices. Self-centredness and the fulfilment of natural impulses mark early childhood. Later, people tend to focus on obedience to parents, authority or law. Those who progress further attain a more abstract and universal approach to making choices through principles and a sense of justice. Some, it would seem, never reach this more abstract level of thinking and judging.

Piaget (1965) believed that individuals develop and refine their sense of morality through their interpersonal interactions and their struggles to determine fair solutions to issues and dilemmas. Kohlberg is, of course, renowned for his theory of moral development, which identified the structure of moral reasoning underlying choices of action. His theory was based on six stages of moral reasoning in three levels, each of which denotes a clear development in the moral reasoning of the individual. In the first 'preconventional' level, he claimed that an individual's moral perspective tended to be self-centred and concrete in nature (not too concerned with the perspectives of others). In the second 'conventional' level, individuals modify their self-centred tendencies with an understanding that self-identity needs to be redefined, taking into consideration the norms and conventions of the group, and within the framework of what society identifies as 'right' (greater development of trust, respect, loyalty, gratitude, especially at family, group and later societal levels). In the third 'post-conventional' level, an individual's reasoning is based on principles, especially those of ethical fairness, justice and human rights from which moral laws are grounded.

Gilligan (1982, 1989, 1997), offering a perspective based on her research into women's experiences, argued that a morality of care, empathy and responsibility are essential components of moral reasoning and should replace Kohlberg's morality of justice and rights. She argued for care ethics, which included considerations of personal relationships and emotional responsiveness to others (especially feminine qualities) as the moral equal of more traditional justice-oriented moral theories and also advocated for alternative moral frameworks to those based on utilitarianism and Kantian ethics (Friedman, 2000).

Noddings (1984), Noddings et al., (1996) and Noddings et al., (1999) all focused on a feminist approach and argued the centrality of caring and relationships to ethics. Noddings suggested that caring which is deeply 'rooted in receptivity, relatedness, and responsiveness' is a preferred approach to ethics (p. 2). Ethical caring essentially means that a carer acts from a belief that one of the best ways of relating to others is to genuinely care for them.

Turiel (1983) presented a modification of Kohlberg's theory in his 'domain theory'. This suggested a distinction between a child's concepts of 'morality', which involves a consideration of the effects their actions can have on the wellbeing of others (e.g., can cause them harm), and those based on social knowledge or social convention (agreed on and predictable rules for behaviour and interaction), which help ensure smooth functioning social exchanges. Turiel, in other words, suggested that Kohlberg's single developmental framework needs to be expanded to include both moral and social meanings of particular dilemmas, choices and courses of action. He further qualified Kohlberg's theory in his book on the culture of morality (Turiel, 2002) when he suggested that the lament, especially by politicians, of the decline in ethical and moral standards among young people has to be carefully examined against contemporary cultural contexts and emerging patterns of social and moral development, and not against some simplistic, nostalgic view of the past.

The need for a method

A challenge for educational leaders in ethical decision-making is the general lack of clarity about how to make ethical judgements. When faced with complex ethical situations, many people just do not know where to start or how to proceed. This is a problem of method which involves: steps to be taken; questions to be asked; values to be clarified; alternatives to be considered; and decisions to be made. To be consistent and coherent in approaching ethical decision-making, leaders need to have some method of working with and through the issues that face them.

One advantage of the virtues approach is that it takes note of the complexity of ethical issues and offers suggestions about the need for rational wisdom and a more detailed consideration of the circumstances involved. The importance of the application of rational wisdom to complex, tension-filled situations is highlighted time and again in the interviews with leaders reported in this book. This is true particularly with questions of leadership responsibilities. Taking into consideration a number of the points raised in these discussions, a method of decision-making in difficult ethical situations is presented in the following section.

Method for ethical decision-making

Educational leaders require methods and processes that will assist them to probe 'the ethical depths of each situation that calls for a judgement' (Rebore, 2001, p. 31). They need these methods more than ever before as they enter a period of great change, uncertainty, and ethical relativism. Too few educational leaders today have a background or formal formation in ethical decision-making.

To assist leaders to consider the ethical dimensions of tension situations and make informed and wise choices in such challenging situations as those discussed in chapters 2 and 3, the following ethical decision method is proposed. It is best if such a method is used within a group context so that responsibility for the final solution to an ethical tension is shared. Also, most, if not all of the steps in the proposed method, lend themselves to collective dialogue and serious discussions among key stakeholders, a point that will be more fully developed in chapter 7.

Making ethical judgements when facing complex ethical situations is hard enough already, without adding the problem of not knowing where to start or how to proceed. The following ten steps will help leaders to make more effective decisions in situations of ethical tension.

1 Determine the nature and significance (importance, urgency) of the situation.
2 Clarify the facts, as far as possible.
3 Identify the players and consider the possibility of multiple perspectives.
4 After conscious reflection and courageous conversations, identify possible options for action.
5 Evaluate these options using different ethical approaches and standards.
6 Choose the best option(s), considering the circumstances, and ensure there is appropriate evidence for it.
7 Explain your choice and be able to defend it publicly, if necessary.
8 Work out the details of implementing the option (how, with whom?).
9 Take action carefully and ensure it is ethical, moral, and resolves the tension situation.
10 Reflect, learn and improve your approach.

Each step is explored in more detail below. It should be noted that, while described sequentially, some of these steps when resolving tension situations will occur in parallel and others may be dealt with somewhat perfunctorily, depending on the circumstances.

Step 1: Determine the nature of the situation. Does it constitute a conundrum between right-and-right, a dilemma between wrong-and-wrong, or a moral temptation between right-and-wrong? What 'contestable values dualities' are involved? (See discussion in chapters 3, 4 and 5.) How important is it to resolve this tension immediately (soon)? Does it appear urgent but is it significant? What might be the consequences of delaying its consideration?

Step 2: Clarify the facts. Ethical decision-making relies on a thorough collection and understanding of the facts. Remember that assumptions (including your own) and hearsay are not the same as facts. Also, there may be disagreements about the meaning of the facts of the case. No amount of careful reasoning or emotional investment will rescue a judgement based on erroneous information. There is sometimes a danger in ethical discussion that we can get involved in an argument on some issue without fully understanding what the issue is really about. Just listen to some dinner table discussions about controversial issues like the cloning of humans, stem cell research, life-sustaining treatments, death with dignity, or abortion, and then reflect on how well the various speakers really understand the issues. In other words, we may get involved in debate without an adequate knowledge or understanding of the facts.

One of the most important things about making an ethical decision on complex issues, like those discussed in chapter 3, is to begin with a thorough interrogation of the facts. Sometimes this will require undertaking research to find out what is really at the heart of the issue. As was made clear in the case cited earlier on the purported use of drugs by girls in a school, the facts of the case were in dispute. In real-life situations the facts are often hard to determine; different people will have their own versions of them and may also interpret them differently. For educational leaders who have to make decisions in such uncertain and contested circumstances, they need to understand as best they can the 'reality' of the situation for all key stakeholders. It will be necessary to know who the central players are, why they might be involved, and what their interests might be. Without knowledge of these one can hardly be said to have a grip on the facts of the issue.

Step 3: Identify the players. Determine, as far as possible, the intentions and interests of the key players, especially those with a stake in particular potential outcomes and be aware of the peripheral but possible influential players in the situation. Consider the appropriateness of actions in the context of who did, does or will do them. An important educational decision ought to be made by the appropriate person or people, with the relevant information, authority and expertise. In the case cited in chapter 3 of the young boy who attacked another boy, kicking him, it is an important fact that the attacker had been diagnosed with a medical problem and was on medication. It would seem sensible to involve this boy's doctor in any consideration on his future. In this case parents and teachers got emotionally involved and took sides. Some were considerate of the boy's medical condition while others were adamant that the aggressive behaviour required the boy's removal from the school. The wise course of action would be to engage in dialogue with key stakeholders, try to establish some common ground, and draw on the wisdom of the group for the decision.

Motivation, or the intention underlying the action or decision, is also important in helping to evaluate the ethics involved but this may be quite difficult to ascertain, since it is often impossible to know why people act or decide in the manner they do. Educational leaders need to get to know the people they work with, especially what normally motivates them. A teacher who constantly acts in the interests of students, for example, is likely to be acting from this value position with regard to any particular decision. The important point here is that the ethical reality may not be adequately addressed by the simple description of the action involved. In other words, our understanding of the ethical tensions and realities of a particular situation will be assisted by a better knowledge and understanding of the people involved.

Step 4: Think of several appropriate options for action. When trying to come to grips with the full reality of an ethical issue, educational leaders also need to check whether there are viable options or alternatives. The same end may be achievable by less harmful or intrusive means, for example, an offer of voluntary redundancies rather than mass sacking. Consider multiple ways to resolve the situation, and the likely consequences of each. You will need, of course, to consider any legal and/or regulatory codes or constraints as well. It is important to ask, 'Is the proposed action the only way to handle the situation?' Thinking seriously about alternatives and their possible consequences can help ensure that narrowly-based solutions are avoided. For example, in the case in chapter 3 involving a 'disadvantaged student' who had received a 'blue slip' for misbehaviour, the principal and the executive considered different alternative solutions to the problem. The problem was that one week prior to the athletic event he earned, fairly, his first 'blue slip' which would normally preclude him from participating in external events. Technically the full week was up the day after the carnival. The dilemma of allowing this child a chance at the carnival was taken to the executive who decided that he should participate.

Although the principal involved does not describe the specific alternatives in this case, the executive most likely canvassed a number of them and weighed up their consequences. The principal suggested that they consider the possible longer-term consequences for the student if he were banned from competing in the sports event at which he excelled, and that it was 'a once-in-a-lifetime opportunity for the student'. He also stated that executive members were clear that choosing to allow the student to compete set an uncomfortable precedent, and that other students and their parents might query its fairness, because other students in similar circumstances had been prohibited from participating in similar events in the past.

The principal in this case decided to discuss the possible alternatives and the solution of the problem with his executive group. Given the complexity of the challenges and tensions discussed in chapters 3 and 4, sharing the responsibility for their resolution seems like a sensible approach. In fact, a strong trend emerging in educational systems and schools is for educational leaders to share their leadership responsibilities with other key stakeholders. In the next chapter, I will argue that it is an ethical imperative for formal leaders to share the burdens and responsibilities, as well as the satisfaction and excitement, of leading their school communities.

Step 5: Evaluate options using different ethical approaches. The major ethical approaches have been explained and discussed earlier in this chapter. A brief summary follows:

- Deontological or rules-based approaches suggest that in choosing an option we should do our moral duty through rational reflection.
- Utilitarian approaches suggest that the option chosen should produce the greatest balance of benefits over harm.
- Care-based approaches suggest that we primarily follow our duty of care as a fellow human being and a professional educator.
- Principlism approaches suggest that the option should, as far as possible, enable people to make the decisions that are rightfully theirs, contribute to the greater good of the community while minimising harm to individuals, and treat all people justly.
- Rational wisdom approaches suggest that the decision should be based on wise reasoning combined with practical judgement, or a 'wisdom way of knowing', and exhibit those virtues that reflect human beings at their best and lead to the living of a 'good life'.

In many of the tensions discussed in chapter 3, principals were concerned with the consequences of their decisions and actions for both individuals and groups. No one can say they have captured the full reality involved in choosing an option or making a decision until they have examined the foreseeable consequences. Educational leaders are ethically responsible for those under their care and it is ethically unacceptable to ignore the reasonably foreseeable consequences of an option or decision. There may well, of course, be consequences that are beyond their foresight and control.

There were definite consequences, some foreseen and others unforeseen, in the case in where the grandfather spoke to his granddaughter at school with the principal's permission and then arranged to pick her up from the park on the Saturday and take her to her aunt's house. The principal had information that the girl's mother, a single parent, was having a problem with drugs and that the girl was increasingly being neglected by her mother. The primary concern was that if no actions were taken the consequences for the girl would be very negative. This is why the principal allowed the grandfather to speak directly to his granddaughter even though the rules stated clearly that only the mother had such direct access. He was aware that the consequences could be very negative for him if the mother made a formal complaint to the proper authorities. The unforeseen consequence for him in allowing the grandfather to speak on the phone to his granddaughter was that he arranged to pick her up from the park and, without her mother's permission, took her to her aunt's place where he knew the girl would be well cared for. In a strictly legal sense, this constituted kidnapping and the principal, unwittingly, was party to it.

In the end, the mother accepted the action that had been taken and no negative consequences eventuated. The principal, who had the child's interests as a priority, later regretted his decision even though it had a positive outcome. He stated:

> I was fortunate that the repercussions of my actions, and inactions, were positive. If I were faced with the same situation in the future, I would hope that I would handle the situation with a much greater sense of professionalism. In fact, I am confident that I would handle the situation differently.

Beware! Claiming ignorance or inexperience is no excuse for getting it wrong.

Step 6: Choose the best option. This best option is likely to be the one that caters for the values and ethical standards you believe to be important. *Both/and* thinking is recommended. Remember you need to exercise good judgement based on well-considered reasoning processes and on defensible ethical standards or principles. Struggling to come to grips with the full reality of a tension situation in order to make some detailed evaluation of possible alternatives places educational leaders in a better position to reach an informed ethical decision. The judgement reached may be a certain and confident one, but it will sometimes be tentative and open to revision. A tentative judgement may, in the particular circumstances of a case, be the best that can be managed. Through no fault of their own, leaders often do not have a mastery of all the facts and may not be able to foresee all the consequences, but they have to make a decision anyway. While mistakes of judgement will inevitably be made, if leaders are confident that they have done their best to work through the issues in a thorough manner, then it can be argued that they have done all that can be demanded of them from an ethical point of view.

Differences of ethical judgement can, however, become a problem when it comes to decisions where there are irreconcilable differences of opinion in a group situation. If it is a matter of a group decision and unanimity is not possible, then some form of integrity-preserving compromise will need to be reached. Some people are immediately troubled when they hear of compromise in ethical matters. It can seem to be the abandonment of principle for the sake of group cohesion and harmony. Accusations of abandonment of principle can be extremely troubling to conscientious individuals and may be seen by some as compromising their integrity.

A reasonable compromise can sometimes be reached using a creative imagination and a desire to obtain the best practical outcome in a complex situation. It will, however, require some relinquishment of one's views and values. At times, an individual will be able to do this in the search for the overall good, but, at other times, the sacrifice of values will be too great, and some may be unable to compromise on particular values of personal importance. In the case in chapter 3, the principal who decided to support the redundancy application of a staff member, even though he believed that a dismissal process was a more appropriate option, was opting for a reasonable compromise. He had concluded that with dismissal being a prolonged and time-consuming process, he could see his time used more productively:

> I weighed up the time and effort involved in trying to bring an unwilling and uncommitted staff member up to speed against the other priorities I had, together with the emerging initiatives and projects which were in the planning stage. I also thought very carefully about where my time would be better spent in terms of staff development, change management, redirecting the organisational culture and re-positioning the school for the future. I also know what it is like to prove incompetence in the area I work in. I believe I made the right choice.

Obviously, the principal in this case considered at least two, if not more, alternatives.

Step 7: Explain and defend your choice. Demonstrate to yourself or others why you have chosen this option and why it is a better resolution of the issue than the other options – reflect on how you would defend it publicly. It is a good idea to document your thoughts as an aid to memory. Verbalising and/or writing down your justification, especially if it is a decision of considerable import, will assist you to see any gaps in your reasoning and give you an opportunity to receive constructive criticism from others. Having a close network of colleagues to give you honest feedback is desirable.

Step 8: Work out how to implement the option. Sometimes the devil is in the detail. What will make this option work? What might undermine it? Who will you need to engage in the implementation to get buy-in and ownership of the option? Develop a well-thought-out plan for taking appropriate action and anticipate possible obstacles or bottlenecks. As with any change process, open dialogue and collaboration with those who are responsible for implementing the option is essential. Many excellent decisions have failed at the implementation stage because of poor planning or because key personnel were not invited to participate in their implementation.

Step 9: Take action carefully and morally. If the action taken involves a change in people's behaviours, then special care must be taken to ensure that their anxieties and fears are considered and addressed. Don't ever underestimate the trauma that some go through when they are required to change long-formed habits and behaviours. Look for honest feedback and keep an open mind. Modify the implementation processes if they are causing harm or having an unreasonable impact on the people involved. Also, be prepared to change the decision if new facts or unexpected consequences come to light. There will, of course, be times when the decision has to be implemented or the action taken in the interests of the common good even if some of those affected are opposed to it. In the end, common sense and good judgement are required in such situations.

Step 10: Reflect, learn and improve. Make sure you critically reflect on the whole process and its outcomes, and note what you have learned from it. Reflection and feedback are essential components of any effective learning process and should occur throughout the decision processes. It is also important to apply this learning to improve or refine your decision-making for the future, taking into consideration the particular context in which you lead.

Concluding comments

This may seem like a daunting set of steps, but most wise educational leaders already operate this way. They may not follow each step in detail, but they flash through the thought processes quickly – after all, thought travels much faster than the speed of light. Applying the steps should become a habit of mind (Costa & Kallick, 2008). While some may perceive the method as too time-consuming, without such a considered approach much more time can be wasted picking up the pieces after a disastrous decision.

A number of other considerations can guide educational leaders when trying to make an ethical evaluation of a particular tension. Factors such as their own feelings or past experiences can be quite useful. Feelings can easily prejudice judgement, but they can also be a good, almost instinctive, guide to right and wrong. An immediate feeling of rejection or revulsion for a proposed line of action should at least give pause, and suggest that the whole issue needs closer examination.

In the case of the students in chapter 3 who were asked by the teacher to enter other students' marks into a computer, one of the girls instinctively felt that it was wrong and checked her concern with her father who recommended that she discuss the issue with the principal. If educational leaders instinctively feel that a decision about redundancy or expulsion of a student is unjust, then it may well be worth searching to see if there are other alternatives. If past experiences, either their own or that of others, suggests that a certain decision will cause more harm than good, then leaders should at least reconsider.

Ethical principles and careful attention to reasoning and argument help us in our evaluation process. No simple application of principles, steps or template to a problem will resolve the issue, but basic principles of justice, fair play and human decency are likely to help us make a more balanced and just evaluation and decision. We need to think through the issues and work with them, not just opt for a simplistic solution. As indicated earlier, leadership involves the application of a 'wisdom way of knowing', a rational but practical wisdom, to complex and contested situations.

In the end, the resolution of complex multidimensional ethical situations requires the use of good judgement based on a sound knowledge of the facts of the case and an understanding of ethical theories and principles. The laws and customs of our society also serve to guide decision-making. These may not be designed for simple application, but they are worthy of consideration and care to see if, and to what extent, they may have implications for the final decision. Leaders must remember, however, that laws or system regulations may not be the final word in discussing the ethics of an option or decision. Their implications must at least be examined, and educational leaders must realise that if they break laws or go against guidelines in the search for a higher ethical value, then they are liable to bear the consequences for that action. There may be circumstances in which violation of the letter of the law may be justified (such as the case where the principal allowed the grandfather to speak with his granddaughter) but one ought to proceed with extreme caution with an awareness of possible negative consequences.

Key ideas for reflection

In situations involving ethical tensions, educational leaders need a set of core inspirational values and knowledge of ethical principles and theories to make wise decisions. They need to incorporate ethical analysis as part of their thinking and reasoning because ethics is at the core of decision-making in many of the challenging situations they face, such as those discussed in chapter 3. Ethical decision-making requires educational leaders to be sensitive to the implications and consequences of particular choices. It also requires a knowledge of how to apply different ethical viewpoints in everyday decision-making.

Discussing ethical issues with other key, relevant stakeholders is usually a wise strategy. However, it must be recognised that ethical dialogue usually reflects a variety of voices, all of which have a right to be heard and believe they are right. Once we start discussing and debating values, we have to confront the fact that, in a multicultural society, there may be no essential agreement on these values.

In some instances, they may have to settle for 'integrity-preserving compromise', even though this might be regarded by some as abandonment of principle and relinquishment of values. Compromise can be seen as 'sitting on the fence' or worse 'selling one's soul' for the sake of group harmony and cohesion. It can also be regarded as ethical relativism or as lacking in moral courage. Compromises can be all these things, which is why it is so important to compromise only when such a compromise preserves integrity.

Questions for reflection

In the case cited earlier in this chapter on the principal's decision to compromise by supporting an application for a voluntary redundancy package when he personally believed that initiating a dismissal process was the 'right' option, reflect on the following questions.

1 Was this compromise justified, in your opinion?

2 What might other key stakeholders think of his compromise?

3 What have you done in similar situations?

4 What advice would you give to a new principal, if and when they had to deal with a similar situation?

Alternative reflection

Revisit the critical incident or case that you described at the end of chapter 4 and try to apply the different ethical approaches described in this chapter to it. Most likely, you will find that no one approach provides you with a complete resolution of the tensions involved. However, the questions that follow will assist you to see how each approach contributed to your thinking:

1 What was the relevance/usefulness of rule-based thinking in the situation?

2 What consequences (ends-based thinking) did you consider when examining different choices in the situation?

3 In what ways were care and compassion (care-based thinking) considered and for whom?

4 To what degree did elements of autonomy, common good and justice (principlism) influence the choices made?

5 How did your decision-making processes involve the use of wise reasoning and practical judgement (rational wisdom/virtues approach)?

Chapter 7

Building a collective ethic of responsibility for leadership in schools

Maximising leadership influence in schools is a collective responsibility. This challenge, which was discussed briefly in chapter 2, is well recognised in the literature on educational leadership, as well as by many influential educational policy makers and practitioners (e.g., Duignan & Cannon, 2011; Walker, 2011; Sharratt & Fullan, 2009; Hargreaves & Fink, 2006; Caldwell, 2006; Davies, 2006). An emerging view from research and literature on school leadership is that school principals will have to broaden their perspectives on what it means to be a principal and on what they should do to be effective educational leaders in the future.

A number of studies and commentaries have suggested that the time is right for rethinking the way the principalship, as the primary focus for school leadership, is conceptualised and practised because it is no longer meeting the needs of schools, individuals in the principal's role or aspirants to the role (e.g., Duignan & Cannon, 2011; Pont et al., 2008b; Boris-Schacter & Langer, 2006; d'Arbon, Duignan, & Duncan, 2002). Many of these studies have recommended that rethinking or redesigning the principalship may be necessary in order to attract quality applicants to, as well as retain those already in, the principalship.

There is a growing belief that single-person leadership, such as that of the principal, is insufficient when it comes to leading learning and teaching in a complex organisation such as a school, especially in today's challenging educational environments (Boris-Schacter & Langer, 2006). From their examination of the changing demands on school leadership in twenty-two countries, Pont et al. (2008b) report that the effectiveness of the principalship is of widespread and growing concern.

This chapter focuses on the reasons for, as well as the ways and means of, making a move from principalship as an individualistic or, at best a small executive group view of leadership, to a greater collective responsibility for leadership in schools. It supports the conclusion of Pont et al. (2008b) that 'a commitment to greater leadership density and capacity within schools' (p. 31) is required if school leadership is to have maximum influence on the quality of learning, teaching and student outcomes currently and in the future. This is also a conclusion of the research on different forms of principalship conducted by Duignan and Cannon (2011) and discussed later in this chapter.

Why, then, are so many in the relevant literature suggesting that the principalship needs a bypass, if not a transplant? In the next section, consideration is given to a number of possible limitations of the principalship and what remedies might be available.

Traditional focus on the principalship

Educational leadership literature has been preoccupied, according to Hargreaves and Fink (2006), with 'the leadership of principals [and with] the assumption that school leadership is synonymous with the principal' (p. 96). They say that the research still 'equates leadership with principalship. Leadership starts in the principal's office' and in many forms of distributed leadership it is the principal mostly who does the 'distributing of leadership or creates the culture in which distribution emerges. The primacy of the principal is assumed, not investigated' (p. 101). In this chapter, the primacy of the principalship is investigated, challenged and alternative models proposed.

In recent times, the role of principal and its effectiveness in the leadership of schools to meet the contemporary and future challenges in education has also been critiqued. Pont et al. (2008b) conclude that 'as the expectations of what schools should achieve have changed dramatically over the years, countries need to develop new forms of school leadership better suited to current and future educational environments' (p. 31). One of the suggested reasons for the ineffectiveness of the principal as the primary source of school leadership is that the expectations for the role are too great for any one person. In a school community setting the principal is expected to be legal expert, health and social services coordinator, fundraiser, diplomat, negotiator, adjudicator, public relations consultant, security officer, technological innovator and top-notch resource manager, whose most important job is the promotion of teaching and learning (Flockton, 2001). Other relevant labels are confidant, marriage counsellor, architect, engineer, and sanitary contractor (Duignan & Cannon, 2011). Given these expectations, and the very heavy workloads reported by incumbents in the role, it would seem both sensible and necessary for them to engage with others in meeting the expectations for the job.

As an internationally recognised expert in the area of distributed leadership, Spillane (2006) claims that a quick inventory of the principal's responsibilities 'indicate that school leaders need to know something about content knowledge, pedagogical knowledge, curriculum knowledge, knowledge about students, and knowledge about adult learning' (p. 88). He also concludes that they need to have:

> some level of competence, not just in a single subject area but in several [so that] they can make wise choices about hiring teachers, facilitating the selection of curricular materials, observe instruction, and make informal judgments about its quality. This is all too much for one person (p. 88).

It would seem that the lone-ranger view of the principal's role is no longer, if it were ever, desirable, practical or effective.

In fairness to school principals, they are called on to exercise a range of responsibilities which requires expertise that no one leader could be expected to possess. Pont et al. (2008b) suggest that many of the current responsibilities tend to be managerial in nature, thereby taking principals away from what they do best, leading teaching and learning in their schools. These authors claim that many of their responsibilities tend to increasingly involve:

> establishing budget and accounting systems, choosing and ordering materials, setting up relationships with contractors and vendors, designing recruitment schemes for hiring teachers, to name just a few ... (p. 23).

These activities, they say, are often exercised at the expense of improving teaching and learning.

Another macro challenge, briefly discussed in chapter 2, is that the requirements of external standards and regular standardised testing has changed the accountabilities of the principal:

> from being accountable for inputs to being accountable for the performance outcomes of teachers and students ... In their planning processes, school leaders are increasingly expected to align local curricula with centrally mandated standards' (Pont et al., 2008b, p. 24).

As well, they are held accountable for:

> raising the levels of student performance, closing the gap in achievement between student populations, providing inclusive education services for such populations as students with special needs and immigrant children, reducing dropout rates and achieving greater efficiency (p. 25).

Is it any wonder then, that the evidence suggests that many who should be aspiring to the principal's role are not applying for it, thus leaving many system leaders with leadership succession concerns?

As many aspirants to the principalship observe the ever-increasing complexity of, and unrealistic demands on, the role, they decline to apply for the position (Caldwell, 2006; d'Arbon et al., 2002). For many 'it has become a very unattractive job' because there are too many negative images associated with it (Pont et al., 2008b, p. 30). There is considerable research evidence to support such negative images and the conclusion that the role is characterised by '... overburdened roles and working conditions, lack of preparation and training, as well as inadequate salaries and rewards [which are] among the top factors discouraging potential candidates from applying' (pp. 30–1).

Others point to a lower than the required quality in the pool of potential applicants. Caldwell (2006) reports that the interim results of a two-year study conducted by the National College for School Leadership in the UK and the Hay Group found that 'the number of quality candidates to choose from [for headship] is often seen as too small or nonexistent' (p. 184).

If the shortage of applicants is associated with potential applicants' negative perceptions of the role of principal, then the role needs to be examined and analysed in the light of these criticisms and the changing pressures of the educational context. The issue of the continuing relevance and effectiveness of the traditional school leadership focus on the principalship for contemporary schools needs to be explored.

Critique of the role of principal and principalship

A review of literature indicates that there are concerns in a number of countries that the role of principal, conceived for needs of the past, is no longer relevant or effective. These concerns have made the need for effective and influential school leadership a new priority in education systems in order to enhance the quality of teaching, learning, and student outcomes. There also seems to be a concern that the principalship is redundant in the current education context as it was 'designed for the industrial age [and] has not changed enough to deal with the complex challenges schools are facing in the 21st century' (Pont et al. 2008b, p. 16). Their report, based on nineteen OECD countries, concludes that many of these countries are seeking '… to develop new conditions for school leadership better suited to respond to current and future educational environments' (p. 16).

From their research with school principals in the US on how they view their roles, Boris-Schacter and Langer (2006) came to some startling if not surprising conclusions about principals' perceptions of the limitations and key obstacles to their leadership. They report that 'regardless of the school's geographic location, level, size, or socioeconomic status and the principal's race, gender, or tenure, the principals overwhelmingly identified similar barriers to their professional effectiveness and satisfaction' (p. 84). The essence of these obstacles was that:

1 work responsibilities infringe on personal lives;

2 personal life defines professional boundaries;

3 roles, responsibilities, and numbers of hours spent working increase yearly;

4 gender bias endures in the principalship;

5 life circumstances and professional experience frame the concept of life–work balance;

6 the community's vision of the principal is bound by tradition, preventing flexible models [of leadership] from being developed and implemented;

7 too much time is spent on administrative tasks and paperwork, especially since the passage of the *No Child Left Behind Act* of 2001;

8 although central to school improvement, staff evaluation is too time-consuming; and

9 too little time is allocated to instructional leadership and professional development (pp. 84–5).

This is a formidable list of challenges and one that is not easily changed or eliminated. While recommending a number of remedies for this state of affairs, Boris-Schacter and Langer suggest that appealing to principals' reasons for entering the profession is a good starting strategy. They report that 'principals said that they entered the position primarily to help students and to assist teachers …

In rethinking the principalship, we need to implement changes that allow school leaders to provide the service they deem integral to effectively run a school' (p. 88).

This service, which they regard as integral to their effectiveness as leaders, must be inspired by the moral purpose of schooling to enhance the quality of learning environments, teaching, learning and student outcomes. This moral purpose is a powerful source of both a personal and professional ethic of responsibility for improving learning conditions and learning outcomes. It is moral purpose that provides meaning and direction for their work and makes them passionate as educators and educational leaders (Duignan & Gurr, 2007). It is this passionate commitment to moral purpose that inspires a culture driven by a collective ethic of responsibility for leading quality learning (discussed later in this chapter). It is generally accepted in a variety of recent relevant literature that school leaders can contribute to improved student learning by shaping the conditions and climate [culture] in which teaching and learning occur (e.g., Dinham, 2009; Robinson, 2008; Townsend, 1998, 1999). This shaping involves commitment to a visionary, collective intent and action in order to provide teachers and their students with every opportunity to maximise learning outcomes.

An important consideration is that this leadership influence is largely 'mediated through other people, events and organisational factors such as teachers, classroom practices and school climate' (Hattie, 2009; Robinson et al., 2009; Marzano et al., 2005a; Leithwood & Jantzi, 2000). Research on distributed leadership adds support for this view by advising that by sharing leadership with a number of key stakeholders, principals can better influence the quality of their learning environments and enhance the quality of student outcomes (Harris, 2006; Spillane, 2006). Some of these mediating factors include: supporting and developing teacher quality; helping develop challenging and engaging learning environments; setting directions and goals; establishing high expectations; monitoring students' progress and providing them with feedback for improvement. While many of these studies focus on the influence of teachers on student achievement, they all recognise that school leadership plays a key role in helping to create favourable conditions for quality learning and teaching.

Principals positively influence learners and their learning

The critique of the principalship in this chapter is not meant to suggest that principals do not positively influence learning environments and student outcomes. They do! There is much research to suggest that they make a positive difference. Pont et al. (2008b) point out that despite the constant changes in education and in educational contexts and the increasing complexity of the role, 'the position of the principal remains an essential feature of schools in [many] countries' (p. 31).

Marzano et al. (2005a) conclude from their research findings that 'leadership is vital to the effectiveness of a school' (p. 4), and that '… given the perceived importance of leadership, it is no wonder that an effective principal is thought to be a necessary precondition for an effective school' (p. 5).

Quoting from a Senate Committee report in the US, Marzano et al. (2005a) maintain that 'it is the principal's leadership that sets the tone of the school, the climate for teaching, the level of professionalism and morale of teachers, and the degree of concern for what students may or may not become' (p. 5). Dinham (2009) supports this positive view of the leadership influence of principals in their schools and concludes from his research that the degree of positive influence of principals 'was somewhat surprising' and 'based on these findings and the literature in general, principals can create key roles in creating and maintaining the conditions and environment where teachers can teach effectively and students can learn' (p. 59).

These conclusions on principals positively influencing the quality of teaching, learning, learning environments, and learning outcomes are also well supported by other influential writers on educational leadership (e.g., DuFour & Marzano, 2011; Robinson et al., 2009; Mulford et al., 2009; Leithwood & Mascall, 2008; Davies, 2006). A key point in research is that principals can enhance their positive influence if they develop intentional collective strategies to strengthen their fields of influence through a deliberate focus on students and their learning.

It would be remiss, however, to single out the positive influence of principals and neglect that of teachers. Teachers occupy a very special place in influencing the quality of learning and student outcomes.

Teachers strongly influence learners and their learning

In many ways, high-quality teachers are the lifeblood of an education system. Most teachers become teachers because they want to make a difference in the lives of their students. When I first became a teacher I passionately believed that I had a 'calling' because I had a vocation to be a teacher. Teaching is a vocation because it is sacred work, so far as teachers have the awesome responsibility of influencing and shaping the lives of the children in their care. What a responsibility. What a privilege.

Few other professionals in society have such privileges, and they are actually protected by law. Teachers are given the special status under common law of being *in loco parentis,* substituting for, or acting on behalf of, parents. From this perspective, teachers have a duty of care for students under their care. This special relationship gives teachers privileged possibilities for influencing students and their learning. Great teachers always matter in the lives of their students and most students will tell you this.

The idea that teachers definitely matter in helping shape and mould students and the quality of their outcomes in education is well-recognised (Darling-Hammond, 2010; Hattie, 2009; Caldwell, 2006; OECD, 2004). Darling-Hammond points out that:

> study after study of educational reforms – whether of school design, instructional programs, curriculum, assessment, or parent involvement – has discovered that the success of the innovation depends on the capacity of teachers to carry it out... (p. 110).

In a specific case study of 'reinventing' a traditional school and transforming it into a learning environment to accommodate the needs of twenty-first century children, Degenhardt and Duignan (2010) conclude that while many changes are required for success in such a venture, including structures, processes, procedures, physical plant and resources, it is the positive attitudes, passion, commitment, hard work, and high performance of staff, and especially the leadership of teachers, that lead to the success of the innovation.

As Hattie (2009) points out, however, it is not the teacher or, indeed, teaching that makes the difference but excellence in teaching, and he explains that the 'current mantra that *teachers make the difference* is misleading' because 'not all teachers are effective, not all teachers are expert, and not all teachers have powerful effects on students' (p. 108, italics in original). He concludes from his synthesis of over 800 meta-analyses relating to student achievement that it is not just any teacher that makes the difference to students and their achievement but:

> it is teachers *using particular teaching methods*, teachers *with high expectations for all students*, and teachers *who have created positive student-teacher relationships* that are most likely to have the above-average effects on student achievement (p. 126, italics in original).

What matters, he says, are not the personal and professional attributes of teachers but 'the quality of the effects of teachers on learning' (p. 126). It is, essentially, the quality of the teacher's teaching that counts. In fact, it is well-recognised that a key reason for Finland's high standing with regard to the quality of its education and student outcomes is the quality of teaching from high-quality teachers (Darling-Hammond, 2010; OECD, 2008; Caldwell, 2006). These positive influences are considerably strengthened when *some teachers become leaders of learning* by helping to create a supportive and enabling can-do culture for other teachers and their students.

Teacher leaders have enhanced influence on learning

Recent research points to the central role of teachers in influencing student performance and outcomes in schooling (Crowther, 2010; Darling-Hammond, 2010;

Harrison & Killion, 2007; Silins & Mulford, 2004; Andrews et al., 2002; Crowther 2002; Crowther et al., 2002a, 2002b). Duignan and Cannon (2011) claim that 'teacher leadership is seen as a means of raising the morale of teachers, gaining greater commitment from teachers in carrying out the goals of the school and assisting other teachers in improving their practices by having teacher-leaders plan with them, demonstrate lessons and provide feedback' (p. 103). They also point out that giving teachers opportunities and responsibility for leadership, 'can also be seen as enhancing teacher professionalism, and empowering teachers' (p. 103).

Effective teacher leaders assume a wide range of roles, according to Harrison and Killion (2007), who suggest that teachers:

> exhibit leadership in multiple, sometimes overlapping, ways [and] the variety of roles ensures that teachers can find ways to lead that fit their talent and interests. Regardless of the roles they assume, teacher leaders shape the culture of their schools, improve student learning, and influence practice among their peers (p. 76).

In some contexts it is suggested that, as a result, teaching has gained increased recognition and acceptance as a profession (Institute for Educational Leadership, 2001, p. 6).

Drawing on the research findings of Leithwood and Jantzi (2000, p. 56), Hargreaves and Fink (2006) conclude that a greater distribution of leadership activities among teachers has '… a positive influence on teacher effectiveness and student engagement' (p. 100). Reporting on the research findings of Silins and Mulford (2002), Hargreaves and Fink (2006) also argue that 'student outcomes are more likely to improve when leadership sources are distributed throughout the school community and when teachers are empowered in areas of importance to them' (p. 101). However, they bemoan the 'lack of leadership opportunities for teachers and the silencing of their voices', and report that most of the literature on teacher leadership concludes that 'more teacher leadership … is better leadership that will lead to better schools' (p. 103).

What is required is an enabling framework for teachers to have a greater voice and an opportunity to contribute their talents to the leadership of their school. Andrews et al. (2002, p. 25) developed a teachers-as-leaders framework that highlights the importance of two key factors: teachers' values with regard to enhancing teaching and learning; and the capacity of teachers to create new meanings, especially for students, in the learning process. They make an important distinction between teachers as leaders in a specialised area such as pedagogy and discipline (e.g., subject leadership) and leadership that contributes to whole-school reform and improvement. In other words, while teachers should focus primarily on leading improvement in pedagogy and curriculum, it is best if this is done as a whole-school initiative. Together with the principal they can help ensure that this larger school orientation is achieved.

This focus on school improvement was central to a Federal Government trial project of a shared leadership approach in schools in Australia (Chesterton & Duignan, 2004). Entitled the 'IDEAS Project', it included a philosophy and framework based on the concept of 'parallel leadership', which encourages teachers to take on leadership responsibilities for curriculum and pedagogy, 'in parallel' with the principal and the executive, but within a whole-school improvement framework (Crowther et al. 2002a, 2002b). It involves teachers working together in teams across grades and subjects in order to overcome their often isolationist habits and practices. It also places their leadership of curriculum and pedagogy within the larger vision and purpose of the school as a whole. Teachers in this project grew as leaders once they were given the opportunity and they helped to motivate their colleagues to accept responsibility for the leadership of learning as well.

Crowther et al.'s work is influential in the growing body of literature that supports various approaches to shared leadership. In their view, teachers should be actively engaged in decisions about learning and teaching. Of course, students, parents and the community are also stakeholders and, as such, should have an input into such decisions, but teachers, as educational professionals, must be in the front line in determining the nature and content of curriculum and the approaches to and processes of pedagogy, learning and teaching.

For educational leaders to develop and foster the growth of shared leadership in their schools they need to assist teachers in developing collaborative and shared mental models and meanings that bind them together as a learning community. The key emphasis is on learning together, sharing and creating processes and conditions that encourage everyone in the school community to learn, grow, and be creative together. This is, in essence, what is meant by sharing leadership in a school community and it involves growing, nurturing and supporting competent and capable teachers to become key leaders themselves, especially of curriculum and pedagogy. An emerging view in relevant literature is that school leadership influences on student outcomes will be stronger if leadership is widely but judiciously distributed among key stakeholders.

Is distributing leadership responsibilities the answer?

The increased complexity and multidimensionality of the principal's role as well as the increasing responsibilities and accountabilities are creating opportunities for the distribution of leadership, both within and across schools (Caldwell, 2006; Harris, 2006; Spillane, 2006). To achieve a more effective distribution of leadership responsibilities, the traditional mindsets and practices of principals and teachers must change toward more inclusive, collaborative and distributed interpretations of school leadership.

To facilitate this development, school system policies must evolve so as to promote and support a strong commitment to sharing leadership responsibilities and encourage greater leadership density and capacity within schools from which future high-level leaders can emerge. Focusing on system leadership in a number of countries, Pont et al., (2008a), conclude that a '… collective sharing of skills, expertise and experience will create much richer and more sustainable opportunities for rigorous transformation [of leadership and schooling]' (p. 11).

Davies (2006), however, recognises that a shift in leadership emphasis is already occurring in many schools. He suggests that traditional views where '… headteachers provide the leadership and middle managers administer [the] curriculum area have changed radically to a model of distributed leadership over the last decade' (p. 166). He claims that increasingly head teachers in the UK are developing a new mental model of leadership where '… instead of seeing themselves as leaders of curriculum they … see themselves as *leaders of educational leaders*' (p. 166, italics in original). What he means is that educational leaders are focusing their efforts more on working closely with other key stakeholders, especially teachers, to help them become influential leaders of learning.

The OECD report (2008) on educational developments in a number of OECD countries focuses especially on how educators can build deep, rich, active and engaging learning environments, and its conclusions have significant implications for teachers as leaders and for school leadership generally. When discussing the role of key agents in change processes in education, the report claims that an innovation's success is, for the most part:

> determined by the social interaction of group members through the successive stages of: awareness, expression, interest, trial and evaluation, and adoption … its implementation will depend on the ability to solve problems and establish spaces for participation (p. 17).

Such championing and supporting of social interaction and the establishment of spaces for participation in innovation imply a collaborative, shared approach to leadership in schools.

In chapter 8 of this OECD report (pp. 175–202), which focuses on the dynamics of educational innovation in a number of countries, Aguerrondo (2008) explores the dynamics of the processes of educational innovation and change and concludes that the driving forces of successful innovation are usually located within '… groups directly interacting in the current situation … Innovations demand one or more actors – whether individuals or groups – to become **bearers of change**' (p. 179, bold type in original). He also claims that these bearers of change engage in purposeful collective and collaborative leadership to enhance the success of the change or innovation.

Harris (2002, 2006, 2009), too, argues for school leadership practices to be distributed among a number of individuals and groups. She suggests that even though principals are:

> important sources of leadership in schools there are compelling reasons to investigate other forms and sources of leadership. For example, there is growing evidence to associate distributed forms of leadership with certain organisational benefits and student outcomes … (p. 38).

She quotes directly from Leithwood et al. (2006) to argue that distributed leadership:

> *assumes a set of direction-setting and influence practices potentially enacted by people at all levels rather than a set of personal characteristics and attributes located in people at the top* (Harris, 2006, p. 38, italics in original).

Harris (2009) also claims that a distributed view of educational leadership:

> recognises that leading and managing schools involves multiple individuals and that the practice of leading and managing is more important than the nature of the roles and responsibilities associated with leading and managing (p. 3).

She recommends that instead of studying the tasks, responsibilities and experiences of individual leaders in schools, such as principals, it is more productive when trying to understand school leadership to 'examine the ways in which leadership practices are shared, negotiated and constructed in schools' (p. 38). Taking some cues from Spillane (2006), she concludes that in order to get away from narrow perspectives of school leadership, such as those premised on the principal or principalship:

> the challenge is to analyse leadership at the combined and collective level, to move beyond the actions of the individual leader and to look more closely at the collaborative and shared practices that contribute to organisational knowledge and improvement (p. 38).

In fact, Harris supports Spillane's (2006) view that distributed leadership implies '… a way of understanding leadership that focuses upon interaction and the exploration of complex social processes' (p. 39). She proposes that school leadership can be best understood as 'practice distributed over leaders, followers and their situation and incorporates the activities of multiple groups of individuals' (p. 20).

Similarly, Hargreaves and Fink (2006) argue for a collaborative and distributed form of leadership to bring about sustainable leadership change in order to better influence the quality of learning environments and student outcomes. They claim that distributing leadership within and across schools and other organisations '… isn't just common sense; it is the morally responsible thing to do' (p. 97). Drawing on the research findings of Leithwood and Jantzi (2000, p. 56), they conclude that a greater distribution of leadership activities among teachers increases the quality of teaching and student engagement. They recommend that the findings of large-scale research studies such as Leithwood and Jantzi (2000), and Silins and Mulford (2002), regarding the effects of educational leadership, 'provide clear indications that some elements of shared, collaborative, or distributed leadership is strongly associated with effective leadership in schools' (p. 101).

Among the foremost experts on distributed leadership internationally, Spillane (2006) argues that:

> individuals who single-handedly try to lead complex organizations like schools set themselves up for failure [and that a] distributed perspective makes it possible for the work of leadership to be manageable' (pp. 87–8).

He claims that 'it is unrealistic to expect any school principal to know everything about leading complex organizations like schools' (p. 88). Adopting such a distributed perspective, he says, '… shifts the focus from leaders to leadership practice … leadership practice is the vital concern [and] practice gets defined in the interactions of leaders, followers, and their situation' (p. 89).

A key challenge, according to Spillane, is to determine how best to distribute leadership. This involves, he says, determining '… the extent to which leadership is distributed in different routines, who is involved in the co-performance of various routines, and how the situation defines leadership practice' (p. 95). Further, he argues that it is important to better understand '… how leadership practice takes shape among the practices of [different] leaders' because influential leadership practices are made up of patterns or '… a collection of interacting component parts in relationships of interdependence in which the group has distinct properties over and above the individuals who make it up' (p. 160). Harris (2009) takes a similar view when she argues that 'the impact of distributed leadership on the organisation depends upon the pattern of leadership distribution' (p. 8).

Drawing on the research findings of Leithwood and Mascall (2008), Harris suggests two essential conditions for the distribution of leadership responsibilities. First, 'leadership needs to be distributed to those who have, or can develop, the *knowledge or expertise* required to carry out the leadership tasks expected of them'; and second, that 'the initiatives of those to whom leadership is distributed need to be *coordinated*, preferably in some planned way' (p. 8, italics in original).

The first of these conditions should be easily met in most schools because there are many knowledgeable, talented and expert professionals in schools. Caution, however, should be exercised over the second condition because innovative professional educators, especially teachers, need space and reasonable degrees of professional autonomy in order to blossom and flourish and create exciting learning environments for their students. Certainly patterns of practice need to be coordinated for the sake of coherence, but coordination with supervisory overtones may kill the seeds of innovation in the ground. It is often better to encourage professionals to self-select and self-regulate by having them engage in dialogue, partnerships and networks with colleagues who have a similar passion and commitment for learning and for children.

It seems that Caldwell (2006), in his work on reimaging schooling, thinks in a similar fashion when he recommends the need for leaders to interact and network with each other within and across schools. He claims that effective leadership of innovative learning calls for leadership to be distributed across schools and within schools. From his research and worldwide knowledge of school networking, he recommends leaders operate 'in a network of schools, or across a system of schools, in a particular area where a leader, or her or his school, has expertise, as in the twinning of schools in efforts to raise the achievement of one' (p. 188). Getting together with colleagues with similar challenges within or across schools that have the expertise and passion to find collective ways of improving learning, is commendable.

In a report on system-driven models of innovation for education, Bentley (2008, pp. 205–29) claims that a commitment to openness, collaboration, participation and networking is a key reason for the success of the Finnish system. He suggests that their world-recognised success has not come from standardised measures, accountability from above or from the heroics of individuals, including school principals but, instead has come from structures and processes for schooling that:

> promote a specific combination of universal participation, specialist knowledge and flexibility. What drives it is the interaction between a deep investment in participation ... and the culture of open, network-based interaction ... (p. 228).

He rightly concludes that while we are unlikely to be able to replicate what Finland has done in education in many other countries, we can at least learn from them '... to apply the lessons of open systems' (p. 228), and a much greater commitment to meaningful participation, collaboration, collegiality and sharing in education and educational leadership in our schools.

While distributed approaches to leadership can generate positive effects when professionally applied, many claim that it is not sustainable if it lacks ethical and moral fibre as well as soul. Too frequently in education systems and schools, we get the rhetoric of distributed leadership but, essentially, it is simply a variation on an old theme, new wine in old bottles. It is still the principal who 'giveth' and who can just as easily 'taketh away'. A collective ethic of responsibility for sharing leadership will not emerge simply from rhetoric or arguments that it is good for us all. Some motivating force much deeper is required.

Where commitment to a collective ethic of responsibility for leadership doesn't already exist, we owe it to our children and grandchildren to take the lead in promoting and supporting it. A starting point is to create school cultures where every stakeholder feels a deep moral and ethical responsibility for the quality and effectiveness of the overall leadership of the learning agenda and is willing to promote and support a collective vision to achieve it. Ethical responsibility based on moral purpose is the key to influential collective leadership.

Developing a collective ethic of responsibility for leadership

In attempting to recommend an alternative to the traditional approaches to school leadership, Boris-Schacter and Langer (2006) recommend 'not merely a redistribution [of leadership], but a rethinking' of it (p. 82). Based on their research on alternative models of principalship in the contemporary context of education, Duignan and Cannon (2011) agree. These authors share the view that such a rethink of leadership in schools involves all stakeholders believing in, committing to, and taking responsibility for the leadership of learning in their school community. While this perspective seems admirable and worthy of careful consideration and action, there is a need to deconstruct it to determine what 'the language of responsibility' (Moran, 1996) actually means for those who have the responsibility for achieving it. Individuals and groups (the collective) have their own special responsibilities for creating a culture where leadership is genuinely shared.

Williams (2009) argues that individuals and groups are judged as responsible, depending on the degree to which they discharge their responsibilities and we often praise some people as responsible and criticise others for being irresponsible. In this sense of the term, responsibility can be regarded as a personal virtue or a morally valuable trait.

From another viewpoint, we can ask, 'For what is a person responsible?' In answering this question, responsibility can be viewed and judged as *retrospective*, in which praise or blame is given for past deeds, or as *prospective*, which is closely related to how well one does their duty or acts in a morally virtuous way (Williams, 2009). In recommending an ethic of responsibility for school leadership we are, in a sense, urging individuals (or groups) to 'perform as a morally responsible agent' (Starratt, 2004, p. 47) for what they have done (*retrospective*) or for what they intend to do (*prospective*).

The question arises as to whether collective responsibility is simply the sum of the responsibilities of these individuals or if it has character and nature all of its own? Williams (2009) sees this as a vexed question and one that has been somewhat neglected by philosophers and poorly understood by practitioners. Instead, he suggests that if we think more in terms of collective moral responsibility, we may develop greater clarity around this question. While many moral philosophers would argue that groups cannot strictly be held accountable for the morality of bad collective decisions, others suggest that specific groups develop cultural, group or social norms that can help moderate and inspire individual and group behaviour. Individuals may still be the ones held directly accountable but so too can groups (they can be dissolved, disbanded, disenfranchised) for gross neglect of moral standards. As Riser (2010) suggests, this is a hotly debated issue, but the stance taken here in relation to collectives in schools is that groups can develop a powerful positive culture for good, based on moral purpose and high ethical and moral standards. This position focuses on a group's positive contributions to the common good and not on what they can be blamed for, even though groups (a school's staff) should be held accountable for inflicting harm on others, just as individuals often are.

The point is that, in practice, it is possible to conceive of collective responsibility and collective moral responsibility as much in organisational and cultural terms as in individual terms, and we know a great deal about culture building, reculturing, group and leadership capacity building, growing professional learning communities and communities of practice, and sharing leadership roles and responsibilities in schools (Duignan & Cannon, 2011; Degenhardt & Duignan, 2010; Hargreaves, 2009; Sharratt & Fullan, 2009; Caldwell, 2006; Eaker et al., 2002; Wenger, 1998). School leaders at all levels engage in the practicalities of culture-building and in creating conditions for collective responsibility every day in classrooms, in their schools, and in their school communities. What is required is a culture that promotes and supports strong core values and high ethical standards and has zero tolerance for unethical conduct.

In the London riots, O'Donohue's editorial in the *Observer* (14 August 2011) took an interesting perspective with regard to reasons for, or causes of, this 'spiralling social disorder'. While personal moral failings and a general lack of moral compass were highlighted, equally the failings of the 'grand bargain' inherent in the social rules and the social contract in the public realm were blamed. Why, O'Donohue queried, given the opportunity, did many on the streets 'trash the principles on which it [contract] is based'? The answer given is that when some members of a social group feel excluded, alienated, treated unequally and unfairly, they may ignore or 'trash' the core tenets on which the contract is presumed to rest. What is most interesting for our discussions here is that the leader of the opposition, Ed Milliband, didn't just blame the perpetrators of the mayhem when he recommended that, in order to avoid repetitions and to repair the tattered social fabric in the UK, there is a need for 'a new ethic of responsibility', one that is needed from 'top to bottom in our society'. He also suggested that ethical standards need to rise dramatically, 'from the benefits office to the boardroom'.

While individuals certainly must be ethically responsible, Sachs (2005) reminds all leaders that they are judged mostly by the quality of their relationships with others (in families, communities, and societies) and that these relationships are based on ethics that are derived from the lives they live together and goods and services they share. He notes that on their death individuals are usually praised for the virtuous quality of their relationships and for what they contributed to the common good (loving husband/wife, parent, or loyal friend) and not for their position, possessions, or individual profiles.

What holds true for communities and societies with regard to an ethic of responsibility has implications for smaller groups, like school communities. Within a school context, a collective ethic of responsibility will rely on both individuals and on the spirit of their relationships. Leaders can play an important role in determining the quality of these relationships and their ethical veracity. While it is useful, even necessary, for leaders to think about and understand cultural dynamics, collective characteristics, and ethical responsibilities, Starratt (2004) argues that there is an 'ethic of responsibility' (p. 49) within educational settings that has considerable ramifications for educators at all levels of education systems and schools. He proposes that educational leaders 'must be morally responsible, not only in preventing and alleviating harm but also in a proactive sense of who the leader is, what the leader is responsible as, whom the leader is responsible to, and what the leader is responsible for' (p. 49).

While Starratt is referring to individual leaders, these same dimensions of responsibility can be applied to the collective leadership of a school if we believe that everyone in a school community should commit to being ethically and morally responsible for its success as a community of learners. Indeed, all leaders should deliberately intend to:

> transform the school as an organisation of rules and regulations and roles into a much more intentional self-governing community [where] initiative and an interactive spontaneity will infuse bureaucratic procedures with human and professional values (Starratt, 2011, p. 103).

Discussing the importance of the virtue or ethic of responsibility for leaders, Starratt recommends a 'value-added moral leadership' for schools in order to create learning opportunities and environments that inspire teachers and students to achieve their full 'human fulfillment' within what he calls 'the drama of [their] human adventure' (p. 103). It is, essentially, the community of teachers, students and leaders who must take ethical responsibility for the quality outcomes of this adventure.

When discussing ethical responsibility for leadership of schools, Starratt's (2004) dimension of 'responsible for' is especially pertinent to the discussion in this chapter. He suggests that while all leaders are responsible for 'developing and sustaining working relationships' with all key stakeholders, they are especially responsible for 'cultivating a caring and productive learning environment' for both teachers and their students, as well as for the quality of the learning outcomes from these environments (p. 55).

Within this responsibility framework, it is not sufficient for individual teachers to suggest that they take responsibility only for their own students – those in their classroom(s). They must also take responsibility for the classroom(s) next door. Who is my neighbouring teacher or classroom? This question should be answered similarly to the classic scriptural question, 'Who is my neighbour?' Within a school community context the answer will be all of the teachers, students, and parents.

From this perspective, it is not ethically good enough to ignore students' misbehaviours in school corridors, other classrooms, or on the playground simply because they are not 'my students'. Similarly, all teachers must take collective ethical responsibility for the quality of learning and learning outcomes in their school. To stand by and do nothing when they are aware that students are being short-changed in their educational experiences because of underperforming teachers in other classrooms is, according to Starratt (2004), unethical. It is also inexcusable and unprofessional for those with a vocation to do this.

In chapters 1 and 2, the key importance of leaders having a deep sense of moral purpose was discussed and it was suggested that their passion for leadership comes from deep inside and is inspired by their core values, professional principles and ethical standards. It is not good enough, however, for educators simply to have the rhetoric of moral purpose in their school; there must be a commitment to and ownership of it and, ultimately, it must be enshrined as the norm within a shared sense of community responsibility (Bezzina & Tuana, 2011). As will be discussed in chapter 9, authentic leaders know that the ethically responsible thing to do in order to properly serve the needs of twenty-first century children is to provide them with excellent teaching within technologically charged, rich and engaging (interactive) learning environments. The ethically responsible thing to do is driven, primarily, by moral purpose which inspires both individual passion and commitment, as well as a collective ethic of responsibility that fires the spirit, imagination and vision of the school as a community of learners and learning; a community with an uncompromising moral purpose that fuels an unrelenting drive for excellence.

Developing a collective ethic of responsibility for quality teaching and learning

Greater involvement of a variety of stakeholders in key decisions on curriculum, improvement of pedagogy, assessment and student outcomes usually leads to the development of a greater sense of commitment and ownership of these decisions. It has been long recognised in research and literature on educational change that it is wise to engage those affected by a decision or a change in its formulation because they are more likely to implement it effectively. The collective engagement and involvement of colleagues based on moral purpose is also more likely to build a positive culture of trust where people feel valued, motivated, and passionate about serving their students' needs. It also creates energies and synergies that raise group members up to higher levels of aspiration, performance, and morality.

The moral purpose of educational leadership at all levels must, therefore, be to promote and support the conditions for excellent learning and teaching. Southworth (in Davies, 2005) sees the purpose of leadership for schools in the future as being more collaborative, with a much stronger focus on leading quality learning. He refers to this as learning-centred leadership and he recommends that formal school leaders need to work more closely and collegially with teachers in order to have greater influence on the quality of student outcomes. He argues that: 'If leadership is second only to the effects of teaching on students' learning, how much more powerful will leadership be when it works in combination with teaching?' (p. 76).

For teachers or other educational leaders simply to proclaim a new focus on students and their learning will not necessarily make it happen. It is only when this focus becomes a collective professional, ethical and moral imperative that the teaching and learning landscape is likely to change. The language of reform has been replete with such well-intentioned aspirations, but often nothing really changes in classrooms. What is needed is a renewed sense of vocation for educators and a collective and passionate commitment to creating learning environments and cultures that will help transform the lives of learners and their learning (LTLL, 2006–2011). Collective or distributed approaches to leadership should embody such passion and commitment. Southworth asks the question, 'If leadership is to be more widely distributed than in the past, what is it that is to be distributed?' His answer is that we need a form of leadership that ensures schools have 'as many leaders as possible making a positive difference to what happens in classrooms' (Southworth in Davies, 2005, p. 89). As discussed earlier, Starratt (2011) points out that the differences that need to happen in classrooms should ensure that teachers' and students' experiences provide 'enhanced opportunities for human fulfilment [by] transforming the mundane work of learning into something that engages the deeper meanings behind the drama of the human adventure' (p. 103).

Having a collective commitment to creating these enhanced opportunities for teachers and students is the raison d'être for leadership and for a school's existence. It is not a fad to believe that collective responsibility for action helps create a supportive and facilitative culture for educators and their students. A collective ethic of responsibility requires all members to interrogate the very reason they became teachers in the first place. It constitutes an appeal to them to query their vocation, their calling, and their teaching if they are falling short or avoiding their professional responsibilities. Their vocation demands that they fully share their gifts, talents and expertise in the interests of their students and for the common good. From this perspective, committing to an ethic of responsibility for the lives of all students within their spheres or fields of influence is not an option for teachers, it is an ethical and professional imperative and can be classed as a professional virtue (Starratt, 2011).

It is not just that a collective ethic of responsibility for leadership will more strongly influence student learning but that the deep moral purpose of schooling itself – maximising opportunities and outcomes for all learners and transforming the lives of learners and the quality of their learning – is the driving force for this approach. From this perspective, it is the professional, ethical and authentic thing to do if children – as we normally say – are at the core of our moral purpose, values and belief systems in schools. When the seeds are planted in the fertile soils of what really matters in schools – excellence in learning and teaching – students will grow and blossom into beautiful collections of flowering personhood. While each flower will have its own unique grace and beauty, it is in the bouquet (the collective) that we can see the dazzling reflections of our moral purpose.

Concluding comments

An emerging perspective in the literature on school leadership recommends that school principals should broaden their perspectives on what it means to lead a school. Constantly increasing external and internal pressures makes it impossible for them to adopt a lone ranger stance. It would appear that the traditional model of the principalship is no longer capable of responding effectively to these pressures or, indeed, meeting the needs of schools, individuals in the principal's role, aspirants to the role, or the learning needs of many students. Even distributed forms of leadership often do not seem to be a viable alternative.

Increasingly, alternative school leadership perspectives are being proposed based more on the moral purpose of education and schooling and the ethical responsibility for achieving it. While it is wise for any formal educational leader, such as a school principal, to tap into the expertise and wisdom of their colleagues when attempting to resolve contentious challenges and tensions, co-responsibility for making decisions in such situations will also help generate greater ownership of the decisions and deeper passions over their implementation. When attempting to resolve ethical tensions, it is essential to listen to diverse viewpoints, engage in dialogue with significant others, even pursue integrity preserving compromise, and then take ethically responsible collective action.

What is proposed as a leadership option is the building of organisational cultures that are driven by moral purpose and that encourage and support a collective ethic of responsibility for school leadership. Such cultures help enhance professional dialogue between and among diverse groups of stakeholders and promote learning environments where leadership and decision-making are focused on transforming the lives of, and the learning outcomes for, all students.

Authentic influential leadership is the key to such developments. In the next chapter, the key ingredients of such leadership – presence, relationships, influence fields – are discussed and explained.

Key ideas for reflection

One key way to enhance collective ethical responsibility for leadership in schools is to rethink what educational leadership actually means and involves – its definition, moral purpose, scope, depth and breadth.

A collective ethic of responsibility for leadership can enhance professional dialogue and create an environment where core educational and pedagogical decisions are seen as a collective and professional responsibility. This approach helps identify the contours of expertise within the school community and harnesses the talents of all key stakeholders for the purpose of improving the processes, content and outcomes of teaching and learning.

While the reasons for a collective ethic of responsibility for leadership in schools are many, the obstacles to its implementation need to be explored and better understood. Educational leaders have the challenge of creating conditions in which the key school community stakeholders are willing and able to collaborate, focusing all efforts on achieving the moral purpose, shared vision and goals of the school community. In this sense, leadership is the ethical responsibility of everyone involved.

Teachers especially need to trust and support one another in a collegial learning environment in order to optimise learning opportunities and outcomes for all their students. However, many teachers may have to overcome a culture of individualism, privacy, professional isolationism and idiosyncratic institutional practices. Research indicates that for teachers to share in the leadership of curriculum and pedagogy, there needs to be a focus on whole-school improvement in learning and teaching as opposed to piecemeal change in a department, subject area or teaching technique.

A commitment to collective ethical responsibility for leadership will not come about for schools with closed professional cultures, just because literature recommends it or some school stakeholders 'talk it up' as a good idea. Changes in attitudes and mindsets are difficult to achieve but are necessary before such changes in practices can occur. A useful starting point, perhaps a turning point, is to encourage courageous dialogue and discuss ways to drive commitment to a collective ethic of responsibility for leadership and quality learning, as well as to identify the strategies and actions necessary to achieve such change.

Questions for reflection

1 What ethical assumptions and values underpin an approach to leadership that is based on the idea of a collective ethic of responsibility for leadership in schools?

2 What moral purpose should it serve?

3 What are some of the key obstacles to its achievement?

4 What assumptions and mindsets need to be challenged to achieve it?

5 What strategies and processes need to be put in place in schools to get commitment to its implementation?

6 What changes to position, status and personal and professional relationships might be required to realise its full potential?

Chapter 8

Authentic leaders use the power of presence, authentic relationships, and influence fields

> If ever you become discouraged and doubt that you are positively influencing others, then know that
> part of you will be flying with every pilot, building with every architect, diagnosing with every doctor,
> creating with every artist, fashioning with every craftsman, and teaching with every teacher. More than
> that, part of you will be woven into the fabric of every sound marriage and every good home.
> You are making your way into the hearts and minds of the children and youth you teach and lead. You
> are leaving a very valuable legacy for future generations (Cardinal Williams, New Zealand, 2000).

I have used this inspirational quote time and again with principals and teachers to remind them of their vocation to inspire and transform the lives of students within their fields of influence. These are very evocative and motivational words that capture the potential that teachers and all educational leaders have for positively influencing all those with whom they relate and engage.

In this chapter I discuss the importance of leaders influencing others through their authentic presence in relationships and connect these, especially, to three macro challenges discussed in chapters 2 and 3; namely, leading in complex and dynamic organisations, leading a paradigm shift in education, and leading change. Leadership, it is argued, is essentially an influence relationship and authentic leaders generate powerful fields of influence through the quality of their presence in morally purposeful and uplifting relationships. Leadership has long been regarded as relational but there is more to it than simply cultivating harmonious relationships. Leaders can best influence others by being fully present, to and for them, in relationships that are authentic and have a clear and mutually beneficial moral purpose.

I argue for an authentic approach to education and to educational leadership and will first briefly address the idea of an authentic school as an enabling context for authentic leadership. I then explore the meaning of authentic leadership as an influence relationship with special focus on the centrality of presence, with its many powerful forces and facets.

I explain that the concept of presence requires more of a leader than merely being there, physically, for others in any specific moment in time. Presence has a number of facets and qualities that help enhance the purpose, quality and depth of relationships and can, thereby, greatly increase the potential for leaders to influence what really matters and make a difference. They can greatly strengthen their influence relationships by conceptualising them as 'fields of influence' and by developing deliberate leadership strategies to encourage and support authentic teaching and learning in their schools.

An authentic school

The discussions on authentic leadership are set within a perspective of the school as a place for authentic teaching and learning. While the many dimensions of authentic learning environments and their implications for authentic leaders are discussed in detail in chapter 9, a brief discussion of the nature and characteristics of an authentic school sets a framework for the discussions in this chapter.

An authentic school has a clear moral purpose driven by core values and a passionate commitment to a collective ethic of responsibility that places the wellbeing of students front and centre. The school's values should guide and inspire everyone (all key stakeholders) and everything (policies, processes and practices) within its fields of influence. Moral purpose and values act as a charter for strategic thinking, planning and action for leaders and decision-makers at all levels. They are also the source of meaning, purpose and inspiration for every leader to enhance the quality of their presence in their relationships and, thereby, maximise influence in order to make a difference in the lives of teachers and their students. A commitment to moral purpose and values can be both aspirational and inspirational.

An authentic school has many characteristics, including:

1 a foundation built from moral purpose and core values lived each day by everyone, which focuses, primarily, on students and their learning;

2 a sense of being a learning community with a commitment to high-quality practices, which gives the school its mandate and vitality;

3 a close match between rhetoric and reality because if there is not it can lead to frustration, cynicism, even anger and alienation;

4 teaching that is authentic, serving the needs of twenty-first century children (discussed later in this chapter);

5 learning processes and content that are authentic in that they engage and connect with students and are deeply meaningful to them in terms of the trajectory of their lives (discussed in chapter 9);

6 leaders who are authentic personally and professionally, are educative in intent, processes and outcomes, and share a collective ethic of responsibility for the transformation of learners, learning and learning outcomes; and

7 an environment that is 'healthy'; meaning that it is safe, welcoming and supportive intellectually, emotionally, spiritually, physically, where students are prepared for living a satisfying and fulfilling life.

These characteristics of an authentic school provide a platform or springboard for authentic leaders to shape and influence the life of the school and its community.

Authentic educational leaders

Authentic leaders have clear moral purpose, a well-developed set of core values, and a passionate commitment to a collective ethic of responsibility for the wellbeing of their school community, the quality of its leadership, the authenticity of what happens within the learning environment, and the quality of learning outcomes. While it is easy to make statements about moral purpose, core values and ethical standards and believe in them, the real challenge is in translating them into practice. Starratt (2011) claims that while, overall, we have described the ethics of educational leadership quite well, we have not done 'a good enough job of describing what the proactive pursuit of those goods of learning might look like' (p. 90). He argues that this pursuit of learning involves virtues 'associated with the professional practice of education' which, in turn, 'reflect leadership virtues' (p. 90). The virtue of authenticity is, he claims, central to the promotion and sustainability of authentic teaching, learning and leadership. He points out that the virtue of authenticity 'implies being true to oneself, owning oneself in one's professional practice, in one's working relationships' (p. 91). When leaders do this others will:

> sense that they speak themselves truly – that is, they are as they appear to be; there is little contrivance about them; they are relatively transparent and not afraid to be so. By and large, when they are with people, others are comfortable being authentic themselves (p. 91).

This is essentially saying that by acting in authentic ways leaders bring out the best in others.

The author started researching authentic leadership over fifteen years ago (see Duignan & Bhindi, 1997), and concluded from the start that authentic educational leaders help infuse educational practice with a higher purpose and meaning. They help *everybody* within a school community to be *somebody*, reducing feelings of anonymity and impotence and helping develop a sense of hope and of possibilities (Starratt, 2004). They especially pay close attention to the quality of learning environments and the impact of teaching on students' learning. They create the conditions within which teachers and students take considerable responsibility for the quality of learning and learning outcomes (addressed in more detail in chapter 9).

While authentic leadership focuses on ethics and morality in actions and interactions, authentic *educational* leadership strongly promotes and supports the core values of schooling. They challenge others to participate in the visionary activity of identifying in curriculum, teaching and learning what is worthwhile, what is worth doing and preferred ways of doing and acting together. They encourage both teachers and students to commit to educational and professional practices that are, by their nature, educative. They are acutely aware that reflective teaching is the key to quality improvement in schools and they encourage teachers to reflect on the quality and effectiveness of their teaching, also providing them with opportunities for such reflection by allocating time for it in the timetable. They encourage and support group dialogue on the issues that really matter to the quality of learning, set clear goals and high expectations for learning (Robinson, 2008) and support this through developing teams focusing on creative and innovative teaching and learning approaches and promote, support and celebrate the efforts of those whose performance upholds the values of their school's culture.

Authentic educational leaders build leadership capacity through the promotion and support of shared leadership practices based on a collective ethic of responsibility and they engage teachers in key decisions related to the promotion of authentic learning based on their knowledge of the contours of expertise in their schools (Duignan & Cannon, 2011).

They encourage all who are engaged in the educational enterprise to commit to quality professional practices that are, by their nature, ethically, morally and educationally uplifting. They also support teachers in bringing about change and innovation, especially through collectively responsible action for creative and novel teaching approaches, and they provide resources to enhance collaborative planning for teaching and learning processes and practices.

Authentic educative leaders should be judged on their ability to create ethically-driven, deep, rich, engaging and high-performing learning environments (Starratt, 2011; Degenhardt & Duignan, 2010; Duignan, 2009; LTLL, 2006–2011). To achieve this end, they need to have the capabilities to:

1 generate a clear moral purpose from which collectively clear goals and high expectations for quality teaching and learning are derived;

2 develop and maintain an effective inquiry and problem-solving culture in their organisation;

3 respect and tolerate different points of view and accept critique as essential in knowledge growth;

4 adapt to contemporary challenges and provide for change through participative feedback and reflection;

5 ensure that people have the freedom to fully participate in processes of learning and growth;

6 defend their decisions on the basis of their contribution to long-term, value-added learning;

7 promote and support high standards of performance and transform learning and learners within their fields of influence;

8 actively promote and participate in their own and especially their teachers' learning and development; and

9 nurture and support the growth of colleagues and enable others to become authentic and influential as leaders.

In summary, authentic educative leaders promote, support and celebrate the collaborative efforts of staff and others whose performances reflect, in positive ways, activities that are valued in their school's culture; for example, reflective critique, authentic learning, and quality teaching processes. They focus their energies and efforts on creating learning environments that maximise opportunities and outcomes for all students. They do this within ethically and morally inspired contexts using collective and collaborative structures and processes. They create such learning environments by developing and nurturing authentic influence relationships and strong fields of influence that include targeted strategies that have the greatest impact on the quality of teaching, learning, and student performance.

Leadership is an influence relationship

Many researchers and writers on leadership contend that effective leadership is, essentially, an influencing process and/or an influence relationship (Neck & Manz, 2007; Duignan, 2006; Hargreaves, 1995; Hargreaves & Fullan, 1991; Johnson & Scull, 1999; Rost, 1993). Rost made a seminal contribution to this view of leadership in a major review and critique of definitions of leadership when he suggested, 'if there are few other unifying elements to our collective thought about leadership, the notion of leadership as influence is one that clearly stands out' (p. 79). Based on his comprehensive critique, he proposed that leadership is ' … an influence relationship among leaders and followers who intend real changes that reflect their mutual purposes' (p. 102). Maxwell (2005) argues that 'the true measure of leadership is influence – nothing more and nothing less' (p. 4) and again '… in leadership – no matter where you are in an organization – the bottom line is always influence' (p. 13). A typical definition of leadership is that it is simply 'a process of influence' (Neck & Manz, 2007, p. 1).

Significant researchers and authors in the area of distributed leadership have taken a similar perspective. Spillane (2006) concludes that 'the term *leadership* is reserved either for activities that administrators and teachers design to influence others or for activities that administrators, teachers, or students understand as influencing them, all in the service of the organization's core work' (italics in original). Harris (2006) argues that distributed leadership *assumes a set of direction-setting and influence practices potentially enacted by people at all levels rather than a set of personal characteristics and attributes located in people at the top'* (p. 38, italics in original).

Others to propose leadership as an influencing relational process include Bass (1990) who sees leadership as a relationship with social influence in a group setting. He points out that 'leadership occurs when one group member modifies the motivation or competencies of others in the group' (p. 20). Begley and Johansson (1998) also conclude that leaders influence the practices of others in order to achieve key social objectives. Hoog et al. (2003) claim that leaders operate from a value set, which they use to influence the thoughts and actions of others.

Leadership is, essentially, an influencing process because effective leaders have the capability to *influence self, others and each other* in order to attain worthwhile and agreed goals; engage in meaningful, authentic relationships to generate and live a shared vision; and elevate the spirit and commitment of colleagues through actions and interactions that are ethical, moral and compassionate (Duignan, 2008).

If influencing is central to leadership, then one key way to influence others is by developing mutually rewarding and productive relationships with them. A simple connection among these concepts would suggest that without relationships there is not going to be much influence, and without influence there is unlikely to be leadership in the way we have defined it here.

Cultivating authentic relationships

Numerous writers on leadership over the years have pointed out that leadership is essentially relational (e.g., Duignan & Gurr, 2007; Duignan, 2006; Fullan, 2005; Halpern & Lubar, 2003; Sergiovanni, 2000, 1992; Starratt, 2004; Senge et al., 2004). However, many educational leaders tend to neglect this leadership imperative because they operate in highly challenging, complex and paradoxical managerial, political, legal and economic environments where attention to social, relational and people concerns are often deflected or ignored. They are too frequently distracted by the hectic pace of life and work and eschew opportunities for reflective analysis on the quality of their relationships and on the deep learning required to bring about transformation in self and others.

Many find it difficult to engage more fully with others in their workplace because they lack the emotional intelligence to be open, trusting, and authentically reciprocal in their relationships. Those driven by corporate, bureaucratic, hierarchical and other imperatives may have no room in their hearts for valuing and respecting the integrity of others and engaging with them to enhance the common good. Slavish adherence to managerialist approaches and an obsession with performance outcomes may rob them of the generosity of spirit that is a hallmark of authentic relationships and transforming leadership. Of course, organisations have to be managed efficiently and effectively and organisational members must be held accountable for the quality of their performance, but it doesn't mean that all this cannot be achieved within an ethical, professional, respectful and compassionate environment.

Developing relationships based on integrity, trust and respect for the dignity and worth of others is a prerequisite if leaders hope to maximise their influence on those who engage with them within their fields of influence. To do this well, leaders need to be, first and foremost, capable or 'real' human beings (Duignan, 2006). As Scharmer (in Senge et al. 2004), reporting on leadership wisdom derived from Confucian masters in China suggests:

> if you want to be a leader, you have to be a real human being. You must recognize the true meaning of life before you can become a great leader. You must understand yourself first (p.186).

After all, it is this self we bring to the relationship table and it is through the quality of our engagements that we project, maintain and sustain our presence and thereby our influence with and on others.

Presence is the key to influence relationships

The focus on presence in leadership relationships is relatively new in the leadership literature (Starratt, 2011; Duignan, 2006; Starratt, 2004; Senge et al., 2004; Halpern & Lubar, 2003). It has emerged, however, as a powerful concept that helps generate coherence between and among the concepts of influence, relationships and leadership. Presence does not only mean being there physically for, and being attentive to, others in the present moment; it is, in fact, a complex, multifaceted concept that deserves close analysis and critique because it is a central concept of leadership as an influence relationship.

While undoubtedly presence can be interpreted as being physically present, 'fully conscious and aware in the present moment' (e.g., Senge et al. 2004; Halpern & Lubar, 2003), O'Donohue (1997) captured its real essence when he stated, 'presence is the way a person's individuality comes toward you. Presence is the soul texture of the person' (p. 173). Tolle (2005) refers to presence as 'still and alert attention', a type of consciousness that causes you to awaken to yourself and to the other in your relationships. He sees still and alert attention as a special form of awareness, which '… is the power that is concealed within the present moment. That is why we may also call it presence' (p. 78).

Being present means being there for others in the sacred space that exists at the core of trusting relationships. Tolle states that 'being present is infinitely more powerful than anything one could say or do, although sometimes being present can give rise to words or actions' (p. 176). Sitting and sharing your presence with others and others sharing their presence with you, all within the sacred space and stillness of the present moment, is at the very heart of authentic human relationships.

A focus on quality presence also helps keep ego in check and the bigger picture in focus because, as Tolle (2005) cautions, it is authentic presence, or an altered state of consciousness, that can free us from the attempts of the ego to use the present moment for its own ends. He suggests that:

> only presence can free you of the ego, and you can only be present Now, not yesterday or tomorrow. Only presence can undo the past [ingrained ego and habits] in you and thus transform your state of consciousness (p. 78).

He also argues that:

> a genuine relationship is one that is not dominated by ego with its image-making and self-seeking.
> In a genuine relationship … there is alert attention toward the other person … That alert attention is
> Presence. It is the prerequisite for authentic relationship (p. 84).

Starratt (2004) also suggests that there is a special quality to presence beyond physically 'being there'. Presence, he says, means being there, in numerous ways, for self and others, and it implies attention and sensitivity to others and each other so that 'our presence activates our authenticity and the authenticity of others' (p. 91). In other words, our authentic presence can bring out the very best in ourselves as well as in others.

Presence, it would appear, has special dimensions or facets and is endowed with moral purpose and special meaning that is not egotistical and self-serving but is exercised in the service of others for the common good. A selection of these interconnected facets of presence, including dignity, integrity, trust, spirituality and ethics is now explored.

Dignity, integrity and trust

Presence has a special dignity and integrity, which elevates it to a pre-eminent position in human relationships. O'Donohue (1998), an internationally renowned theologian, philosopher and poet, highlights these facets when he exhorts us to 'awaken to the mystery of being here and enter the quiet immensity of your own presence … May your outer dignity mirror an inner dignity of soul' (p. 99). He also captured the transcendent essence of presence when he suggests that dignity '… is a special quality of presence. It is wonderful to behold a person who inhabits [their] own dignity.' Your presence will likely reveal how you regard yourself because 'if you do not hold yourself in esteem, it is unlikely that others will respect you either' (p. 69).

Integrity is also seen as closely associated with honesty and with consistently acting according to one's core values and ethical standards. It is a measure of how well our actions accord with our beliefs. Shaw (1997) suggests that it reflects a:

> wholeness or coherence in our philosophies and values, in our public and private statements, and in
> our actions across a variety of situations … In sum, we trust those who are honest in what they say and
> consistent in how they act (p. 61).

We may not always agree with them but we tend to admire them for their honesty and trust them as a result.

Tschannen-Moran (2004) argues that it is important for leaders to understand and appreciate the transformational nuances of trust in order to 'foster and maintain trust in their schools' (p. 41). Trustworthy leaders, she suggests, 'assist their schools to develop authentic and optimal levels of trust' and a positive culture of trust is likely to emerge when 'people have grown to have a deep and abiding trust in one another'. Each person in trusting relationships:

> relies on the other in a full and complete way, resting in interdependence and vulnerability without anxiety … [and there emerges an] empathy with the other party's desires and intentions, and mutual understanding such that each can effectively act on the other's behalf (p. 55).

In school settings, Parks (2005) argues that a student finds authenticity, integrity and trust by gaining an 'insight into the power of one's internal reality' through reflective learning that gives meaning and connects to their lives both inside and outside the school. This insight leads students to a greater appreciation of the power of their own affective lives and encourages them to see:

> how the strength of their inner resources, their sense of purpose, and knowing themselves more deeply all contribute to their ability to be present on behalf of the common good of the group (p. 110).

Such students sing their own song, stand on their own feet, and own who they are and what they do. They are their own person and can engage with confidence, courage, maturity and trust with others to make their school and community a safe and better place.

What is true for students with regard to authenticity and integrity also applies to educational leaders. We all want leaders of honesty and integrity who have discovered their inner self and engage authentically with others through their quality presence, and thereby 'foster the building of a collective strength' (p. 100). Based on the integrity of their presence, leaders enhance their 'ability to attract and hold attention, to convey trustworthiness and credibility, to inspire and call forth the best in others'. Presence based on one's integrity constitutes 'the meeting place between the inner life of the person and the outer life of action in the world' (p. 100). This inner life draws its energy and inspiration from moral purpose, core values and one's deep spirituality.

Presence and spirituality

There is a spiritual dimension to one's presence in the sacred space of authentic relationships. Being fully present with others can give us a deeper appreciation that there is purpose and meaning to life beyond the narrow confines of the self. Our presence is animated, at least partly, from the depths of the soul because, as O'Donohue (1998) so elegantly puts it, 'It is the art of belonging to one's soul that keeps one's presence aflame' (p. 68).

Spirituality entails 'living out a set of deeply held personal values, of honouring forces or a *presence greater than ourselves* (Block, 1993, p. 48, italics in original). Above all, life is a spiritual quest or journey in which we attempt to capture a sense of the sacred in everything we do every day of our lives, in our work, and, above all, in our relationships. Flintham (2010) suggests that through its spiritual dimension leadership is:

> concerned with the often intangible aspects of inter-personal engagement and quality of relationships, particularly when these are tested by the pressures of external events [such as those discussed in chapter 2] and their preservation through a clearly articulated structure of moral and ethical values (p. 111).

In this sense of presence through relationships, authentic leaders can be regarded as 'spiritlinking' that, according to Markham (1999), involves:

> building a circle of friends, fostering networks of human compassion and interweaving teams of relationships through which new ideas are born and new ways of responding to the mission take form and find expression (p. 5).

Webs of meaning are created and enhanced and a common perspective of moral purpose and direction is created, shared, and pursued through experiences within teams and networks of relationships,

A leader's spirituality is developed and honed from a variety of sources, not the least of which are life's experiences – the school of hard knocks. Lessons wrought from the cut-and-thrust of life's journey are often the most influential ones in shaping who we are and what we stand for. These are character-forming, leaving their indelible marks on our minds, hearts and souls. Bogue (1994) captures this sentiment very well when he argues that authentic ideals often find their highest promise in the lives of those people who have:

> spiritual scars and calluses on their characters, the evidence of their having struggled with difficult moral issues, weighted contending moral calls that defy neat solution, agonised over the conflict between their own conscience and the judgment of an opposing majority (p. 146).

Many of the most meaningful character-forming experiences are embedded in the ordinary, everyday encounters with others that help us discover our own spirituality, our purpose in life, as well as the significance of our self in relationships.

It is in our interdependent and supportive relationships that we are most likely to discover our spiritual needs. We cannot live a spiritual life alone because, as Nouwen (1994) reminds us, 'the life of the soul is like a seed that needs fertile ground to grow. This fertile ground includes not only a good inner disposition, but also a supportive milieu' (pp. 81–2).

A problem for many contemporary leaders is that within the busy context of their lives in the workplace it is difficult for them to capture, or recapture, the spirit dimension of life. It often takes crises or tragedies, like deaths, floods or earthquakes to bring out this spiritual essence of our being, bonding people together and creating new and enduring bonds through a collective spirit, thereby encouraging them to live a more meaningful, relational and balanced life.

Ethic of presence

Presence also means taking responsibility for what is happening within one's fields of influence. There is an ethical imperative to presence so far as leaders must be sensitive to the needs and aspirations of others and take responsibility for any inequitable or unjust policies and practices. They should also feel obliged to use the resources under their control wisely, ensuring there is no undue wastage. If they do not allow others to participate, to contribute, to feel a sense of ownership of what is happening within their fields of influence, then they could be accused of being wasteful of the talents of the people around us. The Jesuit philosophy of leadership is instructive. It selects talented people and then values and uses their talents. As Lowney (2003) points out about the successful leaders of the Jesuits, 'they saw each person as endowed with talent and dignity' (p. 176), and their ethical responsibility was to use these talented people to provide leadership throughout the Jesuit world.

Presence through authentic relationship is at the heart of leadership as an influencing process. As already suggested, physical presence is a prerequisite for influencing but it is not sufficient and does not guarantee it. There are at least four reference points for presence that are central to leadership as an influencing relationship. These include: presence and self; presence and others; presence and groups; and presence for influential leadership.

Presence and the 'self'

When discussing influence and influencing there may be a tendency to focus on others and neglect the fact that we need to also be present to and influence our 'selves'. Being authentically present to self may not be as easy as it seems because, as Butler (in Neck & Manz, 2007) reminds us:

> there is a person with whom you spend more time than any other, a person who has more influence over you, and more ability to interfere with or to support your growth than anyone else. This ever-present companion is your own self (p. 1).

Getting to know this self would seem to be essential if we are to develop influential authentic relationships.

In complex, paradoxical and often hectic environments, it may be a challenge to get to know self through inner analysis and quiet reflection. Many leaders in today's demanding workplaces live such busy lives they are often caught up in sweeping, powerful currents of superficial activities and vain attempts to manage crises and conflict. As a result, knowledge of personal and professional self in relationships may also be superficial.

Believing that merely being superficially aware of yourself in the present moment is sufficient to get to know your 'self' may be overly simplistic because, as

Tolle (2005) cautions, we should not 'confuse knowing *about* yourself with knowing yourself' (p. 193). He argues that most people 'define themselves through the content of their lives', which involves, among other things, combinations of their age, health, jobs, salaries, bank accounts, material possessions, and relationships. He says that these facts are 'all about you but are not you'. The real you, he argues, awakens when you are aware that these things are *about* you and not you; when you realise that the essence beneath, the inner space or consciousness that exists despite 'the clutter of thought and turmoil of emotion' of everyday life, is the real you (p. 177).

Indeed, he suggests, the constant stream, the clutter, of ever-changing thoughts, create an illusory perspective of your 'self', a self that is constantly being reshaped and reconstructed to meet the never-satisfied demands of the selfish ego. This shifting and often illusory view of the self is well described by Scharmer (in Senge et al., 2004) when he suggests that 'embedded in our constant flow of thoughts' are 'habitual patterns of thinking' that shape our 'standard notion of self,' which we take to be the real self. But he argues that 'thoughts are not a person', and the real authentic self emerges only when 'we penetrate through everyday thoughts to our deeper experience'. When this happens '… you get rid of the habitual view of the self' (p. 189).

The busyness of contemporary lives and our preoccupation with the content of our lives can thwart the emergence of authentic self and Tolle cautions that the:

> collective disease of humanity is that people are so engrossed in … the content of their lives, that they have forgotten the essence, that which is beyond content, beyond form, beyond thought. They are so consumed by time that they have forgotten eternity, which is their origin, their home, their destiny (pp. 219–20).

He is not recommending that we withdraw from the world of materialism and opportunities but is strongly urging us to dig deep and find the essence, the deep still space within, from which we can source our moral purpose, commitment, passion and energy to engage meaningfully and proactively with this world so as to make a difference to/in it. Scharmer captures the essence of the problem facing many leaders when he claims that the most difficult challenge in discovering your 'self' is to:

> slow down and look deeply into yourself and the world until you start to be present to what's trying to emerge. Then you move back into the world with a unique capacity to act and create (in Senge et al., 2004, p. 191).

Discovering and then influencing self (improving self) is a prerequisite for developing and nurturing authentic relationships and influencing others. Usually when we think of influencing we tend to immediately focus on the other(s) as the one(s) needing to be changed. While we know from the discussion so far that this is only part of the picture, it is a very important part because it is central to our capacity to influence what others do and the quality with which they do it.

Presence and others

Presence, according to Starratt (2011), is both 'a psychological disposition as well as a virtue acquired through moral discipline' (p. 93). While Tolle (2005) suggests that it means being at least superficially aware of your self with the other(s) in the present moment, its deeper meaning involves:

> taking the other inside ourselves, looking at the other really closely, listening to the tone of the other, the body language of the other … [It also means] … coming down from the balcony where one was indifferently watching others' performance and engaging them now with a full attention and risking the spontaneity of the moment to say something unrehearsed, something that *responds* to the authenticity of the other from your own authenticity (Starratt, 2001, p. 93 italics in original).

Being authentically present in the spontaneity of the present moment can make us vulnerable, but it is through such episodes that we build organisational cultures and communities of cooperation, truth, respect and trust where 'the excellence of each community member contributes to the excellence of the whole' (Strike, 2007, p. 17). Authentic presence is the glue that bonds together people who are engaged in influencing relationships. In our presence to others, we can be affirming, enabling, or critical (in a positive sense) but our presence can, of course, be negative and destructive (Starratt, 2011). Authentic leaders try their utmost to model positive presence because they are aware that such a stance is not only ethically and morally the right thing to do but because it is uplifting and inspires and motivates others to achieve greater things. Being authentically present to and for others is a prerequisite for leaders who wish to positively influence the direction and intensity of change in their schools (Degenhardt & Duignan, 2010).

There is a large amount of leadership and change literature on leaders influencing others through mutually authentic relationships. Almost every book on leadership and leading change has some advice in this area, so I will simply propose a number of principles or rules for presence and engagement that have worked for me over the years. They are derived from my research, readings, observations on and experiences of, leading in different organisations in different countries. They are presented to leaders as advice on how to become more authentic in relationships and practices.

1   I often tell educational leaders that, like many of them, I have travelled this world a few times and have yet to meet anyone who doesn't like to be respected. Respect is the good oil of authentic influential relationships.

2   The quality of your presence in a relationship projects to others whether or not you respect them. Remember, if you do not first respect yourself then it is unlikely that you will respect others. Treat groups with dignity, respect and trust just as you would individuals. Levels of respect and trust are a barometer for the quality of a group's relationships and the degree of members' mutually supportive presence for each other.

3   Engage with others with maturity and be aware and attentive in your relationships.

4   Connect to the minds, hearts and souls (spirits) of others. The heart is aroused through mutually responsive, positive and compassionate engagement. The soul is nourished by the sacred stillness created through our awakened and conscious presence in authentic relationships. As Tolle (2005) put it: '... when you feel loving kindness toward another, sense the inner spaciousness [the soul or spirit] that is the source and background to that experience' (p. 235).

5   Break down the barriers, especially those in your mind, that separate you and may cause you to exclude others. Overvaluing position and status can feed the ego, leaving little space for discovering authentic self or for developing authentic relationships.

6   Avoid narrow perspectives and prejudices that may arise from an over-investment in and slavish service to ego. Your ego can trap you within narrow habitual ways of knowing self and blind you to what really matters in life.

7   Maintain the highest ethical standards in everything you do and always act with integrity and authenticity.

8   Practice communicating with moral purpose and do what you say you are going to do. Educational leaders, especially, should have little difficulty in identifying moral purpose, as it will always be closely related to students and their learning. The focus should be on investing time, energy, passion and commitment into maximising opportunities and outcomes for all students.

9   Being present in authentic relationships does not make one a soft target; in fact, the opposite is true. When we operate from a set of core values and a clear moral purpose, we are ethically bound to set high ethical, moral and performance standards and hold ourselves and others accountable for achieving them.

10 Work collectively and collaboratively when appropriate (in groups and teams) to influence what really matters, because it is through a collective ethic of responsibility that influence relationships grow stronger and take shape as emergent influence fields.

Presence and groups: generating influence fields

An important insight when attempting to understand complex systems such as schools is to focus on the multiple connections between and among organisational members and not just on singular linear connections. The human world is not usually as neat, rational, logical and linear as we would like to believe. It doesn't operate with the clockwork precision that managerialist approaches seem to assume. In fact, it tends to be messy, full of human frailty and emotion as well as relational, cultural, social and political turbulence.

Schools are complex and dynamic organisations and leaders may have their strongest influence on what happens on a daily basis through what can be called their influence fields. In seminal work on the dynamic and interconnected characteristics of organisational life that has still to be improved on, Wheatley (1994) suggests that some of the best ways to create and lead change in organisations is through the use of forces that many scientists class as fields or 'invisible forces that structure space or behaviour' (pp. 12–13). For example, moral purpose, values and vision can be seen as a generative force 'of unseen connections that influences employees' behaviour – rather than as an evocative message about some desired future state' (p. 13). This concept of field helps explain the influence of 'action-at-a-distance' (p. 48) or how a force emanating from one source, such as leadership, acts on another, such as student learning and achievement. Fields, therefore, become obvious to us mainly through their effects.

There are unseen forces that leaders and others use to infuse their organisations with life, including the forces of culture, visions, values and ethics. Leaders constantly create collective expectations for the type of organisation they desire, based on their values and beliefs; for example, in schools authentic leaders try to create safe, caring spaces for all the staff and children. Wheatley (1994) illustrates the difference between seeing vision as a field instead of as a linear process and argues that in linear processes, we tend to conceive of vision as 'thinking into the future, creating a *destination* for the organization' and we believe that 'the clearer the image of the destination, the more force the future would exert on the present, pulling us into that desired future state' (pp. 53–4). If, however, we regard vision as a field, 'we would do our best to get it permeating through the entire organization so that we could take advantage of its formative properties' (p. 54) and influence everyone through the vision. In fact, she says, 'vision statements move off the walls and into the corridors, seeking out every employee, every recess of the organization' (p. 55).

Wheatley's work in this area of organisational fields is formative, inspirational and helps present the dynamics of leadership as an influence relationship in a different light. The implications for me are that mutually supportive presence in authentic relationships constitute dynamic influence fields pulsating with energy, promise, hope and possibilities. Each individual adds to a group's dynamics by contributing a complex combination of their unique mental, emotional, physical and spiritual endowments. It is not the roles or positions individual group members hold that determines a group's dynamism and capacity to influence and make a difference, rather it is the gift of mutual presence within a group that creates morally uplifting and inspiring fields of conscious influence, a unity of hope and spirit that impels group members toward realising the vision, mission and core values of their organisation.

Vision, then, is a driving force, not some desired future state and Tolle (2005) advises that, 'whenever you interact with people, don't be there primarily as a function or a role, but as a field of conscious presence' (p. 109) because in relationships and group settings it is important that people:

> not appear to be more than they are but are simply themselves … are the only ones that truly make a difference in the world … Their influence … goes far beyond what they do, far beyond their function. Their mere presence – simple, natural, unassuming – has a transformational effect on whoever they come into contact with (p. 108).

A key understanding of our capacity to generate positive influence fields within groups is that it is not merely the things we do or processes we enact that make the greatest impact on others, but the way we do them and the degree to which we are present to and for each other in the sacred but conscious space that is authentic relationship. As a group we have to search for this still and sacred space together even within the busyness of the work environment by finding the reflective space to discover and share the deep moral purpose and spiritual bonds that bind us together for the common good. Leaders, especially, have a special obligation to assist groups in finding this still, reflective space within mutually respectful, rewarding and influential relationships.

Presence and authentic relationships for influential leadership

Leadership is defined as an influence relationship and leaders are more likely to maximise their influence with others when they are fully present in their relationships with them. Leadership presence is a central element of leadership, which Halpern and Lubar (2003) defines as '… the ability [capability] to connect authentically with the hearts and minds of others' (p. 228). While presence is multifaceted and complex, its quality can determine the depth and extent of influence a leader will have in a group and community setting. Some exceptional leaders seem to have a 'presence' about them; they exude a sense of presence. The good news for the rest of us is that if we work consciously to enhance the quality of our presence in our relationships we can build 'communities of trust' (Strike, 2007) and through them become more influential. A key question is: Can leaders develop and enhance their presence or are people born with it?

In interviews, conversations and workshops with a number of admired leaders over the years, I am convinced that almost all of them had to learn how to be present and most worked hard to improve their presence in their relationships and leadership. Leaders with this type of authentic presence have exhibited a number of characteristics and/or qualities, including:

1 They are, first and foremost, present to themselves; they know who they are, what they stand for (i.e., their core values), and where they want to go in life; they take the time to reflect on the quality of their actions and interactions.

2 They are awake to the quality and authenticity of their presence in their relationships and they work hard to enhance the quality of their presence.

3 They listen with attentiveness, understanding, compassion and are sensitive to those who are vulnerable, hurting, and in need of support.

4 They are principled people and act with moral courage; they are prepared to speak their minds and make the tough decisions in the interests of moral purpose and core values; they challenge unethical, inauthentic and unjust behaviours and practices, such as bullying.

5 Their respect for others is derived from an unconditional acceptance of the other as a fellow human being with dignity, worth and integrity.

6 They are centred, calm and composed; they inhabit their own dignity and this outer dignity reflects a deeper inner dignity of heart and soul.

7 They form deep spiritual bonds based on respecting the dignity and worth of fellow human beings; theirs is a life-filled path, a spirit-filled way of living, which takes them away from the superficial into the depths, from the 'outer person' into the 'inner person'.

8 They ensure that they are sensitive and responsive to talent and potential around them; they nurture and grow others, as persons, so that they become wiser, more capable, and more likely themselves to become influential leaders.

9 They help create 'no-blame environments' that are secure and safe for reflection, critique and feedback; they encourage others to take informed risks and when mistakes are made to learn from them.

10 They are able to let go of entrenched habits that limit or inhibit the development of authentic presence and influence relationships; they are alert to their own prejudices and hang-ups and help others to do the same.

11 They deliberately identify and implement strategies for enhancing their presence and building influence relationships, starting with reflection on self.

12 Through their influence relationships and fields of influence, they help transform others to higher levels of motivation, morality and performance; they raise the ethical bar for all those they touch through their relationships; and they build cultures of respect and trust that encourage 'can do' attitudes and creative and innovative actions.

13 They usually behave as if they're leading leaders and not followers; they demonstrate the Jesuit qualities, which Lowney (2003) describes as:

> The *vision* to see each person's talent, potential, and dignity;
>
> The *courage, passion, and commitment* to unlock that potential; and
>
> The resulting *loyalty and mutual support* that energise and unite teams (p. 170, italics in original).

Lowney's conclusions seem to provide a powerful statement of what leaders who want to influence through their presence in relationships can and should do. Philosophically, they regard themselves as surrounded by potential leaders who, if given the space, freedom, encouragement, nurturing and support will, themselves, become influential leaders. These leaders will not only make a big difference in their fields of influence, *they will be the difference.* Lowney states that the way in which individual Jesuits beheld the world around them changed not only the way they looked at others but what they saw as their vision became 'more acute, their eyes open to talent and potential' (p. 170). Another way of saying this is that Jesuits generate presence in their relationships based on their trust that those around them in their organisation have the talent and potential to be leaders themselves, and they then engage actively with them as colleagues and as capable fellow human beings.

Linking authentic leadership to authentic learning

A core focus for authentic educational leaders needs to be on the enhancement of authentic teaching and learning. This focus challenges them to be more fully present to the transformative possibilities of students' learning and to be more proactively responsible for inviting teachers to create learning opportunities and experiences for their students that will help transform their lives (discussed in more detail in chapter 9).

That is why the corporate–managerialist approaches to educational leadership often fail to transform educational environments and the quality of teaching and learning outcomes. This distinction between educational leaders and business leaders was highlighted by Gross and Shapiro (2005, p. 2) when they argued that educators and educational leaders 'have a very different set of values from those who focus on corporate life'. Educational leaders are accountable, not to shareholders, but to stakeholders who are, essentially, students, their families and their communities. Shapiro points out that *'while business is transactional, our work is transformational'* (p. 2, italics in original).

The work of authentic educational leaders is transformational so far as they promote and support transformational teaching and learning for their students. To do this they must bring their deepest principles, beliefs, values and convictions to their work. The ethics of authenticity and responsibility are at the very heart and soul of educational leadership as it points the way toward a more self-responsible form of relationships and leadership. Authentic educational leaders always act with the good of others (e.g., students, teachers, parents) as a primary reference point.

It is this engagement of the 'self' with the 'other' that provides authentic educators and authentic educational leaders with a deep sense of responsibility for what is happening to the other. They feel responsible for the authenticity of teaching and the quality of student learning in their schools. They engage in personal reflection and whole-school dialogue on the degree to which the conditions necessary for authentic teaching and learning are present. They name, challenge and change, if at all possible, teaching practices that promote inauthentic learning (e.g., teaching narrowly with an undue focus on tests) and they have the courage of their convictions to stand up for what they see as ethically and morally right, especially with regard to the ways in which teachers and students engage with learning content and processes.

Concluding comments

Our understanding of leadership as an influencing relationship and the key contributions of presence to the development of strong influence fields is an emerging and exciting area of exploration and research in leadership. The argument in this chapter is that leadership is an influence relationship and influential leaders generate dynamic fields of influence through mutually respectful and morally purposeful authentic relationships. Leadership has long been regarded as relational but there is more to it than simply being physically present in the present moment with others. Authentic presence constitutes deep engagement with the other(s) that awakens one to the sacred and reflective space that exists between oneself and the other; to the possible precious field of conscious and positive presence at the heart of relationships; to the difficult challenge of looking deeply into one's 'self' and then moving back into the real world with a renewed capacity to be influential and to be the essential difference.

In a number of the cases discussed in chapter 3, the principals involved were both personally and professionally present to and for those who were affected by the conditions of each case. In the case of the girl whose grandfather took her to live with an aunt, the principal was sensitive to the circumstances of the child (whose mother, a single parent, was on drugs and not able to care properly for her at the time) and managed the situation in a way that focused on the girl's needs. Similarly, in the case of the disadvantaged boy who received the blue slip for discipline problems just before the athletics carnival, the principal was present for that child and supported his inclusion in the event. In the case of the elderly teacher with early dementia, the principal was greatly concerned for her welfare and was present for the teacher and her husband as well as the students at the school. Being present in cases like these means that principals and other leaders are fully aware of the details of the situation and are sufficiently concerned and motivated to take action to help it.

Leadership presence demands personal formation and growth that makes taking responsibility for nurturing the growth and development of others natural. Their presence activates a deep sense of their own authenticity and that of others. Injustice offends their ethic of authenticity and generates a response that is consistent with the person I am, the values I embrace, and my commitment to others as a human being (Starratt, 2004).

Key ideas for reflection

Analysing your leadership authenticity

The purpose of the following short instrument (table 8.1) is to help you reflect on your own authenticity as an educational leader and on how evident the conditions for authentic leadership for learning are in your school. The instrument is a tool to provide information about current conditions for authenticity and authentic learning in your school, and to encourage reflection on them as a basis for action and professional formation.

The scores are meant only as indications of strengths and areas needing attention. The idea is to generate discussion among staff so as to sustain and build

Educational Leadership

Table 8.1: *Leadership authenticity*

Authenticity demands that we act in truth, honesty and integrity in all our actions and interactions as humans, educators and educational leaders (adapted from LTLL Project, 2006–2010).

INDICATOR	EVIDENCE	RATING			
As a leader I:	(What are the visible signs that this indicator is present in my school?)	1 – Not at all evident to 4 – Strongly evident			
		1	2	3	4
1 reflect and act upon my moral purpose, values and ethical standards					
2 encourage others to reflect upon and discover their own authenticity					
3 encourage and support authentic presence in mutually beneficial relationships					
4 engage with others in such ways that all are raised to higher levels of motivation and morality					
5 work hard to create conditions of integrity and authenticity in the workplace					
6 demonstrate passion and commitment to the promotion and support of authentic teaching and learning					
7 help transform learning and learners so that they can lead more responsible, productive, meaningful and fulfilling lives					
8 seek to make a positive difference in the lives of all those I (we) touch					
Total of ratings					
* Mean score for authenticity (Total/Number of items)					

* A total score of 16 or below, or a mean score of 2 or below, would indicate a need to pay closer attention to developing your leadership authenticity and that of the school's culture. Examining each item's score will indicate which areas are strong and which need improvement.

Table 8.2: *Leadership presence*

The concept of presence challenges us to engage purposefully and meaningfully with others in ways that are authentic, inspiring and morally uplifting (adapted from LTLL Project, 2006–2010).

INDICATOR	EVIDENCE	RATING			
As a leader I:	(What are the visible signs that this indicator is present in my school?)	1 – Not at all evident to 4 – Strongly evident			
		1	2	3	4
1 value the importance of full awareness of self in relation to others					
2 create opportunities for reflection and critique (self and others)					
3 use presence to build relationships and cultures of integrity and trust					
4 value and act on presence that is sensitive to and affirming of others					
5 value and act on presence that is enabling and encouraging of others' capacity for meaningful participation in the life of the school community					
6 appreciate and act upon the spiritual essence of presence					
7 value and act upon presence to students so as to create conditions for their learning, growth and transformation					
8 support formation and development processes that enhance mutuality of presence					
Total of ratings					
* Mean score for presence *(Total/Number of items)*					

* A total score of 16 or below, or a mean score of 2 or below, would indicate a need to pay closer attention to developing your leadership authenticity and that of the school's culture. Examining each item's score will indicate which areas are strong and which need improvement.

on the strengths and develop strategies to bring about improvement in the areas requiring attention.

You are encouraged to add other items to the instrument that are relevant to yourself, school and situation.

The answers to the items on the instrument can help educational leaders decide how to better influence the shape and direction of learning environments. Influence is normally most effective if educational leaders demonstrate their presence to others through their relationships.

Analysing your leadership presence

As with the instrument on leadership authenticity, the previous instrument (table 8.2) is meant to generate discussion and dialogue with a view to enhancing the quality of your presence with others. The scores suggest trends only. You may wish to add additional items to this instrument that are relevant to yourself, school or situation.

To be fully present to others is a great challenge for many educational leaders. They are frequently distracted by the hectic pace of life and work, and eschew opportunities for reflection on their practice and the deep learning required to bring about transformation in self and others. They may find it difficult to engage more fully with those with whom they work because they lack the emotional intelligence to be open, trusting and authentically reciprocal in their relationships. Those driven by corporate, bureaucratic and hierarchical imperatives may devalue the integrity of others by lacking respect for them as capable human beings. The external and internal pressures, discussed in chapters 2 and 3, may very well have robbed them of the generosity of spirit that is a hallmark of authentic educational leaders.

Other questions for reflection
Leadership authenticity

1 What values and qualities define my relationships and my leadership?

2 How can I make a greater difference in the lives of others?

3 What gives me strength to deal with difficult situations involving 'people challenges' and difficult ethical tensions?

4 How well do I reconcile (balance) my sense of 'self' with the demands of my current work 'role'?

Leadership presence

1 In what ways are you 'present' to/for your professional colleagues and your students?

2 Who is fully present to/for you? How do they do this?

3 How could you be more fully present to the challenges inherent in your learning environment?

4 How can you be more fully present to the people you work with and the conditions of their work?

Chapter 9

Authentic
leaders
help create
innovating,
deep, rich
learning
environments

As discussed in chapter 2, currently there appears to be a tension between two educational paradigms with different emphases. One of these paradigms tends to emphasise the centrality of standards, accountability, testing and student achievement as measures of school performance, while the other focuses more on improving pedagogy and, especially, enhancing the conditions for learning and learning outcomes more generally. The focus in this chapter is on an approach to educational leadership that aims at improving the quality of teaching, learning, learning environments, and student outcomes in schools. Authentic educational leaders at all levels promote and support the core values of schooling; that is, quality teaching and learning, and thereby better prepare students for a productive, contributing and fulfilling life.

In this chapter, recent meta-analysis research is discussed and critiqued, especially with regard to conclusions about how teachers and other educational leaders influence student achievement. Then the implications of seeing schools as complex learning communities, and leadership as an influence relationship operating through influence fields, are explained. Drawing on recent OECD research and commentary on educational leadership and innovative learning environments, as well as on other literature and the author's research findings, the nature of deep, rich and engaging learning environments for teachers and students is described and ways are considered as to how such learning environments can be created and sustained, with special emphasis on the forms of leadership that will best accomplish all of this.

Educational leaders influence student achievement

It is widely recognised in relevant literature that effective educational leaders such as principals and leadership teams, influence student achievement in positive ways (Darling-Hammond, 2010; Robinson et al., 2009; Dinham et al., 2008; Robinson, 2008; Mulford et al., 2009; Leithwood & Riehl, 2003). As discussed in chapter 8, leaders – like teachers and others – generate fields of influence, and it is through these that they create the conditions for learning that positively influence teaching, learning and student outcomes. From their research on educational leadership for organisational learning and improved student outcomes, Mulford et al. (2006) claim that school leadership is second only to classroom teaching in influencing what students learn at school. Leithwood and Riehl (2003) conclude from their review of leadership literature that '... leadership variables do seem to explain an important proportion of the school-related variance in student achievement' (p. 13) and:

> in schools that show impressive achievement gains, educational leaders maintain a clear and consistent focus on improving the core tasks of schooling – teaching and learning, and they accept no excuses for failing to improve student learning (p. 25).

To better understand these findings within the context of a school as a complex and dynamic learning system, it is important to explore the nature and impact of both the linear and non-linear dynamics of influencing.

Influence is linear and non-linear

The reason why it is often stated in research findings and educational leadership literature that a principal's influence is indirect (e.g., Leithwood & Riehl, 2003) is because it is usually regarded as involving, primarily, linear processes that are amenable to linear measurement. While there is some substance to this perspective it is important to realise that there are many things that educational leaders do to influence teachers, learning environments and student outcomes that may not be amenable to such measurement approaches.

The key to understanding the many ways in which teachers and principals influence the quality of learning environments and learning outcomes, suggests Senge (1992):

> is seeing circles of influence rather than straight lines [where] … every circle tells a story. By tracing the flows of influence, you can see patterns that repeat themselves, time after time … From any element in a situation [e.g., teacher feedback or direct instruction], you can trace arrows [e.g., relationships] that represent influence on another element [e.g., learning environment or student outcomes] (p. 75).

This is because schools as learning communities are living entities characterised by 'fluid and fluctuating networks of communications' and 'non-verbal forms of mutual engagement' (Capra, 2002, p. 96), which enhance their 'flexibility, creative potential and learning capability' (p. 97). The best way to keep a school community vibrant, alive and flourishing is to collectively build 'self-generating networks of communications' (p. 93) that produce a 'common context of meaning' and a deep sense of belonging (p. 94). These self-generating, fluid and fluctuating networks create interconnected circles of purpose, meaning and positive influences that help create learning environments within which creativity, novelty, and meaningful change can gain momentum and flourish.

If we treat schools as complex and dynamic learning communities, then we need to 'break with simple cause-and-effect models, linear predictability and a dissection approach to understanding phenomena, replacing them with organic, non-linear and holistic approaches' to leading learning in schools (Morrison, 2002, p. 8). Fullan (1999), an internationally recognised scholar and expert on leading change in educational systems and schools as communities of learning, claims that:

> the link between cause and effect [in change situations] is difficult to trace, that change (planned and otherwise) unfolds in non-linear ways, that paradoxes and contradictions abound and that creative solutions arise out of interaction under conditions of uncertainty, diversity and instability (p. 4).

He also suggests that all learning communities are 'webs of nonlinear feedback loops connected to other people and organizations (its environments) by webs of nonlinear feedback loops' (p. 4).

When we read research results that claim principals are second only to teachers in their influence on student outcomes, or when we see from meta-analysis research that principals only have a significant effect-size impact on student achievement in a narrow range of leadership practice areas, we need to consider the implications of these findings from a non-linear as well as a linear perspective.

Educational leaders influencing student outcomes: research findings

Robinson (2008) makes a positive connection between educational leadership and student learning. She conducted a meta-analysis on twenty-seven studies of the various dimensions or practices of leadership that influence student outcomes. The top five practices, in terms of effect size on student achievement, are presented in table 9.1.

The results indicate that when principals actively promote and participate in teacher learning and development they have a large impact ($d = 0.84$) on student achievement. (Hattie, 2009, p. 9 suggests that typically $d = 0.2$ indicates small impact; $d = 0.4$ indicates medium impact; and $d = 0.6$ indicates large impact when judging educational outcomes). Educational leaders have medium impact on student outcomes when they establish clear goals and expectations ($d = 0.42$) and plan, coordinate and evaluate teaching and curriculum ($d = 0.42$). While it is clear from these results that educational leaders, especially principals, influence the quality of student outcomes, it may seem surprising that the influencing factors are so few in number (a narrow range of influences), an issue discussed later in this chapter.

Table 9.1: *Leaders' influence on student achievement (Robinson, 2008)*

DIMENSIONS OF LEADERSHIP PRACTICE	EFFECT SIZE
1 Promoting/participating in teacher learning/development	$d = 0.84$
2 Establishing goals and expectations	$d = 0.42$
3 Planning, coordinating, evaluating teaching and curriculum	$d = 0.42$
4 Resourcing strategically	$d = 0.31$
5 Ensuring an orderly/supportive environment for all	$d = 0.27$

Dinham (2009) has encouraging findings for the influence that educational leaders in schools, especially principals, have on learning outcomes, and based on his research he states that educational leaders play key roles in creating the conditions for quality learning and teaching, '*although the influence of leadership on student achievement has perhaps been underestimated*' (p. 12, author's italics for emphasis). When drawing conclusions from a number of his own studies and from key relevant literature, he concludes that the degree of positive influence of the principal is surprising and while there is little doubt as to the influence of the individual teacher, 'principals can play key roles in creating and maintaining the conditions and environment where teachers can teach effectively and students can learn' (pp. 48–9). Perhaps the results are surprising because many of the most important ways in which principals can influence learning and student outcomes may not be amenable to precise measurement.

We should not underestimate the significant influence principals and other school leaders can have on learning environments, the conditions for learning, the quality of and support for teaching, and the quality of student learning and outcomes. This conclusion is supported by other important researchers on educational leadership (Sharratt & Fullan, 2009; Boris-Schacter & Langer, 2006; Hargreaves & Fink, 2006; Spillane, 2006; Caldwell, 2006; Mulford et al., 2006; Leithwood & Riehl, 2003).

There is also substantial research that focuses on teachers with regard to their influence on student learning and outcomes, and all educational leaders should be familiar with it. An important part of this research measures teachers' influences in terms of their impact on student achievement, which is typically referred to as 'effect size' (the standardised mean difference between outcomes of one approach or practice and another). Significant research in this area uses meta-analysis (e.g., Hattie, 2009), which involves the statistical analysis of a large collection of findings from previously completed individual studies. Typically, findings in this type of research are reported in terms of average effect size, which:

> expresses the increase or decrease in achievement of the experimental group (the group of students who are exposed to a specific instructional technique) in standard deviation units (Marzano et al., 2005b, p. 4).

In a major meta-analysis of thousands of studies worldwide that focused on the linkages between teaching and student outcomes, Hattie (2009) concludes '… excellence in teaching is the single most powerful influence on [student] achievement'. Importantly, he stresses that it is not teachers as such, but excellence in teaching that makes this powerful difference. Hanushek (2011) of Stanford University agrees and suggests that 'good teaching is the single biggest variable in educating pupils, bigger than class size, family background, or school funding'. Education Secretary in Britain, Michael Gove (2011), is unequivocal about what causes quality student outcomes in education when he states that 'an emphasis on better teacher quality is a common feature of all [successful] reforms'. Countries like Finland and South Korea make life easier for themselves by recruiting only elite graduates, and paying them accordingly.

Hattie identified the top ten teacher practices that have the greatest influence on students' achievement as measured by effect size. These are presented in tabular form in table 9.2. While the focus in this chapter is primarily on the influence of leaders on learning environments and student outcomes, all educational leaders must have a deep understanding of this research in order to help create the conditions to enable excellence in teaching. Educational leaders should be familiar with findings such as Hattie's because, even though they provide excellent advice for teachers, they also make a significant contribution to our understanding of the many ways in which leaders can build rich learning environments for both students and teachers. It is with regard to these many ways of influencing the quality of learning environments that we now turn our attention.

Table 9.2: *Teaching practices and student achievement.*
(Influences that have a meaningful effect size on student learning outcomes)

INFLUENCE (PRACTICES)	EFFECT SIZE
1 Feedback	$d = 1.13$
2 Students' prior cognitive ability	$d = 1.04$
3 Instructional quality	$d = 1.0$
4 Direct instruction	$d = 0.82$
5 Remediation/feedback	$d = 0.65$
6 Students' disposition to learn	$d = 0.61$
7 Class environment	$d = 0.56$
8 Challenge of goals	$d = 0.52$
9 Peer tutoring	$d = 0.50$
10 Mastery learning	$d = 0.50$

Leaders influencing the quality of teaching and learning: research findings

Many quantitative studies focus on and measure the linear relationship between certain leadership and teaching practices and student achievement. This usually involves a linear measure based on performance in tests in such subjects as mathematics, science, and a language (more recently, literacy, numeracy, science). Over the years, many such studies included achievement results in one or two of these subject areas and so represent a narrow view of student achievement. Conclusions from the research often indicate that teachers *directly* influence student achievement while leaders have an *indirect* influence. On the surface, these conclusions appear plausible and represent common sense, but the conclusions for leaders is contestable, not in terms of what the research says but what it ignores or neglects to say. Before elaborating on this point, I will first enumerate the strengths and usefulness of these research findings overall.

For example, the findings of such eminent researchers as Hattie (2009), Robinson et al., (2009); Leithwood and Mascall, (2008); and Marzano et al., (2005b) identify and describe practices for both teachers and other educational leaders (especially school principals) that have the largest effect size (or influence) on student outcomes, especially student achievement. This is valuable knowledge and the findings constitute rich sources of recommendations and advice for teachers and leaders wishing to improve the quality of teaching and learning in their schools. Hattie's (2009) contribution to the area in his very influential book *Visible Learning* is exemplary, and should be priority reading for teachers and educational leaders. Educational leaders also need to be familiar with the conclusions of Robinson et al. (2009) regarding how they (can) influence student outcomes. Other authors and researchers discussed earlier in this chapter are also important sources of knowledge and wisdom on this topic area.

There are, however, limitations to this form of research that need to be carefully considered. Some of these limitations are based on the author's critique of this research as well as on a number of those identified and explained in recent OECD reports (Pont et al., 2008b).

Critique of this research

As stated earlier in this chapter, much of the research on which meta-analysis studies are based focus on a narrow range of measures of student learning, often student achievement on test scores in literacy, numeracy, science and/or reading. There are, of course, many more dimensions to student learning and student outcomes than those measured by achievement on tests. As discussed in chapter

2, tests tend to undervalue, even ignore, the qualitative dimensions of human behaviour and performance and fail to appreciate that many of the most significant influences of leaders on student learning may not be linear.

From the research findings of Robinson (2008, see table 9.1), it would seem that there is only one thing educational leaders can do that will have a large effect size on student achievement (promoting and participating in teachers' learning and development, $d = 0.84$). The other influences identified in the table are either small or at the lower end of the medium impact scale (approximately between $d = 0.4 –$ 0.6). Having engaged in workshops and research with thousands of principals over many years, I believe these findings tell only part of the story. In fact, as we shall see, there are a myriad influence relationships and processes educational leaders can use to positively influence the quality of teaching, learning environments and student outcomes.

Admittedly, many of these influence processes may be difficult to measure precisely in the traditional sense, but we can use many of the findings of the research discussed earlier (for teachers and educational leaders) to inform us of ways and means for leaders to strengthen their influence on learning, if they are reinterpreted within a paradigm that treats schools as complex and dynamic learning communities within views of pedagogy that are more suited to the needs of contemporary students. Einstein famously stated that we couldn't solve problems by using the same kind of thinking we used to create them. I believe that we cannot substantially and sustainably change learning environments by using research findings that were generated from the traditional learning environments we are trying to change. At the very least, we need to reconsider the relevancy and usefulness of these findings for an emerging paradigm of learning.

Another issue related to the influence of leaders on student outcomes is that the research concludes that it is indirect in nature. Given this premise and the very narrow range of influencing processes available to principals identified in much of the relevant research, one could wonder why they would bother turning up for work each day. Surely, these findings on leaders influencing student outcomes (narrow and indirect) are problematic and need careful analysis and critique. We will now look more closely at these issues.

Traditional research findings tend to emphasise linear relationships between leadership practices and their effects on learning environments and learning outcomes. Given that principals spend little time directly interacting with students in their classrooms, it is no surprise that findings of the research show that their influence is indirect. However, this perspective may not be very helpful to educational leaders and may cause them to underestimate the strength of their influence. Dinham (2009) hints at this view when he suggests that the influence of leadership on student achievement has perhaps been underestimated. At stake here are assumptions about the nature of influencing processes and strategies.

What if influencing is more non-linear than linear? What implications would this perspective have for educational leaders?

Pont et al. (2008b), drawing on over forty leadership studies in their OECD report on improving school leadership practice, give valuable advice that provides insights into the problematic nature of the issue of leadership influence that we have just highlighted. They note that empirical research on the factors influencing student learning is:

> conceptually and methodologically challenging. Student learning is shaped by a range of extra- and intra-organisational factors including student socio-economic background, abilities and attitudes, organisation and delivery of teaching and school policies and practices (p. 34).

However, they come to the crux of the problem when they conclude that:

> studies measuring the impact of different factors on student achievement *tend to use data sets and methodologies providing limited measures of learning and partial indicators of the range of factors influencing it* (p. 34, author's italics for emphasis).

We have already discussed the fact that the measures of learning are traditionally too narrow (based on tests in a narrow range of subjects) but it is the second criticism that is of greater interest here.

What is meant by the phrase 'partial indicators of the range of factors influencing it [achievement]'? It actually means that the range of leadership influencing factors are, most likely, greater or broader that those normally identified in research. The perspective that the nature of influencing is, primarily, linear (hence the language of direct and indirect influence) is problematic because we have argued throughout this book that schools as communities of learning are often described as complex, dynamic, alive and characterised by networks of relationships, communications, and circles, patterns or fields of influence (essentially non-linear). We will now examine the implications and consequences for educational leaders if they truly believe schools are communities of learning where influencing constitutes a field with both non-linear and linear dimensions.

The power of influence fields

In chapter 2 we discussed the idea of schools as complex and dynamic learning communities, and in chapter 8 we argued that principals and other educational leaders operate through their *influence fields* in order to influence the direction and intensity of positive change in their learning environments. Now we develop specific implications from this perspective for educational leaders who wish to build rich, engaging and technologically-smart learning environments in their schools.

Authentic educative leaders, including teachers, operate through dynamic, integrated and overlapping influence fields as they focus their energies and efforts on improving what really matters – student learning and outcomes (Duignan, 2009). They engage in multiple tasks, relationships, and in positive culture-building in order to create engaging, inspiring, supportive and productive learning environments for their students. Bereiter and Scardamalia (2008) argue that educators who wish to serve the needs of contemporary students need to be able to look beyond the narrow comparisons of effect-size research 'in order to identify approaches that offer promise of making qualitative leaps beyond current outcomes' (p. 83). It is not enough, they say, to identify approaches that are 'not only worth adopting but are worth working to develop in different directions' (p. 83). Practitioners need breakthrough research that 'opens up new possibilities for future advances' (p. 83). These new possibilities include building positive learning environments that excite and engage children, help them build self-belief and confidence, and prepare them for a fulfilling life filled with hope and possibilities.

Schools with deep, rich learning environments tend to do these things but it would appear from literature reviewed in this book, as well as from my own observations and experiences, that too many schools do not serve the needs of their students well enough. As stated in chapter 8, authentic schools have a clear moral purpose and put students and their learning at the core of their endeavours. They work very hard at generating cultures of continuous learning and they put people before structures and processes. They are places where teachers and students engage authentically with each other in mutually respectful and inspiring relationships. Teachers in these schools are very aware that their presence is important to their students, and students commit to and greatly value being present to one another and to their teachers. Students are also trusted to author key parts of their own learning and take a large measure of responsibility for and ownership of this learning. Teachers and other educational leaders are actively engaged with their students in helping facilitate and shape the development of rich, productive and rewarding learning opportunities and environments.

A problem for some innovative educational leaders is that the traditional classroom set-up with desks arranged in rows, an exposed teacher's desk, and a board in the front of the room is no longer effective or viable (Benavides et al., 2008, p. 32). They contrast such 'standard schools' (term used to describe schools with traditional forms of teaching and learning in the report) with those who tend to put the learner centre stage, providing a wide array of learning resources and facilitating individual improvement as well as collaborative learning. They go on to note that these latter schools also aim to teach an integrated curriculum that does not strictly separate traditional subject areas but rather emphasises 'the interconnections between the disciplines' (p. 32).

Learner-centred learning environments tend to invite, even encourage, students to participate in their learning and own it. Sliwka (2008) concludes from her research and review of relevant literature that when educational learning environments:

> combine customised learning with collaborative group learning in authentic, inquiry-oriented projects [they] provide their students with access to diverse knowledge sources and assess them for deeper understanding and further learning [and they can be used as] meaningful models for the renewal of mainstream education across the globe (p. 108).

These environments are also more likely to provide the 'educated graduates' required to drive and inspire an emerging knowledge society.

Educating for the real world

In the context of a knowledge society, '... the memorisation of facts and procedures is not enough for success' (Sawyer, 2008, p. 49) and educated school graduates today and into the future '... need a deep conceptual understanding of complex concepts, and the ability to work with them creatively to generate new ideas, new theories, new products, and new knowledge' (p. 49). Sawyer suggests that they must be capable of critically evaluating 'what they read, to be able to express themselves clearly both verbally and in writing, and to be able to understand scientific and mathematical thinking'. Perhaps, above all they need to:

> learn integrated and usable knowledge, rather than the sets of compartmentalised and decontextualised facts emphasised by instructionism. [All these abilities are] important to the economy, to the continued success of participatory democracy, and to living a fulfilling, meaningful life (pp. 48–9).

Costa and Kallick (2008) are critical of many contemporary systems and schools when they conclude from their research that too many people, including students '... perceive thinking as hard work, and they recoil from situations that demand too much of it' (p. 33). They argue that we need our students to be curious, to meaningfully engage with the world around them and they advise that students should be encouraged to:

> reflect on the changing formations of a cloud, to feel charmed by the opening of a bud, to sense the logical simplicity of mathematical order. [Most educated people, they claim] ... find beauty in a sunset, intrigue in geometric shapes of a spider web, and exhilaration in the iridescence of a hummingbird's wings ... We want students to feel compelled, enthusiastic, and passionate about learning, inquiring, and mastering (p. 33).

Sawyer (2008), too, is critical of much of contemporary schooling and suggests that it is '... particularly ill-suited to the education of creative professionals who can develop new knowledge and continually further their own understanding' (pp. 49–50). In fact, he argues that the effects of much of contemporary schooling on graduates is to provide them with a form of learning that is '... very difficult to use outside of the classroom' and makes it difficult for them to transfer this learning 'to real-world settings' (p. 50). This is a crucial problem and one that confronts many contemporary educators. In order for students to develop such transfer capabilities, learning environments and learning processes must provide them with realistic opportunities to articulate and apply what they are learning.

Application of learning

The importance of the application and transfer by students of their learning is emphasised by Costa and Kallick (2008) when they point out that thinking in everyday life is a different matter to thinking in a classroom. In the real world students will not only have '... to solve problems, [they] also have to find them amid an ongoing, complex stream of demands and distractions' (p. xiv). They claim that while 'high mental ability alone may serve students well sitting at their desks with their pencils poised, they will need a deep understanding of the concepts and ideas learned in order to apply them in the real world' (p. xiv). They remind us that 'a critical attribute of intelligent human beings is not only having information but also knowing how to act on it' (p. xxii).

They argue that schools need to focus on student learning and performance under challenging conditions, such as those characterised by 'dichotomies, dilemmas, paradoxes, polarities, ambiguities, and enigmas – that demand strategic reasoning, insightfulness, perseverance, creativity, and craftsmanship to resolve' (p. xxii). Schools, they say, should be interested in enhancing the ways students '*produce* knowledge rather than how they merely *reproduce* it' (p. 17) because they need to be able to 'abstract meaning from one experience, carry it forth, and apply it in a novel situation' (p. 28).

Schools should promote and support authentic approaches to teaching and learning that engage students in a deeper understanding of their learning, and its relationship to the trajectory of their lives outside school (Starratt, 2004). He states that authentic learning is not only about *taking and processing* new knowledge and skills for oneself but is also about *giving* of one's unique humanity to others and to the community. It involves making a difference in the lives of others. This form of learning engages students in deep and meaningful learning experiences, where teaching and learning processes are constantly constructed and reconstructed to respect the particular needs and circumstances of the learners, with a view to elevating and enhancing their life chances and choices. The key conditions necessary for authentic learning include the need for students to:

1   create personal meaning through their learning (students must be able to connect their learning to the personal circumstances of their lives and gives them hope for a better future);

2 generate greater awareness of relationships between them 'selves' and the subject of study (acquisition of information, knowledge, skills must help them develop greater self-belief and confidence);

3 develop deeper respect for the integrity of the subject of study (the subject matter is *sacred* in that it equips them with tools for living a contributing and fulfilling life); and

4 be transformed into fully functioning human beings – the aim is not just to know more but to be more (Starratt, 2004).

These conditions for authentic learning imply that the architects of curriculum, pedagogical processes and learning environments must place students, their needs and circumstances, at the heart of their design efforts. Otherwise, students are likely to become disengaged and their learning can become hollow and meaningless.

In order to build the type of learning environments that Sawyer, Starratt, Costa and Kallick and other authors discussed in this chapter recommend, we need to create to a much greater degree than is currently the case in many classrooms, learning environments that are more open and risk-free, where students are able to think out loud, engage in stimulating dialogue, and receive constructive feedback on their learning. Such a form of learning is more likely to be realised when learners feel free to express and explore, through dialogue, their embryonic and still-developing ideas and test their understandings in mutually reinforcing feedback loops. In fact, it is likely that deep learning and its application will not occur until students have opportunities to do this.

There is support for these ideas on application from a different but very interesting source, suggesting that what holds true for students also applies to teachers and educational leaders. One of the gurus in the business management area, Charles Handy (2006), reflecting on his learning as a manager and leader, concludes that the acquisition and use of information, knowledge and skills is necessary for success in management and leadership. This is because it helps us to 'access and apply the deeper learning that can enrich our personalities and our lives' and enables us to reinterpret and reconstruct 'what we already knew, privately and subconsciously', in order to better understand it (p. 64). Only then, he argues, can we use and apply our knowledge effectively in the real world.

Handy concludes that experience and learning must go hand-in-hand for leaders, within the same frame of reference because:

> providing the concepts before the experience is to store learning in a mental warehouse in the hope that it will [be] in useful later on. [He claims that in his experience] warehoused learning decays very rapidly. Too often, it is no longer there when you come to need it. We know that to learn a language you have to use it as soon as you can after you learn it. It is no different with anything else (p. 64).

These are demanding learning challenges for schools, and the question for teachers and other educators is to identify ways in which they can support students so they may enhance their capacity for ongoing reflection and application. This support is often referred to as scaffolding learning. Scaffolding refers to the customised assistance provided to students based on their current learning needs and goals. It helps them learn better by empowering them to actively participate and take more responsibility for their own learning. As Sawyer (2008) explains:

> telling someone how to do something, or doing it for them, may help them accomplish their immediate goal; but it is not good scaffolding because the child does not actively participate in constructing that knowledge (p. 53).

Effective scaffolding provides the type of support for learners that helps them engage with, make meaning of, and apply their learning. It also provides opportunities for them to construct and reconstruct their knowledge and learning so they can articulate and apply it better in today's challenging environment outside their school. Tailored scaffolding can only be provided to students if those providing the support (e.g., teachers) know them very well in terms of the current state of their knowledge and skills, as well as their dispositions toward learning and their capacities to reflect on and articulate their learning. This is a challenge for all educators who themselves need to be informed by authentic and smart assessment processes.

The shifting sands of assessment

We discussed in chapter 2 the prevalence of testing in contemporary education systems and schools. How well do these testing regimes help educators construct the type of learning environments to bring out the best in our twenty-first century children? Benavides et al. (2008) conclude that available indicators, such as those generated through the Program of International Student Assessment (PISA) tests, demonstrate that education systems around the world 'are far from providing the learning environments that would facilitate students to achieve to their full potential' (p. 25) and that much of the learning provided by schools is 'not consistent with many of the recent findings from the research of effective learning and teaching' (p. 24).

A report on a troubling pattern with regard to assessment in high schools in the US (Wiggins & McTighe, 2008) concludes that students 'typically perform adequately on test items requiring recall and basic skills but do poorly on items requiring application or careful analysis and explanation' (p. 36). They identified some of the important challenges for high schools in the areas of learning and assessment as students displaying 'boredom, passivity, and apathy' and 'external test pressures that demand superficial content coverage; and students who seem to know the material but don't know how to apply it'. They suggest that the mission of high schools 'is not to cover content, but rather to help learners become thoughtful about, and productive with, content' (p. 36). Its real job is to prepare students for the world outside school, 'to enable them to apply what they have learned to issues and problems they will face in the future' (p. 36). Unfortunately, they point out that the common methods of teaching and testing in high schools tend to focus on acquisition of knowledge and skills at the expense of meaning and transfer. As a result, 'when confronted with unfamiliar questions or problems (even selected-response problems on standardized tests), many students flounder' (p. 37).

Assessment measures need to keep pace with emerging developments in pedagogy but all too frequently they don't. Whereas there is an increasing focus on customising and personalised learning environments for students, current assessment processes assume that every student should learn the same thing at the same time. While schools will still need to measure learning for accountability purposes, they need to balance this with an increased focus on improving learning for individual students and for whole-school improvement. Perhaps the greatest weakness of many contemporary testing systems is that they assess relatively superficial knowledge and do not assess the deep knowledge required by a knowledge society. An important implication of these arguments about testing is that many current assessment approaches may actively support and perpetuate traditional models of schooling. There is a need for the results of testing to be used to construct learning environments, deep learning and its application.

Building rich and engaging learning environments

The models of schooling we offer our students today and into the future should create a dynamic balance between student- and teacher-centred approaches to learning and help reconstruct and customise learning environments to meet students' needs and increase student achievement (Degenhardt & Duignan, 2010). Learning should focus on 'students developing a sense of curiosity, wonderment, and awe; creating, imagining, and innovating; and becoming more metacognitive about what and how they are learning ...' (Costa & Kallick, 2008, p. 45). They recommend that teachers should design learning opportunities that include rich tasks requiring creative and strategic thinking, as well as for:

> resolving discrepancies, clarifying ambiguities, constructing the meaning of a phenomenon, conducting research to test theories, or ameliorating polarities. When students are sufficiently challenged, they give meaning to work [and] produce new knowledge (p. 51).

The real world presents added challenges to educators and educational leaders so far as it is driven to a large extent by increasingly sophisticated technologies. This challenge was discussed in some depth in chapter 2, but I now want to emphasise an emerging dynamic that requires the urgent and creative attention of all educators in systems and schools.

Technological challenges: teaching the iGeneration and screenagers

In chapter 2, I introduced the idea of the emerging generations – *iGeneration* and *screenagers* – for which technology is not just second nature but is their nature. Based on extensive research, Rosen (2011), an expert on net generations, refers to those born during the 1990s as the 'iGeneration', or what Scherer (2011) calls 'screenagers', because of their addiction to internet technologies. To this generation, 'the smartphone, Internet, and everything technological are not "tools" at all – they simply are' and they consume 'massive amounts of media' (Rosen, 2011, p. 12). To the iGeneration, Rosen says, a smartphone is a 'portable computer that they use to tweet, surf the web and, of course, text, text, text' (p. 13). This generation can travel the world with their 'life necessities' – for example, their library, cinema, games, communications, social networking tools – stored in a single electronic device held in the palm of their hand (Gemmell, 2011).

Schools must take advantage of students' cyber skills because 'the creative use of technology for learning enhances the engagement of students' (Rosen, 2011, p. 15). The iGeneration is 'immersed in technology. Their tech world is open 24/7' and schools, therefore, need to take advantage of this love of technology to refocus education. In doing so, we'll not only get students more involved in learning, but also free up classroom time to help them 'make meaning of the wealth of information that surrounds them' (p. 15). This is because they can access and share information outside school hours (e.g., access on YouTube and share on Facebook) and devote more in-school time to making meaningful connections and transforming information into useful and applicable knowledge. We are not talking here about home*work* but seamless learning within digital and socially interconnected *cyber learning spaces*.

Cator, Director of the Office of Technology, US Department of Education, in an interview with Scherer (2011), Editor-in-chief of the ASCD flagship publication, *Educational Leadership*, explains that the 2010 Federal Government's policy on education technology (entitled 'Transforming American Education: powered by technology') aims to create learning environments in schools that facilitate 'communication, engagement, interaction, and understanding' (p. 17). Her definition of engagement involves students not only relating to others, but their 'brain activity. Is each student's brain fully engaged?' She predicts that as we transition to digital learning environments in schools we will be able to 'facilitate personalization, participation, interaction, and collaboration – with people who might be right there in the classroom or people who might be across the world' (p. 18).

In such digitally enhanced learning environments, she says that we will have the capacity to 'incorporate cognitive tutors and integrate simulations, visualizations of complex math and science concepts, videos [YouTube] and animated demonstrations' (p. 18). While the digital divide that separates many teachers must be bridged, and soon, more urgently she suggests, we need to 'address the pedagogical divide' (p. 19) because, as Hattie (2009) clearly points out, the differences in the quality of teaching, pedagogy and learning outcomes are often greater within schools than across schools.

Through this technology policy, the Federal Government in the US is funding a nationwide initiative to design online connected communities of practice where, Cator says, 'people can grapple with a problem together, share what they have learned, develop a solution together, and connect with experts who can provide research, information, and strategies' (p. 20). While she acknowledges that the concept of communities of practice is not new and is a feature in education in a number of countries, the distinguishing and cutting-edge difference with the US initiative is that they are 'focusing on the best ways to leverage online environments and technologies to connect professional educators' (p. 20).

While it is currently trendy in some countries to undervalue US initiatives, this is, nevertheless, a bold and creative initiative with a very large educational footprint. It combines much of *best* and *next* practice in developing technology-rich learning-focused environments. It is far too soon to predict its eventual success, but it represents a US Government response to what they admit is an education system under great stress. It would be encouraging to see the experiment grow into a national success story and we shouldn't underestimate their capacity to deliver on the promise. Remember their successful response to Sputnik!

This technology revolution has been accompanied by a search by many educators for optimum learning spaces for teaching and learning. The focus is on the configuration and reconfiguration of learning spaces, supported by sophisticated interactive technologies, to build learning environments – among other things – to better engage students in their learning and its application to the real world.

Learning spaces for engaged learning

Whitby (2011), director of a Catholic education system in Western Sydney with 80 schools and 45,000 students, is a strong proponent of the need for flexible learning spaces supported by integrating and interactive technologies, and he suggests that 'the classroom as we understand it – kids sitting in rows, a person at the front – is dead'. In an interview with the *Weekend Australian Magazine* (10–11 September 2011) he states that what we are seeing is a 'new way of learning'. He is referring to developments in the structural delivery and pedagogy of learning and teaching of which he is a strong advocate in Australia. These developments, which are also happening in education systems in many countries, are based on technology-smart, agile or flexible learning environments within open spaces, and with an attendant student-enabling pedagogy. While many, including some parents, may think that the new learning agenda is primarily about learning spaces and their use, Whitby says it's all about learning and the nature of learning today. He states that when they took on this initiative system-wide:

> we didn't say, 'let's build schools without walls', we said: 'How do kids learn in today's world? What is the nature of the world that they live in?' [because] kids are going to have two or three jobs before they are 30. They need to be able to learn and relearn (p. 16).

Changing the technologies or the learning spaces alone, he says, will not provide a learning and teaching paradigm shift. First and foremost, we need quality teachers and quality teaching. This requires a battle for the minds of teachers who will have to open up to new ways of thinking and working in order to build their own and the profession's capacity. They require a brand-new narrative as a starting point that has at its centre the simple proposition:

> we need to move from 'I think' to 'we know'. In crafting this new narrative we have to recognise in this age that the role of the teacher is about being a learner and recognising that if the she/he doesn't know how to improve every student's achievement then they have to learn how to do it. (From a written statement by Whitby in response to a request from the author, 13 October 2011.)

Quality twenty-first century schooling, Whitby claims, will be delivered when we have a good teacher in front of every student. This has to be our focus – everything else is only a small part of the process.

Most schools in his system, however, include numerous agile or flexible learning spaces supported by seamlessly integrated high-speed interactive technologies and engaging but personalised pedagogy aimed at consistent learning improvement for all students. There is also a strong emphasis on evidence-based (using the results of smart tests) improvement in learning with the goal of attaining improvement in student learning outcomes. While it is too soon to have definite empirical evidence (proof) of the success of the venture, Whitby (2011) admits that based on Australia's National Testing Program (NAPLAN), 'there has been no great surge in performance', but 'it's not about one test on one day. It's about the vision and belief' (p. 17).

In a recent detailed overview and critique in the *New York Times* (3 September 2011) of the performance of similar schools in the US, Richtel concludes that as yet there is 'a dearth of proof' (p. 2). Cator (director of the US Office of Technology) says she is aware that the results on student performance are mixed because of the effects of technology-intense learning environments (in some schools they go up and in others they don't), but she claims that even if scores are 'flat' you have to look at:

> all the other things students are doing: learning to use the internet to research, learning to organize their work, learning to use professional writing tools, learning to collaborate with others (Cator, cited in Richtel, p. 5).

This article in the *New York Times* on the effectiveness of technology in relation to student performance created a storm, which is typical of the debate generally on this emotional subject. There are those who drag up their own experiences of schools without walls in the 1970s without considering key differences between then and now. We have many teachers today who are better prepared for implementing new pedagogies and technology-enhanced learning in flexible learning spaces. We now know much more about learning styles and developmental stages of learning, especially in literacy and numeracy, and about the configuration of flexible learning spaces to maximise the use of interactive technologies, than we did in the 1970s.

Often when antagonists, even parents, criticise these new pedagogies they do so on the basis that their child is now in a 'class' of fifty, sixty, even 100, but they may not understand or appreciate how personalised learning can be in such environments, especially because of student customised learning pathways (e.g., Fullan et al., 2006) and the sophistication of differentiated learning approaches (Bower, 2011). A recent criticism by a principal on national television in Australia on the damaging effects on students using Facebook (National 9, *Today Show*, 26 September 2011), while insightful about its possible consequences, must be treated with some scepticism as the principal admitted to the interviewer he had never used Facebook. This is not an isolated case. A recent survey of 1600 principals and other educational leaders in Australia by their own peak body found that 54 per cent of respondents doubted their own personal information and communication technology (ICT) capability (Principals Australia Media Release, Canberra, 14 September 2011).

The fact is that the educational context today is very different from that of the 1970s because high-speed technologies have transformed most of our lives in so many ways (e.g., health, business, marketing, communication, access to information, travel, publishing, entertainment) and *it is changing the educational landscape too*. It is here to stay and it is interesting to note that it is not our students that are challenged by technology but some teachers, parents and educators. In the end, technology is simply a resource, a powerful one at that, and it is likely that in the hands of talented and appropriately trained teachers it will make a big difference and lead to high-quality learning outcomes. As the screenagers and iGeneration become the new leaders of education, forms of technology not yet invented will adorn (some might say scar) our educational landscape.

Is education ready for such technologies? Undoubtedly, the context for education has changed dramatically but many believe the reason schools haven't sufficiently embraced technology is because the model of schooling is stuck in the past. In a speech to the Foundation for Excellence in Education Summit in San Francisco (14 October 2011), News Corporation chairman Rupert Murdoch sums up the problem very well when he states:

> Think of it this way. If we attached computers to leeches, medicine wouldn't be any better than it was in the 19th century, when doctors used them to bleed patients. The same goes for education. You don't

get change by plugging in computers to schools designed for the industrial age. You get it by deploying
technology that rewrites the rules of the game by centering learning around the learner.

He suggests that young people who are constantly engaging with smart, interactive
technologies outside school have the experience of going back in time when they
enter their classrooms. He urges educators to do something about it as a matter of
urgency because our children are our destiny.

Protagonists for new technologically-inspired pedagogies must, however, be
careful not to make exaggerated and as yet unsubstantiated claims for its promise,
never mind its success, and they need to better explain these pedagogies, especially
to parents, as to how they will assist the learning of all students. It is not a matter
of mass marketing initiatives but carefully considered and personalised approaches
within specific education contexts, schools, even classrooms. There are many
schools that have been successfully engaging in technologically-enabled, flexible-
learning spaces for some years and these *success case studies* (Brinkerhoff, 2003)
must be carefully documented and the characteristics that especially enhance
student performance identified. While this has already begun to happen, education
systems that champion new pedagogies need to network and compare what works
for them. They can now access some of the most sophisticated networking tools that
have ever existed and they should use them to build up national and international
evidence portfolios (databases) to support those who are involved in these new
initiatives. Of course, trends in test scores will continue to be important evidence for
the success or otherwise of any improvement initiatives.

The principal of one of the schools engaged in Whitby's (2011) new vision for
transforming education provided an interesting perspective on the debate about the
success of technology and learning spaces when he stated that 'education isn't just
spelling and writing and maths but about the whole child'. He asks all his parents
what they want their child to be like after they complete seven years of schooling in
his school and he reports that, overwhelmingly, they say:

> they want their children to be happy. They want them to have made friends. They want to see them
> being creative, and to see the whole child – physically, educationally, spiritually – developing (reported in
> *Australian Weekend Magazine*, 10–11 September 2011, p. 17).

Of course, it goes without saying that they all want their children to perform very
well academically too.

Debate will continue about the longer-term success and sustainability of
educational delivery approaches involving technology and flexible learning spaces
and its critics will continue to be vocal. While the jury on its success may still be
out, there is little doubt that it includes many of the desirable characteristics of the
new education paradigm described in chapter 2 and those of deep, rich learning
environments discussed in this chapter. Whatever the future, we would do well
to remember the advice of Hattie (2009), that it is excellence in teaching that will

make the biggest difference whatever the sophistication of technologies or the shapes, sizes, and variety of learning spaces. For me, Turner (2011), director of a Catholic education system in Australia and a colleague of Whitby's, hits the nail very directly on the head when he states:

> it's all about the teacher, by which I mean, it's about the integrity, the quality and the calibre of the teacher in the class. If you can get that right, you can pretty much teach in a tent (p. 17).

Personally, I hope it is a tent with flexible, agile learning spaces where the children are actively engaged and excited about their learning.

What, then, might be a way for schools wishing to transform their learning environments? Which side of the debate should they heed? As in most things in life, a balanced approach is likely to be the most effective. A number of researchers and authors have recently provided us with improvement frameworks that reflect such a balanced approach.

A balanced approach

Sharratt and Fullan (2009) advocate the necessity of system-wide (every school) and system-deep (every classroom) reform based on *capacity building*, which they define as 'investment in the development of knowledge, skills, and competencies of individuals and groups to focus on assessment literacy and instructional effectiveness that leads to school improvement' (p. 8). While their descriptions of successful system-wide improvements are impressive and should be familiar to all educators, our interest here is on leaders generating deep, rich learning environments within schools and classrooms – deep-capacity building – leading to increased student achievement. The full realisation of deep-capacity building (every teacher and every student engaged and benefiting) involves, they say, 'knowledge building that is universally aligned and coherent, knowledge building that emanates both from the center [system level] and the field simultaneously and in concert' (p. 9).

Full realisation or implementation recommends scaffolding four capacity building stages (pp. 22–3):

1 *modelled practice* (central purpose and vision explained to all);

2 *shared practice* (dialogue and questioning by learners in a safe and supportive learning environments);

3 *guided practice* ('trying it out' and 'talking it out' by learners with their leaders); and

4 *interdependent practice* (system/school/classroom on the same page in thinking and action and learners able to carry the initiative forward with minimal support).

While the details of the realisation processes are beyond the scope of this chapter (see Sharratt & Fullan, 2009; Fullan et al., 2006), the ultimate aim is to encourage and support teachers to:

> use the progression of modeled, shared, and guided practice in all of their teaching approaches to ensure that students experience scaffolded learning and the gradual release of responsibility to become independent [and interdependent] learners (p. 38).

Education reform is, according to Fullan et al. (2006), at a critical stage but many of the components of successful large-scale reform are known (personalisation, precision, professional learning), and the challenge is to combine them creatively. They say that 'this is not simply a job of alignment, but rather one of establishing dynamic connectivity among the core elements' (p. 15). These authors provide detailed descriptions of how such a breakthrough can be implemented in school systems and schools.

Another comprehensive, systematic and balanced educational improvement initiative in the US is what is called the 'Re-inventing Schools Coalition' (Delorenzo et al., 2009). This approach:

> is an integrated standards-based system of education that represents a synthesis of research and best practice about high-performing organizations, educational excellence, the characteristics of effective schools, and fundamentals of human learning, engagement, and motivation (p. 59).

It involves a 'coherent, aligned system' that aims to 'take achievement to new levels' (p. 60) and, according to Delorenzo et al., it is demonstrating sustainable success in terms of results.

There are other exemplary works on educational reform initiatives that focus on integrated and coherent improvement processes to increase student achievement. These include: Hopkins et al. (2011), who urge a move from reform based on school effectiveness research to 'powerful learning' (p. 28) derived from school improvement based on moral purpose, then scaled up to system-level (all schools and all children), and supported by 'powerful professional learning' (p. 49); Darling-Hammond (2010) who presents the best practices from a number of world-class education systems as well as the characteristics of some failing systems; and Gerver (2010) who argues that:

> the traditional models of schooling are no longer fit for purpose [and what we need is] radical transformation which requires two critical questions to define it: first, what kind of future are we preparing our children for? And second, what do we need our children to be like – as human beings, citizens, individuals – if they are going to be able to cope with that future? (p. 87).

As well, Bellanca and Brandt (2010) bring together in an edited volume the inspirational thinking and recommendations of many of the top academics and practitioners in the US focusing on twenty-first century skills and on rethinking how students learn them; City et al. (2009) who elaborate on their *instructional rounds* approach; Hargreaves and Shirley (2009) who recommend a 'fourth way' of educational reform which brings together:

> government policy, professional involvement, and public engagement around an inspiring social and educational vision of prosperity, opportunity, and creativity in a world of greater inclusiveness, security, and humanity (p. 71)

and Eaker et al. (2002) who provide details on how an education system can reculture schools to become professional learning communities.

There is a strong and varied literature based on research findings to help educators and educational leaders transform their schools as learning communities. An important initiative, directed by this author, focused on a cluster of schools whose wish was to transform the way teaching and learning took place in their schools.

Transforming teaching and learning in schools

In 2007, the author was requested by a cluster of eight schools in New Zealand to assist them transform their learning and teaching environments. In preparation for the project, he distilled a number of research findings (see figure 9.1) from recent relevant literature and clustered them under headings that could be used by the practitioners in the project in their attempts to inform their transformation processes. These findings all come from research that focused on what teachers and educational leaders, including principals, do to influence the quality of student or learning outcomes.

Reflecting on the categories and findings identified in figure 9.1, it seems logical to suggest that the category 'paradigm' is not really a separate category but a way of thinking about the other three. The assumptions and mindsets underpinning different learning paradigms vary and educators may implement the findings from the categories *people, purposes*, and *processes* differently depending on their assumptions and mindsets (paradigm) about the nature of teaching and learning, the degree to which students should be engaged in their learning, the nature of teacher–student relationships, and the purposes of assessment.

For example, if we take the finding from meta-analysis research that the provision of feedback from teacher to student has a large effect size, it is likely that a teacher who mostly works through teacher-controlling processes and teaches with a major focus on tests and testing will provide feedback very differently than a teacher working within a more engaging and deep-learning environment. It is also more likely that the latter teacher will treat feedback as being closely connected to other learning environment variables and will think more of creating a learning culture that connects a number of the research findings within the people, purposes, and processes categories.

The teacher in a more standard and traditional learning space is likely to see feedback as a linear, causal influence and try to implement it on its face value in an isolated way. On the other hand, the teacher in the interactive learning space is more likely to naturally use connected and non-linear (even though they may be unable to label it as such) processes within an already dynamic, engaging and inspiring learning culture characterised by respect, trust, and support.

The findings within the *paradigm shift* area in figure 9.1 are enabling factors or forces for leading change and development of deep-learning environments in schools. Simply put, they represent a paradigm shift from the usual assumptions and mindsets on teaching, learning and assessment associated with traditional schools and classrooms. The elements and their interrelationships identified in figure 9.1 constituted the framework for the research work in New Zealand (Duignan, 2009). The research focused, especially, on how educational leaders can

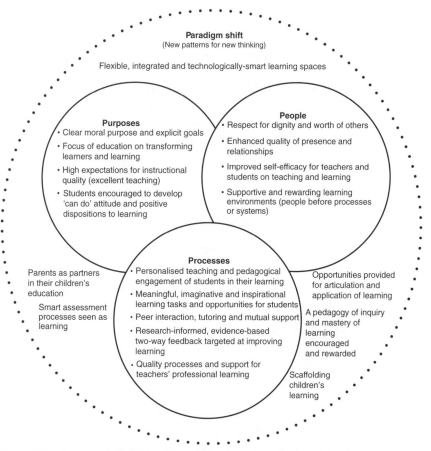

Figure 9.1: *Framework for developing deep learning environments in schools*

use the dynamic connections between the findings related to the paradigm shift with those identified within the purposes, people, and processes categories to help bring about the transformation of learning environments within their fields of influence, in order to enhance the quality of teaching and learning and, thereby, improve the quality of student outcomes.

In the example of transformational change that follows it is important to note that advocating the need for the creation of deep-learning environments is not meant to denigrate academic learning and the need to meet the requirements of external standards and the expectations of many parents and other stakeholders. It is possible to engage students in deep-learning processes, thereby enriching the whole learning process, and still meet and exceed current standards and benchmarks (Sharratt & Fullan, 2009). Indeed, if we are to meet the OECD expectations of qualitative leaps in the quality of student outcomes, we cannot continue with the same old educational processes and environments and expect miracles to happen. The conditions for creating deep-learning environments will not, of course, come about by chance. Improvement changes require leadership and the collective action of all key stakeholders.

Case study: leading sustainable transformational change

In a case study project with eight New Zealand schools (a cluster of seven primary schools feeding into one secondary school) directed by the author, educational leaders used the findings in figure 9.1 as a conceptual framework for leading transformational change in teaching and learning in their schools over a two-and-a-half year period. The author engaged in intensive interactive workshops over the period with leadership teams from each of the schools focusing on:

1 schools as complex and dynamic learning communities;

2 the characteristics of rich and engaging learning environments for contemporary students in their context;

3 leadership as an influence relationship within influence fields that involve both linear and non-linear processes and forces; and

4 the idea that educational leaders (including teachers) should share a collective ethic of responsibility for the leadership of quality learning environments for their students in order to enhance the quality of teaching, learning and learning outcomes.

While the ultimate aim for all schools was to bring about whole-school improvement, it was collectively decided that the conceptual framework in figure 9.1 would be applied to a number of interconnected projects (in excess of twenty overall). The idea was to achieve real change in teacher philosophy, mindsets and teaching practices in a specific area (e.g., provision of effective feedback; enhancing communication with parents; building the self-efficacy of students; assisting teachers to create authentic and deep-learning environments in their classrooms using action research) and then through networked discussions within and across the schools build a critical mass of teachers who were committed to and passionate about transforming their learning environments for their students. Discussion and sharing of project proposals and progress reports within schools was especially important for identifying pedagogical gaps and building on strengths because differences in the quality of teaching and learning outcomes are often greater within than across schools. The cross-school (cluster) dialogue and the sharing of the intentions and progress of the various projects in a moderated open forum also proved valuable in building a knowledge-base on what worked and didn't work.

As the research initiative was funded by the New Zealand Government, it had to conform to the stringent standards of the government-sponsored initiative called 'Extending High Standards Across Schools' (EHSAS), which focused on initiatives to raise student achievement. All projects, therefore, had to include measures of student outcomes as stipulated within the EHSAS guidelines.

The stated aim of the research project was to build leadership capacity within the schools in order to create deep-learning environments and thereby enhance student learning and outcomes for all children. The key question for the research was: *What do leaders do and what can they do to enhance the quality of student outcomes?* (Duignan, 2009).

While it is beyond the scope of this chapter to capture the essence of all the projects, one is singled out as an example of how the conceptual framework in figure 9.1 was typically used in each project. This project in a primary school focused on *enhancing the effectiveness of feedback to students in selected classrooms to improve learning outcomes.*

The aim was to implement this project within a paradigm that regarded their school as a learning community, recognising the fact that teachers influence the quality of student learning by practising their leadership through influence relationship within their influence fields. They also took careful note of Hattie's (2009) explanation that the provision of feedback is a two-way street and that it 'is most powerful when it is from the *student to the teacher*' (p. 173, italics in original). He puts his view on feedback succinctly when he reminds us that:

> when teachers seek, or are at least open to, feedback from students as to what students know, what they understand, where they made errors, when they have misconceptions, when they are not engaged – then teaching and learning can be synchronized and powerful. Feedback to teachers helps make learning visible (p. 173).

He recognises the importance of teachers providing learning-improvement feedback to students, but the important issue for us here is that Hattie opens up a range of possibilities to teachers for feedback to impact positively on student learning and achievement.

This is an important emphasis because many 'traditional teachers' tend to see feedback as a one-way linear process from teacher to student. If they use didactic teaching methods in tightly structured and highly controlled classroom environments, they may simply do more of what they do already, but are unlikely to appreciate the full implications for their teaching of what Hattie is really saying. More of the same will give the same results.

A teacher who already operates in a rich, engaging, and flexible learning environment, where there is a culture of trust and a sense of freedom for teachers and students to explore different learning possibilities and opportunities for students to form and apply their ideas, is much more likely to use feedback processes in the spirit of Hattie's recommendations (both linear and non-linear). Where such cultures exist, not only feedback will be effective but a host of other teaching and learning protocols (e.g., direct instruction, instructional rounds, visible teaching and learning) are also more likely to have largely positive influences.

There are other important considerations when applying the conceptual framework in figure 9.1 to learning improvement initiatives. Again, the focus is on the provision of effective feedback to illustrate these issues as they were addressed in the actual project.

The project team were asked to discuss the findings in figure 9.1 in light of Hattie's advice on feedback and then to position their project within the perspectives of: schools as complex learning communities; their understandings of rich learning environments; leadership as an influence relationship and influence fields involving non-linear processes; and a collective ethic of responsibility for the quality of learning and learning environments. These required the team to consider the interconnectedness and interdependencies of the research findings; patterns of communication and influence; possible implications of the many research findings on teachers and leaders influencing student outcomes from a non-linear view of influencing (there are so many ways to influence); and the importance of collaboration driven by a collective ethic of responsibility for leading learning. The processes followed in the project are illustrated in figure 9.2.

The key message for leaders of educational innovation using research findings like those in figures 9.1 and 9.2 is that they should look at the connectedness and interdependencies of the research findings, and the project teams designed figure 9.2 to remind them of this fact. When considering how to enhance feedback processes, the teams not only looked at research findings directly focusing on feedback (processes category), they also considered (discussed, debated, and

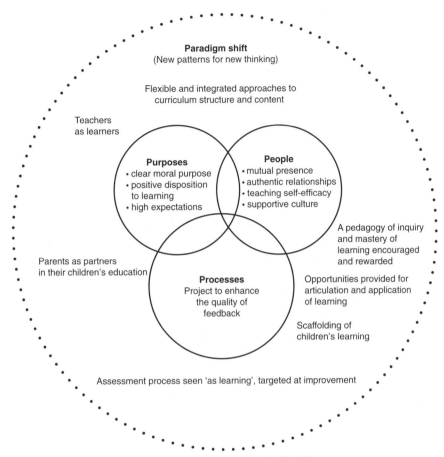

Figure 9.2: *Applying framework to change projects in schools*

came to agreement on) what else needed to happen to help implement the project successfully. They also considered relevant and useful research findings under the *paradigm*, *purposes* and *people* categories that might need to be addressed *at the same time* if they were not already in place. The findings from those categories that were deemed by the project team to be required to meet the aims of their project on feedback are highlighted in figure 9.2. These included:

1 A whole-school discussion on the type of pedagogy that would suit the needs of their students and would help facilitate the provision of positive feedback. This is a crucial step in any teaching improvement initiative because the quality of teaching and the nature of the pedagogy may vary widely within a school and if there is to be a whole-school approach to improvement it is important to surface teachers' assumptions and beliefs about the nature of teaching and learning and then discuss and critique them.

2 Dialogue and debate on what findings from the *purposes*, *people* and *processes* categories (figure 9.1) need to be included to help create the conditions for enhancing positive feedback. The project team identified the need to emphasise the importance of mutual presence, authentic relationships, teachers' positive self-efficacy, and a supportive learning culture as necessary *people* findings. From the *purposes* category they selected clear moral purpose, high expectations, and positive disposition to learning by students, as necessary antecedents.

Other project teams selected those findings from figure 9.1 that suited the focus and intentions of their project.

The reason for considering the interconnectedness of the findings is to ensure that decisions made are appreciative of the complex, dynamic and connected world of schools as communities of learning. There is also recognition that influence processes (e.g., provision of effective feedback) have non-linear characteristics and attempts to focus only on a single linear process (even if two-way feedback) may be insufficient to achieve the desired effects. The same is true for other research findings. Looking for patterns of relationships and connections among the findings in terms of the change being implemented is a key to leading a successful and sustainable change. As was discussed earlier, the most influential things leaders can do to transform learning environments, learning, and learning outcomes is to enable teachers to create the conditions within which teachers can teach effectively and students can learn (Dinham et al., 2008).

The impact of the projects on the participating schools was very positive as reported by the participants. The project teams in each of the schools were supported and mentored by the cluster director and the author of this book. Over a two-year period the participants met with their mentors separately and together. There were a number of workshops at the development phase of the projects and others to help shape, support and assess implementation phases. Opportunities were provided for progress reports and the reorientation of projects if necessary. The cluster director and this author visited the project schools to help the teams with any challenges or concerns.

At workshops, the project teams were required to provide documented (as well as anecdotal) evidence of progress and cross-team discussions ensued. In this way, different teams became resources for each other, especially if progress had some common elements.

In the implementation period (approximately two years) it was difficult to demonstrate any substantial improvement in student performance in test scores even though participants in the projects were, overall, very confident that such increases would occur in the longer-term. The case project suffered, unfortunately, from the shortcomings of many other improvements projects – insufficient time given to be able to determine longer-term improvement in student performance. This was, primarily, for two reasons:

1 the formal project lasted just two-and-a-half years; and

2 just as the schools were gearing up for a transfer of learning from their projects to whole-school improvement the Government terminated most EHSAS initiative funding, causing much disappointment for participants.

This meant that much of the positive evidence for the success of the project and its potential was anecdotal. Recent information (October 2011) from three of the primary principals involved in the project is that their schools have been positively and permanently changed by their experiences and learning in their projects.

One of the principals reported that his school has continued to build leadership capability in a number of ways, including: focusing all efforts on the moral purpose of giving their students the very best education to support a successful life; a team-inquiry approach that has come out of assessment data analysis for improvement of teaching and learning; improved learning links between home and school; and a stronger emphasis on teamwork and a collective responsibility for leading quality learning.

A second principal from the project reported that it has encouraged her to set and articulate a clear common vision within the school and it has enabled her to critique her own practice as a leader of learning and seek feedback from those she leads. For the teachers in her school the most positive and lasting influence of the project is, she reports, their reflective practice with peers which has taken many forms from coaching to the current practice of in-school professional learning communities. Teachers have become researchers in order to find the best way to enhance teaching and learning and have learned to identify needs and research ways to respond positively to these needs as a collective community. The greatest influence has been the very comprehensive analysis of a range of data and using this analysis to plan for better outcomes across her school. This has enhanced student achievement immensely over the length of the project and what is most positive is that 'we as a school have taken collective responsibility for all outcomes. We are truly a team committed to providing the best learning opportunities for all students, which in turn improves achievement and outcomes'.

A third principal reported that within the project the principal and other leaders in her school and network of schools focused on raising the levels of student engagement in order to improve student achievement. Together, they began to examine ways in which they could create the conditions for authentic teaching and learning and strengthen their fields of influence as leaders and teachers. Improving relationships with and between students and colleagues, working more collaboratively to achieve specific achievement goals in literacy, and being present to each other 'has changed the school culture and led to a collective responsibility for student achievement'. The project framework (figures 9.1 and 9.2) encouraged teachers to analyse achievement data, identify learning gaps and strengths, develop strategies to close gaps, and reassess and reflect on findings. Personal goal-setting, learning conversations with students and colleagues, collegial observations, feedback across the school, and three-way learning conferences involving students, parents and teachers are now fundamental aspects of this process. She claims that:

> our work with Patrick [the author] also led us to fine-tune our inquiry framework to focus our reflective actions within our teaching inquiry under purpose, people, processes and paradigm shifts [figure 9.2] [leading teachers to become] more deeply reflective [and changing] the delivery and content of our school curriculum with student input. Students now engage in their own authentic inquiry learning in areas that engage their interest within the curriculum. Teacher–student relationships are more respectful and the learning environments in our classrooms are more student-achievement focused. Our shared vision of achieving the best learning outcomes for all students is evident in our improved school achievement data in Literacy.

Concluding comments

The contemporary tendency in educational leadership to explore and analyse the link between leadership and learning is an important and timely one. The emerging emphasis on sharing the responsibilities for leadership in schools, especially those for improving the quality of teaching and learning, also seems to be closely connected to building this nexus.

In any attempt to transform learning environments, educational leaders need to be more fully aware of and present to the transformative possibilities in student learning and to be more proactively responsible for inviting, encouraging and supporting teachers to cultivate the conditions that encourage and support the deeper dimensions of learning. An authentic approach to leadership in schools requires the energy, commitment and contributions of all who work there – a collective ethic of responsibility for students' learning. Ongoing processes of dialogue, courageous conversations, and integrity preserving negotiation and compromise among all school members are required as they go about the construction and reconstruction of the conditions that promote and support deep-learning processes for improved student outcomes.

To achieve these conditions, educational leaders need to facilitate key stakeholders to learn how to learn together so as to develop collaborative and shared mental models and meanings that ethically bond them as teams within a learning community. The key emphasis is on learning together, sharing and creating processes and conditions that encourage everyone in the school community to be inspirational learning resources for each other.

Teachers, especially, need to be actively engaged in dialogue, debate and critique on key learning and teaching challenges and opportunities. Isolationist attitudes have no place in growth-oriented environments. Of course, students, parents and communities are also stakeholders and as such should be included in key discussions, but teachers, as educational professionals, must be in the front line in determining the nature and content of curriculum and the approaches to and processes of authentic pedagogy, learning and teaching. At the end of the day, the initiative for such transformative change must come from somewhere and educational leaders have a special ethical obligation to step up to the mark.

For many years educators have used the language of learning communities to describe schooling and schools. The time has come to be true to this language. The idea of leadership involving influence relationships, as was discussed in chapter 8, has been emphasised for almost twenty years, since Rost's seminal work in 1993. The view of schools as complex dynamic systems (e.g., Fullan, 1999), characterised by circles and fields of influence (e.g., Senge, 1992 and Wheatley, 1994) are not new to educators and educational leaders and appear to be well accepted at a conceptual level. All these concepts have also been part of many leadership preparation and development programs. A case has been made in both this chapter and the previous one for using these ideas as a conceptual framework for leading the transformation of learning environments. A case study of how this framework was actually used to lead a change intervention was presented using examples from case study schools in New Zealand.

Key ideas for reflection

Activity 1
Which two of the essential characteristics of deep, rich, interactive learning environments would you like to strengthen in your school? Give reasons.

1   Establish clear moral purpose with focus on deep and applied learning.

2   Teachers and students are authentically present for each other.

3   Learning processes/content scaffolded to engage/support students.

4   Learning is personalised for each child.

5   High expectations and standards set for teaching/learning.

6   Other.

Activity 2
What are the key obstacles to building deep and engaging learning environments? Select the two of those most important for you and discuss them with colleagues.

1   Teacher isolationist attitudes in classrooms.

2   Testing dictating curriculum content and pedagogy.

3   Teachers excessively controlling and directing learning.

4 Students' learning needs and styles not understood well enough by teachers.

5 Feedback processes do not lead to improvement of learning or to improved performance.

6 Other.

Activity 3

Select two leadership strategies you can employ to strengthen your influence fields and, thereby, enhance the quality of learning, teaching and student outcomes. Discuss with your colleagues.

1 Create high expectations for teachers and students.

2 Actively promote and participate in professional learning with teachers.

3 Develop a culture of openness, trust and support.

4 Actively participate with teachers in discussions on curriculum and pedagogy.

5 Enhance your authentic presence with teachers and students.

6 Engage in courageous conversations with those whose performance is unacceptable.

7 Other.

Chapter 10

Forming capable and authentic leaders: transformational learning approaches

This chapter focuses on the formation of authentic leaders who deal with complex challenges and lead change and innovation in their systems and schools in an uncertain environment. Educational leaders are expected to respond appropriately and 'adaptively to the depth, scope, and pace of *change* that combined with complexity creates unprecedented conditions' for them (Parks, 2005, p. 2, italics in original). To assist them in their responses they require a type of formation that involves:

> embarking on an internal journey of discovery, challenging [their] deepest assumptions, embracing alternative ways of knowing about the world, tackling past demons and facing fears of the future head on (Hames, 2007, p. 10).

They also have to be prepared to 'throw stuff away', especially the 'cognitive waste in [their] heads that stifles possibilities, ingenuity and progress' (pp. 10–11).

Hames is suggesting that for leaders in today's complex organisations there is a 'critical decision to be made. And it is a moral one'. He says that they can insist on clinging to traditional attitudes and practices by:

> swallowing the blue pill of amnesia [and continue in their] deluded stupor, ignorant of any deeper sense of the human soul and of human destiny – but resigned to a future increasingly spinning out of [their] control (p. 11).

He is convinced that the current knowledge-base of leaders will become 'increasingly redundant as the world becomes more connected and the global economy goes real time and digital' (p. 218). He is, however, optimistic that 'together we possess unbelievable potency to shape better futures' (p. 220).

Through shared reflective activities with colleagues, either in the workplace or in structured formation programs, new leadership strategies and processes can be designed that are 'infinitely richer or more equitable' than many current ones, in order to 'bring clarity from complexity and meaning from chaos' (p. 220). Given the challenging environments now and in the future for leaders, Hames says that a particularly formative approach to leadership development includes the relating, discussion and analysis of 'stories about how the future *might, could* or *should* be in the context of how things actually are' (p. 221, italics in original). This involves the art of strategic foresight – *scenario planning* – which helps us to better understand the nature of the decisions we need to take in the present in order to open up opportunities to 'explore the future, imagine our desired actuality and then reinvent and shape our capability to achieve this' (p. 222). What is required in leadership formation programs is an approach that includes narratives and discourse that are:

> deliberatively disruptive and profoundly disturbing at a world-view level, [that] enable us to grasp how others perceive their world (p. 223) [and] evoke the essence of complex emotional responses, myths, credos, enacted beliefs and other forms of *internal* reality that ultimately give rise to behavioural patterns or compel events to unfold in particular ways (p. 224, italics in original).

Many current leadership development or formation programs do not sufficiently engage participants in deeply personal reflecting on 'the human drama' that is leadership (Starratt, 2011). Educational leadership preparation and formation programs do not typically plan to be deliberatively disruptive and profoundly disturbing, nor do they engage participants in courageous conversations about current leadership paradigm inadequacies or about how the future *might*, *could* or *should* be in the context of how things actually are today. We have to think very differently about the purposes, structures, processes and learning environments of leadership formation programs if we hope for leadership that is moral, ethical, adaptive, inspirational and future shaping. In this chapter, we address many of these challenges.

One such program, conducted by renowned Harvard Professor, Ronald Heifetz, based on case-in-point methodologies, ticks the key boxes (detailed description provided in Parks, 2005).

Case-in-point leadership formation

Educational leaders need to be capable as persons and as leaders if they hope to respond wisely, ethically and influentially to 'adaptive changes' (Parks, 2005). Parks sees a clear distinction between what she calls 'technical problems', which can be solved with knowledge and procedures already in hand, and 'adaptive challenges' or 'swamp issues', which require 'new learning, innovation, and new patterns of behaviour'. She refers to these challenges as swamp issues because they present as 'tangled, complex problems composed of multiple systems that resist technical analysis' (p. 10). She succinctly sums up the content of contemporary and likely future challenges for leaders, which is similar to those challenges and tensions discussed earlier in this book:

> Critical choices must be made within significantly changed conditions, a greater diversity of perspectives must be taken into account, assumed values are challenged, and there is a deeper hunger for leadership that can exercise a moral imagination and *moral courage* on behalf of the common good (p. 2, italics in original).

Preparing and forming leaders in the capabilities required to lead with moral imagination when engulfed with swamp issues is a daunting but exciting challenge. This challenge raises the issue as to whether leadership can be taught, and how. Giving the example of a highly respected Harvard leadership development program, which aims to prepare leaders to deal effectively with adaptive challenges and swamp issues, Parks assures us that leadership *can be taught* and the most effective method is a 'case-in-point approach'. This method has been designed by Heifetz, using program participants' life experiences as the 'case-in-point' (p. 27). It constitutes reflection on 'self' in everyday action, and each participant in this leadership formation program presents a case example of a leadership episode that failed, while other participants act as consultants pointing out how things could have been done differently. The approach is formational in that it challenges the participants' 'habits of thought and action' (p. 45) and encourages them to 'perceive the activity of leadership, and therefore themselves, in a new way' (p. 46). They are encouraged to consider their leadership success or failure in the case as if they were responding to the adaptive challenges required to resolve swamp issues, and this involves 'grappling with competing values, changing attitudes, encouraging new learning, and developing new behaviour' (p. 46).

While the case-in-point learning environment is designed to form a 'crucible for transformational learning', it does so within a safe and trustworthy space that supports 'the difficult and intimate work of changing one's mind' (pp. 56–7). Participants' theories in action (individuals and the group) are placed under the spotlight and critiqued using the theoretical elements of leadership as an adaptive process. These concepts become 'the enzymes for digesting what is happening in the class' and the case (p. 61).

This approach to leadership development is formational in that participants also develop greater insights into their 'internal reality' and then:

> begin to see how the strength of their resources, their sense of purpose, and knowing themselves more deeply will contribute to their ability to be present on behalf of the common good of the group (Parks, p. 110).

Through this crucible of transformational learning 'they discover what it means to have the authenticity and integrity to sing [their] own song, not just the song assigned [to them] in some predetermined [musical] score' (p. 110). It leads to forms of nimbleness in thinking and acting that are necessary to lead when faced with adaptive change conditions.

Heifetz's method, as described and analysed by Parks, focuses on the type of learning leaders require in order 'to work effectively in changing and challenging conditions', and it defines leadership as 'the activity of engaging the important but confounding conditions on multisystemic domains that are necessarily undergoing profound change'. It creates a 'challenging context in the classroom itself that mirrors the larger field of action' and encourages each participant (and the group) to be 'more than a mere consumer of knowledge and technique [as happens in many leadership development programs] and becomes instead an actor in a complex system and an active participant in her or his own learning' (p. 232).

The challenges and problems reported by principals in many of the incidents described in chapter 3 were essentially adaptive challenges and swamp issues within uncertain and unpredictable circumstances that cannot usually be resolved by the application of a set of formulae or the use of learned competencies. Resolving complex problems requires leaders to draw from the heart and the spirit as well as the hands and the head. When facing complex situations involving competing or contested values or ethical principles, leaders need to draw on all their resources – knowledge, skills and wisdom – in order to exercise good judgement. Many of these resources are derived from the lessons of life's experiences and are crafted into capabilities from accumulated learning, or earned with great personal cost and sacrifice from the school of hard knocks.

Leadership capability is primarily concerned with expanding one's own and other people's capacities so that all can lead valued and meaningful lives and, in so doing, make a significant difference in the lives of those they touch. In the case of school principals, it means that they need to be capable and relevant human beings who help create meaning in the lives of those who work and live with them. Capable leaders need to have adequate knowledge, understanding and skills to discharge their responsibilities and resolve complex problems effectively. However, many of these 'skills of doing' can only be applied effectively if people also have the necessary 'skills of being'.

Capable people usually engage with the ethical and moral dimensions of life as well as the cognitive, factual and rational. They go beyond the competent person's rational analyses of facts and situations and develop a 'wisdom way of knowing' that *engages their whole being* (Groome, 1998, author's italics added for emphasis). A wisdom way of knowing elevates mere facts, knowledge and competencies to the loftier heights of human endeavour, involving the whole person in life-giving ways.

A capable leader is, first and foremost, a capable and confident human being. While knowledge and competencies are necessary ingredients, influential leaders also instil a deep sense of values and confidence in all those they touch through their leadership. Their sense of self-efficacy and personal integrity is contagious, thereby creating learning cultures in which all involved believe that they can be whatever they want to become.

Given the nature of the macro and micro challenges and tensions discussed in chapters 2 and 3, principals and other educational leaders in schools will need to be supported and formed in special ways. The short cases presented in chapter 3 represent many of the daily challenges and tensions faced by educational leaders and resolving such tensions calls on more than an educational leader's knowledge and skills: it requires the application of good judgement, intuition, ethical and moral literacy and agency, and wisdom.

In this book it is argued that educational leaders need to have the capacity to:

1 encourage a collective ethic of responsibility for leadership in their school communities;

2 develop and nurture their authentic presence within influence relationships and fields of influence; and

3 lead an education paradigm shift by building rich, engaging, technologically smart and flexibly designed learning environments.

While professional development programs for educational leaders will always have to include support in key areas of pedagogy, curriculum, and management skills, such as strategic planning, budgeting, conflict resolution, negotiation and communication, this chapter focuses, primarily, on ways in which they can be *formed* as capable and authentic human beings. As we saw in chapter 3, the most difficult challenges for leaders usually involve people tensions and problems where there is often a contestation of values, ethics, as well as personalities, and where everyone thinks they are right. Resolution of such challenging tension situations requires leaders to possess a highly developed sense of their presence in relationships as well as strong capabilities in ethical and moral reasoning and decision-making. These are areas in which many educational leaders admit they require better preparation, development, and formation.

Transforming leaders personally and professionally

What it means to be human is the key to understanding and forming educational leaders as capable and authentic human beings. Formational experiences should be uplifting, humanising, transformational, enabling those thus transformed to engage with practical wisdom in mutually inspirational, interdependent and interpersonal relationships. Senge et al. (2004) suggested that one of the oldest ideas about leadership is that 'with power must come wisdom', but that most organisations' commitment to 'cultivate moral development has all but vanished' (pp. 183–4). He defined cultivation as involving 'a capacity for … seeing longer-term effects of actions, for achieving quietness of mind', which both the ancient Greeks and the Chinese believed 'required a lifetime of dedicated personal work, guided by masters' (p. 184).

In attempting to chart a new path for leadership formation, they recommend that there is an urgent need to 'find ways that lead to increasing reliance on enhancing human development and wisdom' (p. 215), which puts an emphasis on the human dimension of leadership as it is expressed in the daily cut-and-thrust of practice, especially in relationships and interpersonal exchanges.

This is not to say that formation approaches should neglect knowledge acquisition and cognitive development. Formation programs for leaders should be intellectually challenging but the real challenge is to combine the intellectual and the moral into frameworks that transcend knowledge generation and skill development, that rise to the challenge of the reflective critique of contemporary dilemmas and tensions, and lead to a deeper exploration of what it means to be a capable and authentic human being in an increasingly secular twenty-first century.

Formation programs should be carefully constructed to ensure that they assist participants to further develop and refine their intellects and adopt an interdisciplinary approach to expand their horizons to enable them to better appreciate that intelligence is holistic, connecting them to a universe of knowledge and to their wholeness as human beings. Such programs should also recognise the realities educational leaders deal with on a daily basis and ensure that assumptions are challenged and existing paradigms critiqued in relation to ethical and moral standards and contemporary knowledge and understandings. Such programs should prepare educational leaders for the future, not the past.

Formation, however, does not mean being shaped by a narrow ideology. It involves both a letting go of outmoded thinking and practices and a 'letting come' (Senge et al. 2004) of new, more appropriate, and useful ones. It constitutes opening our eyes, hearts and minds to new possibilities in ourselves and in others, and to the development of capabilities to frame new paradigms of leadership, based on new orientations to relationships, presence, and influencing.

Authentic educational leaders are in no small way responsible for ensuring that conditions are created in their schools and school communities that challenge students and teachers to explore the essence of their being and to seek the truth about what it means to be human. To meet this challenge, they need a type of formation that is not normally provided by typical educational leadership training and development programs, especially the competency-based training in vogue in many educational jurisdictions.

The intent of formation programs should be to take action to bring about transformational learning and adaptive change; to help raise leaders and others to higher levels of motivation and morality; and to infuse their leadership practices with higher purpose and meaning. Their language of authenticity should not be empty jargon because if it is they will be found out sooner rather than later. Such programs will be judged to be successful if they assist educational systems and schools to develop capabilities in their leaders to make maximum difference in their influence relationships and fields of influence in education and in life (Duignan, 2004). The tensions inherent in the leadership challenges identified in the research study that supports many of the ideas in this book require educational leaders to develop creative frameworks and capabilities for choice and action that transcend knowledge acquisition, competencies and management skills.

Leadership capabilities

Authentic educational leaders require a number of leadership capabilities to deal with the tension-filled environment of contemporary schools. Those described in this chapter are adapted from the work of Duignan and Burford (2002), Spry and Duignan (2003), Spry (2004) and Duignan (2006). These capabilities are not necessarily discrete entities, but taken together form a framework for leaders who are faced with adaptive challenges in situations of complexity, uncertainty, unpredictability and ambiguity. They can also be used as a framework to develop formational learning programs for leaders. Those developing and implementing leadership formation programs can expand and/or modify them to better suit particular contexts and needs. The capabilities are categorised into *personal*, *relational*, *professional*, and *organisational* to give coherence and emphasis to clusters of different capabilities.

A capability constitutes 'an integration of knowledge, skills and personal qualities used effectively and appropriately in response to varied, familiar and unfamiliar circumstances'. It means:

> having justified confidence in your ability to:
>
> 1 take appropriate and effective action
> 2 communicate effectively
> 3 collaborate with others
> 4 learn from experiences
>
> in changing and unfamiliar circumstances (Cairns & Stephenson, 2009, p. 9).

Leadership capability means more than simply possessing particular knowledge and skills and having the potential to do something; it means that you can demonstrate that you can actually do it consistently in changing and unfamiliar circumstances.

Personal capabilities

1 **Is self-aware and reflective**: exhibits habits of critiquing personal assumptions, motivations, beliefs, values and behaviours; takes personal strengths and limitations into account in decision-making; and commits to personal growth and self-improvement.

2 **Cultivates intellectual acuity**: leadership demands a high level of mental acuity and discernment; effective educational leaders need disciplined minds and must be knowledgeable and rigorous in their methods of logical analysis and reasoning.

3 **Projects a sense of self-efficacy and personal identity**: acts from a confident sense of self and with a clear set of values and high ethical standards.

4 **Uses intuition as well as logic and reason**: shows that intuition and practical wisdom are as important as logic and reason, especially in decision-making.

5 **Projects confidence, optimism and resilience**: believes and acts from a clear vision; maintains a positive outlook and views challenges and mistakes as opportunities for learning; shows a sense of optimism and enthusiasm; gets going when the going is tough and consistently bounces back from adversity.

6 **Exemplifies honesty and integrity**: impelled by core values and lives by those values; accepts the personal consequences of difficult choices and decisions; respects the integrity of others; is open and honest in all dealings; applies ethical standards to complex and contested tension situations.

7 **Is ethically literate and morally courageous**: familiar with moral principles and is committed to high ethical standards; demonstrates strength of character and stands up for his/her values even against the expectations, wishes or demands of a popular majority.

8 **Is spiritually connected**: creates an environment rich in spiritual chemistry, based on a deep respect for the dignity and worth of everyone in the organisation and on a sense that there is something purposeful about life and relationships that transcends the narrow boundaries of the self and gives special meaning to one's existence; exhibits generosity of heart and spirit in relationships with fellow humans.

9 **Displays imagination and vision**: imagines what the future could be; articulates a personal sense of purpose and direction and communicates this vision with moral purpose and influence.

10 **Integrates work and personal life**: balances the demands of family, community and personal life with work; maintains good health in terms of physical and mental wellbeing; derives meaning and energy from a balanced and integrated life.

Relational capabilities

1 **Is relationally adept**: develops positive and productive relationships, especially with work colleagues; nurtures authentic interpersonal skills, as well as mutually respectful and rewarding relationships.

2 **Is emotionally mature**: engages with others in mature, interdependent and mutually beneficial relationships; shows sensitivity to the emotions displayed by individuals and groups in given situations and uses emotions appropriately in relationships and decision-making.

3 **Communicates with influence**: displays open, informed, purposeful and meaningful communication with others; gains commitment from others through constructive and courageous dialogue on important challenges and problems; actively listens and allows time for others to provide authentic feedback.

4 **Is authentically present**: demonstrates a genuine interest in and concern for people; acts with the good of others as a primary reference, especially those who are vulnerable or in need of assistance; engages fully with others and is attentive and sensitive to the signals they send out.

5 **Displays a trusting disposition**: accepts a positive human anthropology; seeks out others and values their opinions and ideas; builds an inclusive community by seeking to forge personal and professional bonds with others.

6 **Cultivates collaborative working environments**: committed to a collective ethic of responsibility for collaborative leadership; engages others in mutually beneficial relationships; keeps a common vision, goals and purpose to the fore in all interrelationships.

7 **Engages in positive politics**: identifies the key people or groups affected by a problem or decision; understands the interest of key stakeholders; builds positive relationships, coalitions and alliances; learns from 'the opposition'; deals openly with difference and tries to negotiate win–win (right–right) solutions.

8 **Nurtures leadership capability in others**: builds a collective leadership culture by sharing and distributing meaningful leadership responsibilities; creates an environment where risk-taking is supported and learning from mistakes is encouraged; encourages, nurtures and supports others to become influential leaders themselves.

Professional capabilities

1 **Is contextually aware and responsive**: shows appreciation for the wider context of education and of significant emerging challenges; demonstrates leadership of change in a rapidly changing environment; seeks and implements new ideas and approaches to meet existing and emerging needs; helps shape a future of hope.

2 **Inspires a collegial purpose and vision**: articulates a vision and invites others to participate in communicating and implementing it; seeks to embed this vision in the goals, policies, programs, structures and operations of the organisation; celebrates the vision in the day-to-day activities of the school; encourages and supports professional collegial action and teamwork.

3 **Displays curriculum and pedagogical know-how**: aware of theoretical developments and best-practice in teaching and learning; grows rich and engaging learning environments for all students; supports and/or initiates whole-school improvement in pedagogy and curriculum; uses authentic assessment for the improvement of student outcomes.

4 **Focuses on educational outcomes and accountability**: creates high expectations for all performance; monitors and evaluates teaching and learning with smart evaluative tools; uses appropriate feedback processes and evaluation results to improve teaching and learning; keeps key stakeholders informed of progress.

5 **Engages in and supports professional learning**: shows commitment to continuous growth and learning; plans professional learning opportunities for

self and others; connects professional learning to the core activities of learning
and teaching with a view to improving them.

6 **Demonstrates professional commitment**: serves others (e.g., students, teachers,
parents, community) with passion and expertise; discharges professional duties
responsibly and with care; adopts a lifelong commitment to personal and
professional formation and development; lives by professional codes of conduct
and acts in ways that enhance the image of their profession.

Organisational capabilities

1 **Engages in strategic thinking**: demonstrates an awareness of the big picture;
responds to all adaptive challenges with determination, confidence and foresight;
avoids imposing old paradigms on new realities or constantly recreating the
past; constantly challenges key stakeholders to envision a dynamic future of
hope and possibilities; involves others in contributing to the process of shaping
strategic direction on an ongoing basis; builds on current strengths to create a
desired future.

2 **Enhances organisational capacity to respond to contemporary challenges
and future expectations**: continuously scans the environment and develops
strategic readiness for most eventualities; builds organisational capacity to
respond to contemporary and future adaptive challenges; gives high priority
to creating adaptable and flexible organisational structures and processes to
respond creatively and effectively to rapid and continuous change; demonstrates
the capacity to lead positive change.

3 **Builds a collective and collaborative culture that focuses energies and
talents on achieving high-quality performance and outcomes**: helps create
the conditions for collaborative teaching and learning; maximises engagement
with and involvement of teachers and students in planning and delivering quality
learning experiences; encourages and supports authentic teaching and learning;
implements processes to generate evidence-based outcomes.

4 **Constructs creative designs for the use of people, time, space and
technologies**: critiques current use of these key resources and adjusts
their dynamic balance to maximise learning and teaching effects; matches
the quantity, quality and combination of these resources to the specific needs
and mix of students in a specific learning environment; is technologically
proficient.

5 **Models cultural sensitivity**: shows sensitive discernment with regard to human
and cultural differences; demonstrates consideration and empathy for those who
may not share their perspectives or preferences; draws on talents and expertise
across organisational levels and cultural diversity.

6 **Demonstrates managerial aptitude and proficiency**: possesses and uses knowledge and competencies to manage people and resources in constructive and inspirational ways so as to achieve the purposes, goals and priorities of the organisation; specifically engages in creative job design and formative performance management; prepares budgets for areas of responsibility and employs responsible accounting procedures; builds organisational knowledge and information capability to help enhance teaching and learning for all students; designs and maintains flexible, adaptable and technologically-smart physical learning spaces that promote and support twenty-first century learning environments.

Capabilities as a basis for planning leadership formation programs

The types of leadership capabilities just discussed have also been approximated in other research. Flintham (2003), reporting on his research in England which partly focused on the development of head teachers' capacities to exercise spiritual and moral leadership, identified the following leadership formation areas: growth in confidence; growth in self-awareness; growth in risk-taking capacity; and growth in 'being' rather than 'doing' (pp. 20–1). These growth areas support the idea of a formation approach that includes many of the leadership capabilities just discussed. In the conclusions to his research, Flintham recommends stages of head teacher development (based on the work of West-Burnham, 2002) which progress from '… external authenticity derived from the trappings and symbols of power to internal authenticity' (p. 22) which is, primarily, derived from reflection, moral purpose, wisdom and transcendence, the latter leading to the discovery of the fully authentic self. The work of West-Burnham and Flintham supports a major claim in this book: that educational leaders need, first and foremost, to become capable and authentic human beings.

Possible structures for leadership formation programs

Leaders' capabilities cannot be formed overnight but there is strong evidence that 'leadership can be taught' (Parks, 2005) and that all leaders can be formed or re-*formed* which typically must start with personal reflection and critique, complemented by opportunities to engage with colleagues and mentors in deliberately constructed and creative learning experiences. While some people in leadership positions may have fixed mindsets and paradigms that may be difficult to change, all leaders can with time, effort and sincere commitment greatly improve themselves as human beings, educators and educational leaders.

Effective leadership formation programs engage leaders in purposeful educative processes over substantial time periods. While the right time to start to form educational leaders is when teachers first enter the profession, the focus here is primarily on principals as leaders and on those aspiring to formal leadership positions in schools, for example, deputy/assistant principals, department heads and subject/curriculum coordinators.

Programs should be structured over a period of at least two years, with planned intermittent episodes of face-to-face engagement (two to three days at a time), and action learning periods in the workplace based on experiential learning from problem-based project work (approximately two months each period). These could be supported by the use of customised interactive websites to generate a continuing online dialogue and critique of key issues and challenges; opportunities for participants to partner and network with colleagues both inside and outside their systems; and one or more high profile summits or conferences at which participants can showcase their learning.

Within such a structure, a number of processes can be used, which are particularly well suited to a formation approach for educational leaders.

Possible processes for leadership formation programs

Several processes have been shown to be effective in recent attempts to form leaders, rather than simply train or develop them.

Leaders transforming learners and learning

A leadership development project, 'Leaders Transforming Learners and Learning' (LTLL, 2006–2011), was conducted by the Australian Catholic University in partnership with a number of Catholic education systems in Australia. The first two stages of the project (2005–2009), which involved a mutually negotiated research component, engaged teams of educational leaders from twenty primary and secondary schools in generating and implementing *learning projects* over periods of up to two years. The main focus of this project is on the formation of authentic leaders who help create school cultures within which authentic learning takes place.

During the project period all teams meet as a group in face-to-face sessions on five occasions (to plan, critique, refine and evaluate their learning experiences). Between these meetings the teams are busy implementing their learning projects, and they meet frequently as individual school teams and also with other teams geographically nearby, and with assistance from local school system support staff.

Participants are introduced to cutting-edge research on moral purpose, authentic leadership, authentic pedagogy, and authentic learning. Discussions on ethics and ethical applications are inherent to the processes (Bezzina, 2011).

During the second research phase a website operates to provide a forum for continuing dialogue on and critique of the learning projects. For each of the first two phases the engagement with the university culminates in a conference during which schools present their projects, with a focus on what has changed in teaching and leadership practice, and how experiences in the project have impacted on students. These presentations reflect the findings of interviews and reflection tools utilised as part of the research. Participants, report Starratt and Bezzina, have developed the knowledge and wisdom to transform the teaching and leadership practices in their schools and, in turn, help transform the learning of their students (Starratt, 2012). One of the significant research findings has been the mutually reinforcing nature of an explicit, shared moral purpose, and shared leadership (Bezzina, 2007).

The LTLL project has now moved into a new phase in which the university team is working in a range of different ways to support schools in efforts at renewal and transformation. Perhaps the most exciting of these has been to work with whole staff groups in all the schools of one Catholic school system which includes a number of remote schools. Like the second-phase research activities, this phase has also utilised a website to link schools and gather perceptions. By mid-2012 every member of staff in every school in the system will have been part of a process of reflection, identification of areas of improvement, design and implementation of a school-based initiative based on authentic learning and educative leadership practices.

At the time of writing approximately three-quarters of the schools had completed their cycle of engagement and culminating presentations have impressed system personnel with both the insights demonstrated and the transformed outcomes for staff and students.

Face-to-face sessions for applied ethical inquiry

The concept of 'communities of ethical inquiry' was proposed by Dempster et al. (2001b) as a framework for the professional formation of educational leaders, especially principals, to better prepare them for making ethical decisions in unanticipated, novel or unfamiliar situations. Most principals in another study on leadership development by Dempster (2001) preferred modes of delivery related to ethical decision-making that 'involved interaction with others in face-to-face settings', closely followed by 'professional networking' and 'mentoring' (p. 11). He recommended that principals should engage in face-to-face dialogue on complex ethical dualities or tensions that challenge their professional values and 'test their personal and professional values against real-life scenarios'. A distinctive feature of this approach to leadership formation 'is the use of vignettes of ethical issues ... for the purposes of learning about the processes of applied ethical inquiry' (p. 18).

Apart from experiential learning on the job, leaders are best formed and nurtured in face-to-face situations. The content and processes used in these sessions can then be explored through applied experiential learning in the workplace over time. Educational leaders should again be brought together for face-to-face interactive sessions to provide opportunities to reflect on, critique, analyse and compare their learning. Use of complex case studies involving case-in-point methodology is recommended, which are deliberately constructed from real-life critical incidents in schools, and require real-life leadership attributes and capabilities for their critique, analysis and resolution.

Development and analysis of complex cases

The consideration of cases that highlight value dualities and ethical tensions, similar to those described and discussed in chapter 3, can be key learning tools for educational leaders. Influenced by the research of Dempster et al. (2001a), Wildy et al. (2001) recommend that programs of study and discussions about contestable values dualities help shape the personal and professional values of principals and teachers in their everyday work. Case analysis, grounded in everyday recognisable problems and dilemmas, can stimulate reflective critique with a view to the improvement of practice and can be used within a case-in-point methodology.

The leadership formation program, the Lutheran Leadership Development Project (LLDP, 2005), showed that part of the formation process can be the actual construction of complex cases, drawn from real-life experiences. Small groups of leaders can be encouraged and supported to pool their experiences and craft multidimensional and tension-filled cases. The reflection, critique and analysis of these cases is a productive learning experience in itself and the swapping of these cases across groups for analysis constitutes important collaborative learning opportunities. Cases generated by the participants in formation programs are more relevant and more meaningful to their work situations and to the leadership challenges they face. Such cases and their analysis encourages participants to reflect on their leadership theories of practice with a view to critiquing and, if necessary, refining and or reforming them.

Another formation tool with similar outcomes was used to great effect in the LLDP (2005). It was referred to as a 'leadership development portfolio'.

Leadership development portfolios

The LLDP project focused on profiling aspiring leaders to determine their leadership development needs. They were challenged to construct a *leadership formation portfolio*, which involved a two-month long opportunity to reflect on and critique their leadership strengths and areas needing improvement. Participants were also required to formally analyse two complex case studies generated from real incidents within their schools, and forward their analysis, together with the completed portfolio, to the project mentors.

The portfolio details and the analysis of cases, overall, generated in-depth data, which provided useful indicators of their leadership development strengths and needs. Based on these indicators a development profile was created for each aspiring leader which helped to create customised leadership development pathways and programs for each participant.

The construction of the portfolio – that itself turned out to be a deep-learning experience for participants – was constructed around six key areas. These were:

1 **Personal reflection on leadership experience and achievements**: this included questions about why they chose education as a career; professional experiences and achievements that had given them most satisfaction; educators who had a significant impact on them and why; the special gifts they brought to their leadership; and their major contributions to leadership in their school communities.

2 **Personal reflection on the dimensions of leadership that were part of their system's leadership framework**: this included questions related to visionary leadership; authentic leadership; educative leadership; organisational leadership; and community leadership.

3 **Personal reflection on capabilities required for effective leadership in their school/system**: this included questions related to the capabilities discussed earlier in this chapter. Each of the capabilities listed under the four categories (personal, relational, professional and organisational) was plotted on a 5-point Likert scale and each participant was asked to evaluate whether it was a strength (5 on the scale) or an area needing development (1 on the scale). The results were used to help construct personalised leadership formation programs for each participant in the project.

4 **Reflection on personal experience of best practice**: this included requests for examples of their best practice in leadership and then reflection on this practice to encourage learning about their capacity for leadership or to identify areas requiring improvement.

5 **Reflection on and critique of their priorities for personal and professional leadership development**: participants identified their leadership strengths and personal and professional development needs in terms of leadership attributes and capabilities – this constituted their development profile for planning their leadership formation.

6 **Comment and critique by their school principal on number 5 (strengths and needs)**: the principal, in consultation with the aspiring leader, was asked to analyse the aspirant's profile and make recommendations for his/her future personal and professional development for leadership.

While participants' responses to the portfolio and case studies constitute examples only of simulated performance, they are proposed as a valid approach to evaluate an educational leader's '… capacity to practice and understand his or her craft as well as to communicate the reasons for professional decisions to others' (Clarke et al., 2000, p. 6 based on their use in their research of in-basket and mini-cases). Those in the LLDP project who analysed the cases and completed their portfolios were required to: analyse situations involving conflicting principles, values and ethics; exercise contextualised leadership judgement (in the context of their school); and, as Clarke et al. recommend, 'create an action plan describing the actions needing to be implemented and justify the actions intended to be taken' (p. 6).

Mini-cases and in-basket exercises constitute a valid approach to evaluating a principal's capacity to practise and understand their craft (Wildy et al., 2001). The research team in the LLDP project concluded that this approach, with some modifications (portfolio was substituted for in-basket activities), could generate accurate, relevant, meaningful and useful snapshots of where participants were in their leadership development and what formation support they required.

Individually managed e-portfolios

Cairns and Stephenson (2009) provide an example of how leaders in the workplace can use e-learning based on the development of an e-portfolio to enhance their personal and leadership capabilities. It can be used 'in ways that explicitly support learner managed learning in the workplace' (p. 108). The features of the e-portfolio are as follows:

1 *Control centre*: the learner's personalised home page set-up to access learning resources (it can have conventional home-page elements as well).
2 *Activities*: a repository of recent and ongoing learning goals and activities.
3 *Self-analyses*: links to self diagnostic tools that focus on interests, levels of attainment, learning styles.
4 *Personal log/monitoring*: a diary of events and monitoring of progress toward goals.
5 *Resource library*: repository of useful learning resources constantly updated.
6 *Personal plan*: a futuristic plan of learning for improvement of capabilities and practice.
7 *Help*: a place for confidential exchanges with workplace mentors and academic supervisors (if applicable).
8 *Networking*: links to discussion groups with peers, selected experts, and pooled experiences from relevant communities of practice (Cairns & Stephenson, 2009, p. 109).

This integrated approach to leader learning and development constitutes a 'powerful support for learner managed learning in the workplace' (p. 110) and has the advantage over paper-based learning portfolios of electronically opening up access to a myriad of rich and diverse learning resources.

Analysis of life stories

Many important insights and lessons can be learned from studying the lives of people who have known what it means to struggle and succeed, often against overwhelming odds. In Australia, for example, the ABC network produces the television program *Australian Story* (see <www.abc.net.au/austory>), which features ordinary Australians doing extraordinary things. Usually it depicts 'normal' human beings as they experience the highs and lows, the agony and the ecstasy, the trials and tribulations, the successes and failures in their lives. Most people whose lives are featured demonstrate great moral fibre, authenticity, and resiliency. Their lives are usually inspirational examples of flourishing against all odds, and we all can learn from them how to live more fulfilling lives.

A similar source of inspiration, moral witness and reason for hope can be gleaned from the biographies of people like Mahatma Gandhi, Nelson Mandela, Mother Teresa, Florence Nightingale, Martin Luther King, Rosa Parks and Mary MacKillop. Their stories provide life-inspiring benchmarks to which we should all aspire. Mandela, especially, has taught us that it is important to be humble, tolerant, forgiving, optimistic and hopeful. Rosa Parks, with great courage, exposed the evils of racial segregation in the southern US for what it was, a blight on all humanity.

Numerous other sources can be used in formation programs. Great literary biographies are obvious sources and readers of this book will, no doubt, have their own favourites. A personal favourite is *Lives of moral leadership* by Coles (2000). In his introduction (p. xi) Coles states that we need moral heroes who can inspire us to purposeful action and encourage us to inspire others to be leaders themselves. He concludes that while we need moral leaders and leadership, 'the need for moral inspiration is ever present'.

An older publication, *The book of virtues: a treasury of great moral stories* (Bennett, 1993) presents a large number of inspiring stories organised around the themes of self-discipline, compassion, responsibility, friendship, work, courage, perseverance, honesty, loyalty, and faith. These stories are aimed primarily at children but they provide insights into moral living that can benefit us all. Klein's (2003) book, *A year with C. S. Lewis: daily readings from his classic works*, is also inspirational with numerous topics relevant for leadership formation programs.

There are many other ways and means of engaging educational leaders in leadership formational processes and activities and I have tried in this chapter to provide a philosophy and framework, as well as some suggestions for structure, processes and content. Leadership capabilities constitute a useful starting point for the formation of authentic and influential leaders faced with adaptive challenges and swamp issues, and who are expected to respond with ethical and moral courage to such challenging and uncertain situations.

A future of our own making

There is a new energy abroad that is calling, perhaps crying out, for leaders of our systems and institutions to be more moral, ethical, authentic and capable. A case is made in this book to answer the call. In education we have the insight and the foresight to lead the way and show how it can be done.

Throughout this book it is argued that we need authentically sustainable collective leadership in our schools because traditional leadership approaches are no longer adequately serving our needs. We require forms of leadership that are infused with moral purpose, authenticity, and integrity.

If we don't change from traditional leadership paradigms, then we will be faced with a future that is not of our own making. This would constitute a 'sin' by omission, would be unethical, and may be harshly judged by future generations.

Leadership thinking and actions are needed that are transforming and inspiring, leading to greater human flourishing. We owe it to our children, and our grandchildren …

I leave the last words of this book to Seligman (2011) who suggests that:

> Happiness, flow, meaning, love, gratitude, accomplishment, growth, better relationships … constitute human flourishing. Learning that you can have more of these things is life changing. Glimpsing the vision of a flourishing human future is life changing (p. 2).

What are we waiting for?

Key ideas for reflection

A number of leadership capabilities, grouped into four categories – personal, relational, professional and organisational – were proposed in this chapter to form a basis for leadership formation programs.

Questions for reflection

1 What do you understand to be the distinction between leadership skills/competencies and leadership capabilities?

2 In what ways can educational leaders develop their own leadership capabilities and those of others?

3 What would be some of the key indicators of capable teachers?

4 In what ways can educational leaders assist teachers to become more capable (self-confident, resilient, flexible, adaptable, and professional)?

5 How can educational leaders help transform the collective capacity of their schools and communities to transform learners and their learning?

References

Ackerman, R. H. & Maslin-Ostrowski, P. (2002) *The wounded leader: how real leadership emerges in times of crisis*. San Francisco: Jossey-Bass.

Aguerrondo, I. (2008) The dynamics of innovation: why does it survive and what makes it function? In OECD report 2008 *Innovating to learn, learning to innovate*. Paris: Centre for Educational Research and Innovation, (8) 175–202, <www.oecd.org/publishing/corrigenda> (accessed 7 November 2011).

Andrews, D., Crowther, F., Hann, L. & McMaster, J. (2002) 'Teachers as leaders: re-imaging the profession'. *Practising Administrator* 1, November.

Avolio, B. J. (2010) Pursuing authentic leadership development, in *Harvard Business Press Handbook of Leadership Theory and Practice*. January.

Barber, M. (2011) *How school systems improve*. Presentation at Harvard University, January. <www.youtube.com/watch?v=vTvk95OkErM> (accessed 7 November 2011).

Barseghian, T. (2011a) 'Beyond the bubble test: how will we measure learning in the future?' *Mindshift*, <http://mindshift.kqed.org2011/07> (accessed 7 November 2011).

—— (2011b) 'How educators are finding ways to mix it up.' *Mindshift*, <http://mindshift.kqed.org/2011/07> (accessed 7 November 2011).

Bass, B. (1990) Concepts of leadership in *Bass & Stogdill's handbook of leadership: theory, research, and managerial applications* in Bass & Stogdill, New York: Free Press.

Bazeley, P. & Richards, L. (2000) *The NVivo qualitative project book*. London: Sage.

Beare, H. (2010) *Six decades of continuous school restructuring: swimming through the waves of reform without being drowned*. Australian Council for Educational Leaders, Monograph Series, 46, October.

Beatty, B. (2007) 'Going through the emotions: leadership that gets to the heart of school renewal'. *Australian Journal of Education*, 51 (3) 328–40, November.

Beck, U. & Beck-Gernsheim, E. (2002) *Individualization*, London: Sage.

Beckner, W. (2004) *Ethics for educational leaders*. Boston, MA: Allyn & Bacon.

Begley, P. & Johansson, O. (1998) 'The values of school administration: preferences, ethics and conflicts'. *Journal of School Leadership*, 8 (4) 399–422.

Begley, P. & Stefkovich, J. (2007) 'Integrating values and ethics into post-secondary teaching for leadership development: principles, concepts and strategies'. *Journal of Educational Administration*, 45 (4) 398–412.

Bellanca, J. & Brandt, R. (2010) *21st century skills: rethinking how students learn*. Bloomington, IN: Solution Tree Press.

Benavides, F., Dumont, H., & Istance, D. (2008) 'The search for innovative learning environments'. In OECD report 2008, *Innovating to learn, learning to innovate*. Paris: Centre for Educational Research and Innovation, (2) 45–65, <www.oecd.org/publishing/corrigenda> (accessed 7 November 2011).

Bennett, W. J. (1993) *The book of virtues: a treasury of great moral stories*. Melbourne: Bookman Press.

Bentley, T. (2008) 'Open learning: a systems-driven model of innovation for education. In OECD report 2008, *Innovating to learn, learning to innovate*. Paris: Centre for Educational Research and Innovation, (9) 205–28, <www.oecd.org/publishing/corrigenda> (accessed 7 November 2011).

Bereiter, C. & Scardamalia, M. (2008) 'Toward research-based innovation'. In OECD report 2008, *Innovating to learn, learning to innovate*. Paris: Centre for Educational Research and Innovation, (3) 67–92, <www.oecd.org/publishing/corrigenda> (accessed 7 November 2011).

Bezzina, M. (2007) *Moral purpose and shared leadership: the leaders transforming learning and learners pilot study.* Paper presented at the Leadership Challenge: improving learning in schools, Research Conference, Melbourne, August.

—— (2011) *Moral purpose: a blind spot in ethical leadership?* Paper presented at the 16th Annual Values and Leadership Conference. British Columbia, Canada, September.

—— (2012 in press) Paying attention to moral purpose in leading learning: lessons from the Leaders Transforming Learning and Learners Project. *Educational Management, Administration and Leadership.*

Bezzina, M. & Burford, C. (2010) *Moral purpose in leading for learning.* Paper presented at the 15th Annual International UCEA Conference in Values and Ethics, Umea, Sweden, September.

Bezzina, M. & Tuana, N. (2011) 'From awareness to action: some thoughts on engaging moral purpose in educational leadership'. *Manuscript of Centre for Creative and Authentic Leadership*, Strathfield: ACU, National.

Bezzina, M., Starratt, R. J. & Burford, C. (2009) 'Pragmatics, politics and moral purpose: the quest for an authentic national curriculum'. *Journal of Educational Administration* 47 (5) 545–56.

Birch, C. & Paul, D. (2003) *Life and work: challenging economic man*. Sydney: UNSW Press.

Block, P. (1993) *Stewardship: choosing service over self-interest*. San Francisco: Berrett-Koehler.

Bogue, E. G. (1994) *Leadership by design: strengthening integrity in higher education*. San Francisco: Jossey-Bass.

Boris-Schacter, S. & Langer, S. (2006) *Balanced leadership: how effective principals manage their work*. New York: Teachers College Press.

Bower, M. (2011) *Technology enhanced assessment for learning: developing teachers' ability to differentiate the curriculum using technology*. Sydney: Macquarie University.

Breton, D. & Largent, C. (1996) *The paradigm conspiracy: why our social systems violate human potential – and how we can change them*. Minnesota: Center City, Hazelden.

Bridges, W. (1995) *Managing transitions: making the most of change*. London: Nicholas Brealey.

Brinkerhoff (2003) *Success case method*. San Francisco: Berrett-Koehler.

Burley, M. (2011) 'Different strokes: differentiating lessons within a classroom is still largely unexplored but technology can be a help'. In Bower, M., *Technology enhanced assessment for learning: developing teachers' ability to differentiate the curriculum using technology. Plumpton Education Community*. Sydney: Macquarie University.

Cairns, L. & Stephenson, L. (2009) *Capable workplace learning*. Rotterdam, Boston & Taipei: Sense Publishers.

Caldwell, B. J. (2006) *Re-imagining educational leadership*. Camberwell, Victoria: ACER Press.

—— (2011) 'Unleashing the creative capacities of schools'. Sydney: *Australian Council for Educational Leaders* (ACEL).

Capra, F. (2002) *The hidden connections: a science for sustainable living*. London: HarperCollins.

Catalano, F. (2010) Keynote address at AEP *Content on Context Conference*, Washington, DC: Association of Educational Publishers.

Cator, K. (2011) 'Transforming education with technology: a conversation with Karen Cator'. In Scherer, M., *Educational Leadership*, (68) 5, February, <www.ascd.org/publications/ educational-leadership/feb11/vol68/num05/Transforming-Education-with-Technology. aspx> (accessed 7 November 2011).

Chapman, J. (2005) *Recruitment, retention, and development of school principals*. Paris: International Institute for Educational Planning.

Chesterton, P. & Duignan, P. (2004) *Evaluation of the national trial of the IDEAS Project*. Report to DEST. Sydney: ACU National.

City, E. A., Elmore, R. F., Fiarman, S. E. & Teitel, L. (2009) *Instructional rounds in education: a network approach to improving teaching and learning*. Cambridge, Massachusetts: Harvard Education Press.

Clarke, S.R.P., Wildy, H. & Louden, W. (2000) *Assessing principals' performance: a research agenda*. Edith Cowan University, Mount Lawley Campus WA.

Coles, R. (2000) *Lives of moral leadership*. New York: Random House.

Collins, A & Halverson, R. (2009) *Rethinking education in the age of technology: the digital revolution of schooling in America*. New York and London: Teachers College Press.

Conger, J. A. & Associates. (1994) *Spirit at work: discovering the spirituality in leadership*. San Francisco: Jossey-Bass.

Cooper, R. & Sawaf, A. (1997) *Executive EQ: emotional intelligence in business*. London: Orion Business Books.

Costa, A. & Kallick, B. (2008) *Learning and leading with habits of mind: 16 essential characteristics for success*. Alexandria, VA USA: ASCD.

Covey, S. (1992) *Principle-centred leadership*. New York: Simon & Schuster.

Cranston, N., Ehrich, L. C. & Kimber, M. P. (2006) 'Ethical dilemmas: the bread and butter of educational leaders' lives'. *Journal of Educational Administration*, 44 (2), 106–21.

Crowther, F. (2002) *Developing teacher leaders*. Thousand Oaks, CA: Corwin.

—— (2010) 'Parallel leadership: the key to successful school capacity-building'. *Leading and managing*, Sydney: Australian Council for Educational Leaders, 16 (2) 16–39.

Crowther, F., Hann, L. & Andrews, D. (2002a) Rethinking the role of the school principal: successful school improvement in the postindustrial era. *Practising Administrator* 24 (2) 10–13.

Crowther, F., Kaagan, S. S., Ferguson, M. & Hann, L. (2002b) *Developing teacher leaders: how teacher leadership enhances school success*. Thousand Oaks, CA: Sage Publications.

d'Arbon, T., Duignan, P. & Duncan, D. (2002) 'Planning for future leadership of schools: an Australian study', *Journal of Educational Administration* 40 (5) 468–85.

Darling-Hammond, L. (2010) *The flat world and education: how America's commitment to equity will determine our future*. New York: Teachers College Press.

Davies, B. (2005) (ed.) *The essentials of school leadership*. London: Paul Chapman Publishing.

—— (2006) *Leading the strategically focused school: success and sustainability*. London: Paul Chapman Publishing.

Davis, S., Darling-Hammond, L., Lapointe, M. & Meyerson, D. (2005) *School leadership study: developing successful principals (review of research)*, Stanford CA: Stanford Educational Leadership Institute, Stanford University.

Degenhardt, L. & Duignan, P. (2010) *Dancing on a shifting carpet: reinventing traditional schooling for the 21st century.* Camberwell, Victoria: ACER Press.

Delorenzo, R. A., Battino, W. J., Schreiber, R. M. & Carrio, B. G. (2009) *Delivering the promise: the education revolution.* Bloomington, IN: Solution Tree Press.

Dempster, N. (2001) 'The ethical development of school principals'. Paper presented at the International Leadership Institute, Adelaide, SA, August.

Dempster, N. & Berry, V. (2003) 'Blindfolded in a minefield: principals' ethical decision making'. *Cambridge Journal of Education*, 33 (3), 457–77.

Dempster, N., Freakley, M. & Parry, L. (2001a) 'The ethical climate of public schooling under new public management'. *International Journal of Leadership in Education*, 4 (1) 1–12.

—— (2001b) 'Principals' professional development in ethical decision-making through case study'. Paper presented at the 21st annual conference of the International Society for Teacher Education, Kuwait.

Deveterre, R. I. (1995) *Practical decision making in health care ethics: cases and concepts.* Washington, DC: Georgetown University Press.

Dinham, S. (2009) *How to get your school moving and improving.* Camberwell, Victoria: ACER Press.

Dinham, S., Ingvarson, L. & Kleinhenz, E. (2008) *How can we raise the quality of school education so that every student benefits?* Melbourne: Business Council of Australia.

DuFour, R. & Marzano, R. J. (2011) *Leaders learning: how district, school, and classroom leaders improve student achievement.* Bloomington, IN: Solution Tree Press.

Duignan, P. (2004) 'Forming capable leaders: from competencies to capabilities'. *New Zealand Journal of Educational Leadership* 19 (2) 5–12.

—— (2006) *Educational leadership: key challenges and ethical tensions.* Melbourne: Cambridge University Press.

—— (2008) Building leadership capacity in Catholic school communities. In Benjamin, A. & Riley, D. (eds.), *Hope in uncertain times: leading Catholic schools toward the future.* Melbourne: John Garrett Publishing.

—— (2009) *Developing deep-learning environments.* Research project Wainuiomata Cluster, New Zealand and Broken Bay Diocese, Australia. Sydney: *Leading to Inspire* <patrick@leadingtoinspire.com.au>.

—— (2010) *Educational Leaders Building Innovating and Deep-Learning Environments in Schools.* Sydney: *Leading to Inspire* <patrick@leadingtoinspire.com.au>.

Duignan, P. & Bhindi, N. (1997) 'Authenticity in leadership: an emerging perspective'. *Journal of Educational Administration* 35 (3 & 4) 195–209.

Duignan, P. & Burford, C. (2002) 'Preparing educational leaders for the paradoxes and dilemmas of contemporary schooling'. Paper presented at the British Educational Research Association Annual Conference, UK: Exeter.

Duignan, P., Butcher, J., Spies-Butcher, B. & Collins, J. F. (2005) *Socially responsible indicators for policy, practice and benchmarking in service organisations.* Sydney: ACU National.

Duignan, P. & Cannon, H. (2011) *The power of many: building sustainable collective leadership in schools.* Camberwell, Victoria: ACER Press.

Duignan, P. & Gurr, D. (eds) (2007). *Leading Australia's schools.* Sydney: Australian Council for Educational Leaders.

Eaker, R., DuFour, R. & DuFour, R. (2002) *Getting started: reculturing schools to become professional learning communities.* Bloomington, Indiana: National Educational Service.

English, A. W. (1995) The double-headed arrow: Australian managers in the context of Asia. Unpublished doctoral thesis, University of New England, Armidale.

Flintham, A. (2003) *Reservoirs of hope: spiritual and moral leadership in head teachers.* National College for School Leadership (NCSL): Practitioner Enquiry Report, Nottingham: NCSL.

—— (2010) *Reservoirs of hope: sustaining spirituality in school leaders.* Newcastle-upon-Tyne: Cambridge Scholars Publishing.

Flockton, L. (2001) 'Tomorrow's schools: a world of difference'. Paper presented at the International Confederation of Principals, Kyongju, South Korea.

Fourre, C. (2003) *Journey to justice: transforming hearts and schools with Catholic social teaching.* Washington, DC: National Catholic Educational Association.

Freeman, R. E. & Stewart, L. (2006) *Developing ethical leadership.* Business Roundtable Institute for Corporate Ethics, Virginia, USA, Bridge Papers <www.corporate-ethics.org/pdf/ethical_leadership.pdf> (accessed 7 November 2011).

Friedman, M. (2000) 'Feminism in ethics: conceptions of autonomy'. In Fricker, M. & Hornsby, J. (2000) eds, *Cambridge companion to feminism in philosophy*, Cambridge: Cambridge University Press, 205–11.

Fullan, M. (1993) *Change forces: probing the depths of educational reform.* London: Falmer Press.

—— (1999) *Change forces: the sequel.* London: Routledge Falmer Press.

—— (2001) *Understanding change: leading in a culture of change.* San Francisco: Jossey-Bass.

—— (2003) *The moral imperative of school leadership*. Thousand Oaks, CA: Corwin Press.

—— (2005) *Leadership and sustainability: system thinkers in action*. Thousand Oaks, California: Corwin Press.

—— (2011) *Change Leader*. San Francisco: Jossey Bass.

Fullan, M., Hill, P. & Crévolla, C. (2006) *Breakthrough*. Thousand Oaks, California: Corwin Press.

George, B. (2003) *Authentic leadership: rediscovering the secrets to creating lasting value*. San Francisco: Jossey-Bass.

Gemmell, N. (2011) 'An uplifting download'. *Weekend Australian Magazine*, 24 September.

Gerver, R. (2010) *Creating tomorrow's schools today*. New York and London: Continuum International Publishing Group.

Giddens, A. (1998) *The third way*. Cambridge: Policy Press.

Gilligan, C. (1982) *In a different voice: psychological theory and women's development*. Cambridge, MA: Harvard University Press.

—— (1989) *Mapping the moral domain: a contribution of women's thinking to psychological theory and education*. Cambridge, MA: Harvard University Press.

—— (1997) *Between voice and silence: women and girls, race and relationships*. Cambridge, MA: Harvard University Press.

Gleeson, G. (2005) *Being human*. Sydney: Catholic Institute of Sydney.

Goleman, D. (2006) *Social intelligence: the new science of human relationships*. London: Hutchinson.

Goleman, D., Boyatzis, R. & McKee, A. (2003) *The new leaders*. London: Time Warner Paperbacks.

Gove, M. (2011) 'The great schools revolution'. *Economist*. 17 September, 23.

Greenfield, W. D. (2004) 'Moral leadership in schools'. *Journal of Educational Administration*, 42 (2), 174–96.

Groome, T. (1998) *Educating for life: a spiritual vision for every teacher and parent*. TX: Thomas More.

Gross, S. J. & Shapiro, J. P. (2005) *Our new era requires a new DEEL: towards democratic ethical educational leadership*. Philadelphia: Temple University.

Halpern, B. L. & Lubar, K. (2003) *Leadership presence: dramatic techniques to reach out, motivate, and inspire.* New York: Gotham Books.

Hames, R. D. (2007) *The five literacies of global leadership: what authentic leaders know and you need to find out.* Chichester: John Wiley & Sons.

Handy, C. (1994) *The empty raincoat: making sense of the future.* London: Hutchison.

—— (1997) *The hungry spirit: beyond capitalism.* London: Arrow Books.

—— (2006) *Myself and other more important matters.* London: Random House.

Hannah, S. T. & Avolio, B. J. (2010) 'Moral potency: building the capacity for character-based leadership'. *Consulting Psychology Journal: practice and research*, 62 (4), 291–310.

Hanushek, E. (2011) 'The value of teachers'. *Economist*, 17 September, 33.

Hargreaves, A. (1995) 'Renewal in an age of paradox'. *Educational Leadership*, 52, 14–19.

—— (2003) *Teaching in the knowledge society: education in the age of insecurity.* New York: Teachers College.

—— (2009) *The fourth way of educational reform.* Sydney: Australian Council for Educational Leaders, Monograph Series no. 45.

Hargreaves, A. & Fink, D. (2006) *Sustainable leadership.* San Francisco: Jossey-Bass.

Hargreaves, A. & Fullan, M. (1991) *What's worth fighting for: working together for your school.* Hawthorn, Victoria: ACEA Paperbacks.

Hargreaves, A. & Shirley, D. (2009) *The fourth way: the inspiring future for educational change.* Joint publication with the Ontario Principal's Council and National Staff Development Council. California: Corwin (a Sage Company).

Harris, A. (2002) 'Distributed leadership in schools: leading or misleading?' Keynote paper presented at BELMAS annual conference, Aston University Lakeside Conference Centre, Birmingham, England, 20–22 September.

—— (2006) 'Opening up the 'black box' of leadership practice: taking a distributed leadership perspective'. In *Leadership and Management*, ISEA 34 (2) 37–45.

—— (2009) *Distributed leadership: evidence, issues and future directions.* Sydney: Australian Council for Educational Leaders, Monograph Series no. 44.

Harrison, C. & Killion, J. (2007) 'Ten roles for teacher leaders'. *Teachers as leaders*, 65 (1), 74–77.

Hattie, J. (2009) *Visible learning: a synthesis of over 800 meta-analyses relating to achievement.* London: Routledge.

Havel, V. (2007) 'Our moral footprint'. *New York Times*, A33, September <www.nytimes.com/2007/09/27/opinion/27havel.html> (accessed 7 November 2011).

Heft, J. L. & Bennett, S. J. (2004) *The courage to lead: Catholic identity, diversity.* Washington, DC: National Catholic Educational Association.

Heifetz, R. A. (1994) *Leadership without easy answers.* Cambridge, MA: Belknap Press of Harvard University Press.

Herman, B. (2007) *Moral literacy.* Boston, MA: Harvard University Press.

Higgins, D. (2011) *Lodestones: conversations about leadership.* Bendigo, Victoria: Sandhurst Catholic Education.

Hoog, J., Johansson, O., Lindberg, L. & Olofsson, A. (2003) 'Structure, culture, leadership: prerequisites for successful schools?' International Conference: School Effectiveness and Improvement. Sydney, Australia. January 5–8.

Hopkins, D, Munro, J. & Craig, W. (2011) *Powerful learning: a strategy for systemic educational improvement.* Camberwell, Victoria: ACER Press.

Hursthouse, R. (2010) 'Virtue ethics'. In E. N. Zalta (ed.), *The Stanford Encyclopedia of Philosophy*, winter 2010 edn, Stanford, CA: Stanford University Press.

Institute for Educational Leadership (2001) *Leadership for student learning: redefining the teacher as leader.* School Leadership for the 21st Century Initiative: A Report of the Task Force on Teacher Leadership, Washington, DC, April.

Jackson, D. (2004) *Sustainable school improvement: building a system-wide vision.* Camberwell Victoria: ACER Press, Monographs 15 <http://research.acer.edu.au/apc_monographs/15> (accessed 7 November 2011).

Jansen, C., Cammock, P. & Connor, L. (2011) 'Leadership for emergence: exploring organisations through a living system lens', *Leading & Managing*, 17 (1), 59–74.

Johnson, N. J. & Scull, J. (1999) 'The power of professional learning teams'. *Improving Schools (UK)* 2 (1).

Josephson, M. (2002) *Making ethical decisions.* Los Angeles: Josephson Institute of Ethics.

Keane, J. (2003) *Global civil society?* Cambridge: Cambridge University Press.

Kelly, T. (2000) Researching Catholicity at Australian Catholic University. Draft paper, Sub-Faculty of Theology ACU National.

Kidder, R. M. (1995) *How good people make tough choices: resolving the dilemmas of ethical living.* New York: William Morrow.

Klein, P. S. (2003) *A year with C.S. Lewis: daily readings from his classic works*. London: HarperCollins.

Kohlberg, L. & Turiel, E. (1971) 'Moral development and moral education'. In G. Lesser (ed.), *Psychology and educational practice*. Glenview, IL: Scott Foresman.

Kraemer, M. J. (2011) *From values to action: four principles of values-based leadership*. San Francisco: Jossey-Bass.

Leithwood, K. & Beatty, B. (2008) *Leading with teacher emotions in mind*. Thousand Oaks, CA: Corwin Press.

Leithwood, K. & Jantzi, D. (2000) 'The effects of different sources of leadership on student engagement on schools'. In K. Riley & K. S. Lewis (eds), *Leadership for change and school reform: international perspectives*. New York: Routledge/Falmer Press, 50–66.

Leithwood, K. & Mascall, B. (2008) 'Collective leadership effects on student achievement'. *Educational Administration Quarterly*, 44 (4), 529–61.

Leithwood, K., Mascall, B., Strauss, T., Sacks, R., Memon, N. & Yaskina, G. (2006) *Distributed leadership to make schools smarter*, Research Report. Ontario, Canada: Social Sciences & Humanities Research Council of Canada.

Leithwood, K. & Riehl, C. (2003) 'What do we already know about successful school leadership?' Paper presented at American Educational Research Association Conference, Division A Task Force, March.

Levitt, S. D. & Dubner, S. J. (2006) *Freakonomics: a rogue economist explores the hidden side of everything*. New York: Penguin Group.

Lindholm, C. (2008) *Culture and authenticity*. Oxford: Blackwell Publishing.

LLDP (2005) 'Lutheran leadership development project'. Flagship for Creative and Authentic Leadership, Strathfield: Australian Catholic University, <www.acu.edu.au/316439> (accessed 7 November 2011).

Lowney, C. (2003) *Heroic leadership: best practices from a 450-year-old company that changed the world*. Chicago: Loyola Press.

LTLL (2006–2011) 'Leaders transforming learners and learning'. Flagship for Creative Leadership, Research and Development Program, Strathfield: Australian Catholic University, <www.acu.edu.au/316439> (accessed 7 November 2011).

MacIntyre, A. (1985) *After virtue*. London: Duckworth.

Markham, D. J. (1999) *Spiritlinking leadership: working through resistance to change*. New York: Paulist Press.

Marzano, R. J., Pickering, D. & Pollock, J., (2005a) *Classroom instruction that works: research-based strategies for increasing student achievement*. New Jersey: Pearson.

Marzano, R. J., Waters, T. & McNulty, B. A. (2005b) *School leadership that works*. Alexandria, Virginia: ASCD.

Maxwell, J. C. (2005) *The 360 degree leader: developing your influence from anywhere in the organization*. Nashville, Tennessee: Thomas Nelson.

McAdon, B. (2004) 'Reconsidering the intention or purpose of Aristotle's *Rhetoric*'. *The Rhetoric Review*, 23, 216–34.

Melbourne Declaration on Educational Goals for Young Australians (2008) Ministerial Council on Education, Employment, Training & Youth Affairs, 5 December, Canberra.

Mendonca, M. & Kanungo, R. N. (2007) *Ethical leadership*. New York: Open University Press.

Moberg, D. J. (2006) 'Ethics blind spots in organizations: how systemic errors in person perception undermine moral agency'. *Organization Studies*, 27 (3), 413–28 <http://oss.sagepub.com/feedback> (accessed 7 November 2011).

Moran, G. (1996) *A grammar of responsibility*. New York: Crossroads.

Morrison, K. (2002) *School leadership and complexity theory*. London: Routledge Falmer.

Mourshed, M., Chijioke, C. & Barber, M. (2010) *How the world's most improved school systems keep getting better*. McKinsey & Company Report <www.mckinsey.com> (accessed 7 November 2011).

Mulford, B., Edmunds, B., Ewington, J., Kendall, L., Kendall, D. & Silins, H. (2009) 'Successful school principal in late career'. *Journal of Educational Administration*, 47 (1), 36–49.

Mulford, W., Leithwood, K. & Salins, H. (2006) *Educational leadership for organizational learning and improved student outcomes*. Netherlands: Kluwer Academic Publishing.

Murdoch, R. (2011) 'Let's bring classrooms into the 21st century', Speech to Foundation for Excellence in Education Summit, San Francisco, 14 October.

National 9 *Today Show* (2011) 'Anti-Facebook principal', <www.today.ninemsn.com.au/storyinfo/8351819/monday-26th-september-2011> (accessed 7 November 2011).

Neck, C. P. & Manz, C. C. (2007) 'Self-leadership: leading yourself to personal excellence' <www.emergingleader.com/article4.shtml> (accessed 7 November 2011).

Noddings, N. (1984) *Caring: a feminine approach to ethics and moral education*. Berkeley: University of California Press.

Noddings, N., Gordon, S. & Benner, P. E. (eds) (1996) *Caregiving: readings in knowledge, practice, ethics, and politics*. Philadelphia: University of Pennsylvania Press.

Noddings, N., Katz, M. S. & Strike, K. A. (1999) *Justice and caring: the search for common ground in education*. Teachers College Press, New York.

Nouwen, H.J.M. (1994) *Here and now: living in the spirit*. London: Darton, Longman & Todd.

Nussbaum, M. C. (2000) 'Aristotle in the workplace'. In M. Tobias, J. P. Fitzgerald & D. Rothenberg (eds), *A parliament of minds: philosophy for a new millennium*. Albany, NY: State University of New York Press, 30–45.

—— (2001 updated edn) *The fragility of goodness: luck and ethics in Greek tragedy and philosophy*. Cambridge: Cambridge University Press.

O'Donohue, J. (1997) *Anam cara: spiritual wisdom from the Celtic world*. London: Bantam Press.

—— (1998). *Eternal echoes: exploring our hunger to belong*. London: Bantam Press.

—— (2011) *Observer*, Editorial, 14 August.

OECD (2004) *Teachers matter: attracting, developing and retaining effective teachers*. Paris: OECD.

—— (2008) *Innovating to learn, learning to innovate*. Paris: Centre for Educational Research and Innovation <www.oecd.org/publishing/corrigenda> (accessed 7 November 2011).

Overington, C. (2011) 'Funky school', *Weekend Australian Magazine*, 10–11 September.

Parks, S. D. (2005) *Leadership can be taught: a bold approach for a complex world*. Boston: Harvard Business School Press.

Piaget, J. (1965) *The moral judgment of the child*. New York: Free Press.

Pont, B., Nusche, D. & Hopkins D. (eds) (2008a) *Improving school leadership, vol. 2: case studies on system leadership*. OECD: Paris <www.oecd.org/publishing/corrigenda> (accessed 7 November 2011).

Pont, B., Nusche, D. & Moorman, H. (2008b) *Improving school leadership, vol. 1: policy and practice*. OECD: Paris <www.oecd.org/publishing/corrigenda> (accessed 7 November 2011).

Power, F. C., Higgins, A. & Kohlberg, L. (1989) *Lawrence Kohlberg's approach to moral education*. New York: Columbia University Press.

Prensky, M. (2001) 'Digital natives, digital immigrants'. *On the horizon*. MCB University Press, 9 (5) 1–6.

Principals Australia Inc. 2011, Media Release, Canberra, 14 September, <www.google.com.au/search?client=safari&rls=en&q=principals+australia+media+releas+on+technology+Canberra+14+sept+2011> (accessed 7 November 2011).

Rebore, R. W. (2001) *The ethics of educational leadership.* New Jersey: Prentice-Hall.

Reeves, D. B. (2008) *Leadership and learning.* Sydney: Australian Council for Educational Leaders, Monograph Series no. 43.

Richtel, M. (2011) 'In classroom of future, stagnant scores'. *New York Times*, 3 September.

Riser, D. T. (2010) 'Collective moral responsibility'. *Internet Encyclopedia of Philosophy* <www.iep.utm.edu/collecti> (accessed 7 November 2011).

Roberts, W. R. (1954 transl.) *Aristotle's Rhetoric.* New York: Random House.

Robinson, K. (2011) *Out of our minds: learning to be creative.* Chichester, West Sussex: Capstone Publishing.

Robinson, V. (2008) 'Forging the links between distributed leadership and educational outcomes'. *Journal of Educational Administration*, 46 (2) 241–56.

Robinson, V., Hohepa, M. & Lloyd, C. (2009) *School leadership and student outcomes: identifying what works and why.* New Zealand: Ministry of Education.

Rosen, L. D. (2011) 'Teaching the iGeneration'. *Educational Leadership*, ASCD, February <www.ascd.org> (accessed 7 November 2011).

Rost, J. C. (1993) *Leadership for the twenty-first century.* London: Praeger.

Ryan, W. (2008) *Leadership with a moral purpose; turning your school inside out.* Carmarthen: Crown House Publishing.

Sachs, J. (2005) *To heal a fractured world: the ethics of responsibility.* New York: Schocken Books (a Random House company).

Sawyer, R. K. (2008) 'Optimising learning: implications of learning sciences research'. In OECD, *Innovating to learn, learning to innovate.* Centre for Educational Research and Innovation (2) 45–65 <www.oecd.org/publishing/corrigenda> (accessed 7 November 2011).

Scherer, M. (2011) 'Transforming education with technology: a conversation with Karen Cator'. *Educational Leadership*, February ASCD, <www.ascd.org> (accessed 7 November 2011).

Seldon, A. (2010) *An end to factory schools; an education manifesto 2010–2020.* London: Centre for Policy Research.

Seligman, M. (2003) *Authentic happiness: using the new positive psychology to realize your potential for lasting fulfilment.* London: Nicholas Brealey Publishing.

—— (2011) *Flourish: a new understanding of happiness and well-being – and how to achieve them*. London: Nicholas Brealey Publishing.

Senge, P. (1992) *The fifth discipline: the art and practice of the learning organisation*. New York: Random House.

Senge, P., Scharmer, C. O., Jaworski, J. & Flowers, B. S. (2004) *Presence: human purpose and the field of the future*. Cambridge, MA: Society for Organisational Learning Inc.

Sergiovanni, T. J. (1992) *Moral leadership: getting to the heart of school improvement*. San Francisco: Jossey-Bass.

—— (2000) *The life world of leadership: creating culture, community and personal meaning in our schools*. San Francisco: Jossey Bass.

—— (2007) *Rethinking leadership: a collection of articles* (2nd edn). Thousand Oaks, California: Corwin Press.

Shapiro, J. P. & Stefkovich, J. A. (2005) *Ethical leadership and decision making in education: applying theoretical perspectives to complex dilemmas* (2nd edn). New York: Lawrence Erlbaum.

Sharratt, L. & Fullan, M. (2009) *Realization: the change imperative for deepening district-wide reform*. Thousand Oaks, California: Corwin Press.

Shaw, R. B. (1997) *Trust in the balance: building successful organizations on results, integrity and concern*. San Francisco: Jossey-Bass.

Silins, H. & Mulford, B. (2002) 'Schools as learning organisations: effects on teacher leadership and student outcomes'. *School Effectiveness and School Improvement*, (15) 443–6. September–December.

Singer, P. (1979) *Practical ethics*. Cambridge: Cambridge University Press.

Sliwka, A. (2008) 'The contribution of alternative education'. In OECD *Innovating to learn, learning to innovate*. Centre for Educational Research and Innovation, (4) 93–112 <www.oecd.org/publishing/corrigenda> (accessed 7 November 2011).

Solomon, R. C. (1993) *Ethics and excellence: cooperation and integrity in business*. Oxford: Oxford University Press.

Sommerville, M. (2000) *The ethical canary: science, society and the human spirit*. Ringwood, Victoria: Penguin.

Southworth, G. (2005) Learning-centred leadership, in B. Davies (ed.) *The essentials of school leadership*. London: Paul Chapman (5) 75–92.

Spillane, J. P. (2006) *Distributed leadership*, San Francisco: Jossey Bass.

Spry, G. (2004) *A framework for leadership in Queensland Catholic schools*. Research Project. ACU, National <g.spry@mcauley.acu.edu.au>.

Spry, G. & Duignan, P. (2003) *Framing leadership in Queensland Catholic schools*. Paper presented at the NZARE AARE Conference, Auckland, New Zealand, February.

Starratt, R. J. (2004) *Ethical leadership*. San Francisco: Jossey-Bass.

—— (2011) *Refocusing school leadership: foregrounding human development throughout the work of the school*. New York: Routledge.

—— (2012 in press) *Cultivating an ethical school*. New York: Routledge.

Strike, K. A. (2007) *Ethical leadership in schools: creating community in an environment of accountability*. Thousand Oaks, California: Corwin Press.

Surowiecki, P. (2005). *The wisdom of crowds*. New York: Anchor Books (division of Random House Inc.).

Thomas, D. & Brown, J. S. (2011) *A new culture of learning: cultivating the imagination for a world of constant change*. Charlestown, SC: CreateSpace.

Tolle, E. (2005). *A new earth: awakening to your life's purpose*. New York: Penguin.

Townsend, T. (1998) 'The primary school in the future: third world or third millennium?' In T. Townsend (ed.), *The primary school in changing times: the Australian experience*. London: Routledge.

—— (1999) 'Leading in times of rapid change'. Keynote address at the Annual Conference of the Australian Secondary Principals Association, Canberra.

Tschannen-Moran, M. (2004) *Trust matters: leadership for successful schools*. San Francisco: Jossey-Bass.

Turiel, E. (1983) *The development of social knowledge: morality and convention*. Cambridge: Cambridge University Press.

—— (2002) *The culture of morality: social development, context, and conflict*. Cambridge: Cambridge University Press.

Turner, P. (2011) Interview with C. Overington, 'Funky school', *The Weekend Australian Magazine*, 10–11 September.

Usher, E. L. & Pajares, F. (2008) 'Sources of self-efficacy in school: critical review of the literature and future directions'. *Review of Educational Research*, 78, 751–96.

Vroom, V. H. & Yetton, P. W. (1973) *Leadership and decision making*. Pittsburgh, PA: Pittsburgh Press.

Walker, A. (2011) *School leadership as connective activity*. Sydney: Australian Council for Educational Leaders, Monograph Series, no. 48.

Weber, K. (2010) (ed.) *Waiting for Superman: how we can save America's failing public schools*. New York: Public Affairs.

Wenger, E. (1998) *Communities of practice: learning, meaning, and identity*. Cambridge: Cambridge University Press.

West-Burnham, J. (2002) 'Leadership and spirituality'. National College of School Leadership Leading Edge Seminar Thinkpiece. Nottingham: NCSL, July.

Wheatley, M. (1994) *Leadership and the new science: discovering order in a chaotic world*. San Francisco: Berrett-Koehler.

Whitby, G. (2007) 'Reframing school in the 21st century'. Podcast, Australia Broadcasting Corporation (ABC Radio) <www.abc.net.au/local/stories/2008/08/13/2336236.htm> (accessed 7 November 2011).

—— (2011) Interview with C. Overington, 'Funky school', *The Weekend Australian Magazine*, 10–11 September.

Wiggins, G. & McTighe, J. (2008) 'Put understanding first'. *Educational Leadership* 65 (8), ASCD: Alexandria, VA USA.

Wildy, H., Louden, W., Dempster, N. & Freakley, M. (2001) 'The moral dimensions of school principals' work: standards, cases and social capital'. *Unicorn,* Australian College of Educators, 11, 1–15.

Williams, G. (2009) 'Responsibility'. *Internet Encyclopedia of Philosophy* (2010) <www.iep.utm.edu/responsi> (accessed 7 November 2011).

Williams, T. (Cardinal) (2000) 'The role of the principal in Catholic schools'. Presentation to the Association of Catholic Principals of NSW Annual Conference, Tamworth, May.

Zhao, Y. (2009) *Catching up or leading the way: American education in the age of uncertainty*. Alexandria, Virginia: ASCD.

Index